DATE DUE

MY 2 ='99			

DEMCO 38-296

Small-Scale Model Railroads

Small-Scale Model Railroads

S. Blackwell Duncan

TAB BOOKS

Blue Ridge Summit, PA

FIRST EDITION
SECOND PRINTING

© 1991 by **TAB Books**.
TAB Books is a division of McGraw-Hill, Inc.

Library of Congress Cataloging-in-Publication Data

Duncan, S. Blackwell.
    Small-scale model railroads / by S. Blackwell Duncan.
        p.   cm.
     Includes index.
     ISBN 0-8306-3518-1 (p)
     1. Railroads—Models.   I. Title.
TF197.D86   1990   90-37850
625.1′9—dc20   CIP

TAB Books offers software for sale. For information and a catalog, please contact TAB Software Department, Blue Ridge Summit, PA 17294-0850.

Questions regarding the content of this book should be addressed to:

Reader Inquiry Branch
TAB Books
Blue Ridge Summit, PA 17294-0850

Acquisition Editor: Jeff Worsinger
Book Editor: John Bottomley
Production: Katherine G. Brown
Book Design: Jaclyn J. Boone

Contents

Introduction

*T*here has been a widespread fascination with railroads and railroading in this country almost since the first rails were laid. Railroads are inextricably entwined in the mesh of our national history. They have been a source of wealth and power for a few, a pitfall of greed and corruption for others. They have provided a livelihood for hundreds of workers, transportation for thousands of travelers, a network of social and commercial intercourse for a multitude of communities, and a source of wonder or awe or excitement (or all three) for countless youngsters. Trains are a part of us and have been for generations and are an integral element of our heritage and culture.

Not surprising, then, is the fact that toy trains appeared on the scene not long after the real ones did. Nor is it remarkable that the construction of miniature railroads built to scale also began to appear not long after the toys did. What *is* notable is the steadily growing popularity of model railroading as a hobby over the past 60 or so years, and the size of the support industry that has grown up around it. Today, model railroading as a hobby is enjoying rapidly increasing recognition and participation. It has been estimated that for every thousand people in this country, there is at least one model railroader. That amounts to about a quarter-million folks actively engaged in a pastime that is every bit as fascinating as the real thing—quite possibly more so. And there is probably a greater number than that involved in one way or another.

Model railroading can be a one-person, multiperson, or family hobby, and is wide open to all kinds of interpretations. It is many-faceted; there is an interest area for everyone, and often more than one. This hobby should not be confused with that of just putting together models. Models, except for the self-propelled, radio-controlled varieties, are assembled and set on a shelf as a static collection of nonintegrated and often unrelated objects. Model railroading, however, involves a unified, coordinated system of models that emulates, however loosely, a real railroad in a real setting. Probably the closet comparison to a model railroad is a *diorama,* a cased scenic representation complete with blended-in background, of the sort found in museums. However, dioramas are almost always inanimate and lifeless.

Model railroads, even incomplete ones, never are static; they are dynamic. Locomotives and cars move along the rails. Signal lights flash, semaphore arms wag, figures can be animated. Smoke plumes from steam engines and factory stacks. Crossing gates lower and bells clang. Lights turn on and off in houses and stores. Mournful steamer whistles or raucous diesel engine air horns sound their calls. Locomotives rumble or roar or clank or chug, freight car wheels clickety-clack on the rails. Smells of roasting coffee beans, fresh sawdust from a mill, cannery or stockyard effluvia, or a dozen other aromas can be generated to add to the realism. Sounds of heavy highway traffic, barking dogs, or a cheering football crowd can be programmed in. And with the miracle of video technology, you can even sit in the cab of your locomotive and watch on a screen as your own trackage and scenery unfolds before you, as it actually exists, while you thunder down the tangent. With a bit of imagination and concentration, you can project yourself in miniature right into the cab, Casey Jones at the throttle, an engineer in your own tiny railscape. It's a remarkable sensation.

Truly, anyone with an interest in modelmaking, railroading, or both, (or anyone who would like to engage in an absorbing hobby that incorporates skill, knowledge, manual activity, imagination, and creativity to any level you desire and culminates in highly tangible and satisfying results) would be hard pressed to find a more rewarding pastime.

There are several major elements in model railroading. This allows the participants to concentrate on those aspects that are most interesting to them. For some, building or accumulating the locomotives and cars is the major point while the rest of the layout merely serves as a backdrop. For others, complex and convoluted trackage patterns is the challenge. Many find that creating impressive scenery is their forté, while some prefer to concentrate on extraordinary detailing. Those who are hooked on electrical and electronic controls and systems can have a field day. Actually running the trains on a schedule in prototypical fashion, often in concert with one or two or several other "engineers", is the most satisfying part of the hobby for many. A large share of model railroaders, of course, just enjoy all the aspects of building up a complete and realistic scale layout.

But the big question, especially for newcomers to the hobby, is where do you start? And, after you get started, then what? How do you put all those bits and pieces together and make them work? Good questions, because the truth is even a small model railroad can be a complicated creature. And the larger and more sophisticated the layout (and the ideas and desires of the modeler), the more complex a pike becomes. Many beginners make a hesitant or wrong start and become discouraged. Many modelers with a little experience get in over their heads and end up equally discouraged. And with results that are less than satisfactory, or satisfying, they give up. Even some model railroaders with a fair amount of experience have been known to do that, which is unfortunate. It is awfully easy to get off on the wrong track (sorry, no pun intended), and the reason often is a lack of handy, useful, and comprehensive basic information that will add to the modeler's knowledge and further his or her plans and capabilities.

This is where, and why, How To Build a Small Scale Model Railroad comes into the picture. The book begins with a brief overview of model railroading, including a discussion of the scales used and their pros and cons.

This is followed by a chapter on the most crucial aspect of creating a successful, realistic model railroad, in developing the fundamental concept for a particular layout. Next is designing the layout in detail, an essential preliminary step if problems are to be avoided. Nuts—and—bolts chapters are next; how to build the benchwork, how to lay the track, how to wire the layout and set up the control systems, how to select, build, and place structures, and how to construct the scenery and detail the layout. The last chapter covers selecting and/or building locomotives and rolling stock. The book closes with a glossary of terms.

Thus, *Small-Scale Model Railroads* is a complete basic discourse on the subject, all in one handy volume. The purpose of the book is to introduce you to the hobby and then provide detailed instructions on how to build an operating scale model railroad. The scope of the book is full, ranging from initial idea through the design stages to the last detailing of the pike. It covers all of the main elements of the hobby in sufficient depth that you can use it as a working guide in the reasonable expectation of developing and completing a fine model railroad layout, one that is a unique product of your own ideas, skills, and creativity. Because of its wide coverage and good depth, this information is useful not only to newcomers to the hobby, but also as reference for any model railroader for intermediate or even higher levels of experience and knowledge.

If you've ever wished you could step back a little in time, even if only one year, and recreate a tiny bit of the world as it once was, here's your opportunity.

Chapter 1

The basics

*A*s with any other hobby, model railroading has its own terms, language, and fundamentals. Coming to grips with the most important of this information—and there is a considerable amount—at the outset will enable you to more easily understand what model railroading is all about before you dive in headfirst only to surface in bewilderment. With a modest amount of foreknowledge in hand, you will be able to make more intelligent decisions and selections that will make the hobby much more satisfying and engaging for you.

The glossary will help you with definitions of some of the terms that are common to model railroading and also to real railroads. Which, by the way, are called *prototypes,* because they are the full-sized, real-life originals after which model railroads are patterned. Other terms and language, as well as the basics of model railroading, will be explained as the occasion demands through the following chapters. To begin with, we need to explore the two most basic elements of them all, each of which causes much confusion among those unfamiliar with model railroading, and sometimes even with people who are. Those elements are *scale* and *gauge.* Their pros and cons must be weighed, and you'll have to made a selection from among them; available hobby time and economics play a part here. There are decisions to be made before you can even think about any model railroad ideas, much less plan or execute them.

SCALE

As used in model railroading, and in most model making of any type, the term *scale* stands for a proportion between two sets of dimensions. The first set is of the model, and the second is of the original. All the dimensions of the first set, all the sizes and shapes of the various parts and pieces of the model, are theoretically in direct proportion to the original, or prototype. They are simply smaller, or *scaled down.* The actual scale can be designated in a couple of ways. One is as a ratio, like 1:10, for example. In this case, the model would be 10 times smaller than the prototype. The ratio is also occasionally written as 10:1, but don't be confused. Either way, the "1" represents the full-sized original. Or, the scale might be written as the fraction "1/10," meaning that the model is one-tenth the size, or more accurately, the proportions are 1:10 of the prototype. Put another way, every unit of size of the model equals 10 units of size of the prototype. The units can be any measure—inches, feet, meters, rods, miles, whatever. Sometimes scales are written in terms not necessarily of the ratio, but rather the unit used, and this can be confusing. For example, *½-inch scale* means that ½ inch on the model equals 1 foot on the prototype, and the actual ratio of 1:24 is implied, not expressed.

The intent in constructing a scale model is to exactly replicate the original in a smaller size. If the scale is large enough, this is possible. At 6 inches to the foot you would have little difficulty in exactly reproducing, for example, a 20-by-40-foot house right down to the last nail. But in the small scales used in model railroading, exact replication is a practical impossibility. At ¼ inch to the foot, that building would be 5 by 10 inches, and you would not be putting the latches on the windows and the hinges on the doors. It's important to keep in mind that in the small scales we will be discussing, much detail is lost and much of the detail kept is not to scale. The proportions are off, generally on the high side. Note that one of the crucial factors in working with small scales is to retain the *illusion* of exactitude and realism. In fact, illusory representation of the real world, working with the proverbial "smoke and mirrors," makes up a good part of model railroading. After a while you will become a specialist in chimera and mirage, especially if you select one of the very small scales.

Different fields have different scales that are commonly used. A road map, for example, might use 1 inch to equal 15 miles, a topographical map scale might be 1:24,000 wherein by actual measurement on the map 1 inch equals 2,000 feet or 1 foot equals 24,000 feet. Automotive promotional models appear in ⅟₂₅ and ⅟₄₃ sizes, while auto and boat model kits are made in a variety of scales. Model railroading also has been blessed (or cursed, depending upon your viewpoint) with a number of scales over the years. Fortunately, just a few of them have been more or less standardized and are in widespread use today. Model railroading scales are also unique in that they are specified by certain designations that do not include the actual numeric proportion and don't appear to have any connection with anything. They do have one thing in common: Whatever the particular designation is, it extends to all parts of a given model railroad. Not just the locomotives and cars, but also the ties and rails, the buildings, the people, the trees and shrubs, the roads and vehicles—everything.

Though this book is concerned primarily with only two of the smaller scales, a brief look at all the common model railroad scales (FIG. 1-1) is included to give you a rounded view of the available sizes and a base of reference.

Scales of %₁₆ inch to the foot and up—there are several—are employed by only a few master machinists around the world who engage in building locomotives from scratch that actually run on live steam, along with the accompanying cars.

The ratio of G scale is 1:22.5. This is a European import that has been around for a while but is relatively new to this country. Its popularity is increasing rapidly, especially for outdoor "garden" railroading, though it can be set up indoors as well. Models and equipment are now being made in the United States, and product availability and range is good.

Scale	Ratio	Track Gauge (in.)	Track Gauge (mm.)	Scale Foot (in.)	Scale Foot (mm.)
G	1:22.5	1.772	45.00	0.533	13.55
O	1:48	1.250	31.75	0.250	6.35
S	1:64	0.875	22.23	0.188	4.80
HO	1:87	0.650	16.50	0.138	3.50
N	1:160	0.354	9.00	0.075	1.90
Z	1:220	0.256	6.50	0.055	1.39

1-1 These are the most common scales and ratios.

The ½-inch scale, or ½ inch to the foot, has a ratio of 1:24. It is uncommon, and is used for both live steamers and other models mostly set up and operated outdoors as garden railways. It is a scratch builder's scale; little if any equipment or parts stock is commercially available, except for what few architectural model (which field also employs this scale) bits and pieces can be adapted.

The 7/16-inch scale has a ratio of 1:27.5. There was a brief flurry of activity in this scale a number of years ago, but it has largely disappeared for lack of commercial material and the presence of already better established scales. But it still has its adherents for scratch building, and some interesting advantages.

No. 1 scale is in a ratio of 1:32, and that is equal to ⅜ inch to the foot. This is primarily a European scale patterned mostly after European prototypes, but the system has gained some attention in this country and some products are available.

The first scale on the list that might be familiar to you, and the one that usually is considered the break point between small and large scales, is O. Its ratio is 1:48, and because the scale is equal to ¼ inch to the foot, it is also referred to as the ¼-inch scale. This scale has been popular for many years in both toy trains, (better termed *tinplate*), and scale models. It is occasionally employed in garden railroading, but is much better known as the largest of the small scales commonly used for conventional indoor model railroading.

With a ratio of 1:64, S scale is also a fairly popular size. At 3/16 inch to the foot, many consider it to be an ideal scale to work with. It has been around for decades and was made popular by the AMERICAN FLYER tinplate products. Scale products are available today in a decent selection, mostly craftsman-type kits.

The OO scale at a ratio of 1:76 once had a toehold in this country, but lost out for various reasons and is now about gone.

Next down the line is HO scale, with a ratio of 1:87. Proportions are expressed in the metric system because measuring is easier and more exact at 3.5 mm. (millimeters) per foot. Or you can do it decimally, at 0.138 inch per foot. This is by far the most popular scale for a variety of reasons, including its workable size, availability, and range of products.

TT scale has a ratio of 1:120 and is scaled to 1/10 inch per foot. After a splash some years back with glorious predictions of this being the coming big (small) thing, the scale faded away almost entirely. Now it's only of interest to collectors.

N scale has a ratio of 1:160 and is calculated to be 1.9 mm. or 0.075 inch per foot. Now about two decades old, this scale is gaining rapidly in popularity, and there is an increasingly good range of products available.

Z scale has a ratio of 1:220 and can be scaled at 1.38 mm. or 0.055 inch per foot. This is a European scale that has recently attracted interest in this country, and shows signs of growth. The product line is small but reasonably good.

These are not the only model railroading scales. For example, 0–27 was common for a while in tinplate. There are two other O scales, one at 1:45.2 and one at 1:43, and a TM scale at 3 mm., and No. 3 scale, OO, and E. There are others, too, but they are equally obscure. For practical purposes, the scales to consider for conventional and indoor hobby model railroading in this country number only five: O (¼ inch), S, HO, N, and Z, with G as an added outside possibility. For a handy comparison of the actual sizes of several common elements of a model railroad in various scales, refer to FIG. 1-2.

As of 1990, as a result of various surveys and statistics about the hobby, it is reasonable to assume that approximately 80 percent of all model railroaders work in HO scale. N scale is next at 11 percent, and O scale is third most popular at 6 percent. S scale follows, miscellaneous others are next, and Z fills last place. These final scales together account for the remaining 3 percent of all model railroaders. A graphic representation of the size differences is shown in FIG. 1-3.

Prototype Item	O	S	HO	N	Z
50′ Boxcar	12½	9³/8	6⁷/8	3³/4	2³/4
Ranch House 36′ long	9	6³/4	5	2³/4	2
18′ Auto	4½	3³/8	2½	1³/8	1
2-lane Road 24′ wide	6	4½	3³/8	1³/4	1³/8
GP18 Diesel 56′ long	14	10½	7³/4	4¼	3
2-10-10-2 Mallet 121′ long	30¼	22³/4	16³/4	9¹/8	6⁵/8
Turntable 135′ diameter	33³/4	25³/8	18⁵/8	10¹/8	7³/8
Person 6′ tall	1½	1¹/8	3/4	½	3/8
Tree 65′ tall	16¼	12¼	9	4⁷/8	3½
Track 1′ Mile	110′	82³/4′	60³/4′	33′	24¹/4′

1-2   These figures will give you an idea of how scales compare to each other and to various prototypical elements.

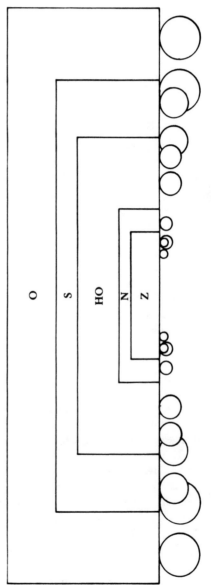

1-3 This is how standard 40-foot boxcars compare in the five most widely used model railroad scales.

How do you calculate scale? Simple. First, choose either inches or millimeters, whichever is more appropriate for the solution to your problem. To calculate the model size for a prototype size, divide it by the model ratio. Thus, a barn 40 feet long would measure 480 inches. Divide by 160 for N scale, and you'll find that a scale model of the barn should be 3 inches long. To reverse the matter and figure, for example, the prototype size of a particular piece of modeling material, multiply it by the model ratio. If you have a piece of dowel 1 inch in diameter and 1¼ inches long, and stand it on end, it could be a tank 7¼ feet in diameter and 9 feet high in HO scale—a small water tank. In Z scale it would be 18 feet 4 inches in diameter and almost 23 feet high—a fuel storage tank.

GAUGE

Along with some strange scale designations, model railroading is unique among model making hobbies by being tied to a series of *gauges*. Unfortunately, the terms "gauge" and "scale" are often used mistakenly as interchangeable to confer the same meaning; for example, an HO gauge layout, or an O gauge depot. One could perhaps speak of an N gauge freight car, but even that is stretching the point. Scale and gauge are two different things, although they must be used together, and that opens up a number of interesting possibilities.

Scale, as explained earlier, is a proportion. *Gauge,* however, is the distance between the railheads of a railroad track. In FIG. 1-4 is a cross section of a railroad track. As you can see, the wheel flanges of the cars and locomotives contact the inside edges of the rails near the rail tops, and this distance between these points is the *track gauge*. This dimension must be kept constant with only slight variations everywhere on the trackage of any particular railway system, whether that is a real railroad or a model layout. In addition, the gauge must be standardized to allow for equipment interchange from system to system.

To better understand gauge and how it applies to model railroading, it is necessary to look at prototypical gauges. In the earliest days of railroading, there was no standard and the width between rails could be whatever the railroad builder happened to like. Within a short time there came to be several "standard" gauges—in New York it was 6 feet, in most of the South it was 5 feet and, in many other areas it was 3 feet. Eventually national standards were set. In the United States, this became 4 feet 8½ inches as standardized

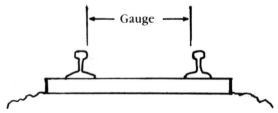

1-4   Gauge is the distance between the insides of the track rail heads, whether model or prototype.

by the Pacific Railroad Act of 1863. Western Europe and England also used this gauge early on, and Japan, China, and other countries eventually came to it. Other standard gauges were established in other countries. However, not all existing railroads converted, nor were new railroads always built to the new standards. Thus, the gauge for some Maine railroads was 2 feet, some in Canada were 42 inches, and many United States railroads remained at 3 feet or 30 inches.

With a very few exceptions, such as some tourist excursion lines, the oddball gauges are extinct in this country. Nearly every line is standard gauge and the same is true in other countries, though their dimensions might differ from ours. But in model railroading, different gauges are still very much alive, and always will be.

In model railroading, it helps to remember that "gauge" refers to track, which is the distance between the railheads and the distance between the wheel flanges of the equipment that will run on the tracks. When you see a reference to HO gauge track, for example, this means track that is manufactured to HO scale size, proportionate to prototype U.S.A. standard gauge (4 feet, 8½ inches). The actual *gauge* measures 16.5 mm. or 0.65 inches; the *scale* is still 1:87 at 3.5 mm. or 0.138 inch to the foot. S, N, and Z scales follow this pattern. To confuse the issue, O scale does not. It is not O gauge track, but rather, gauge O, which is 1¼-inch or 32-mm. gauge. This actually is the correct gauge of track for O17 scale (1:45), which hardly exists, but is conventionally used with O scale equipment. This equipment is scaled at ¼ inch to the foot, which theoretically should be Q scale, using the Q gauge track at 1³⁄₁₆-inch gauge. In any event, each of these aforementioned gauges is called *standard gauge* in model railroading.

However, not all model railroaders want to model in a standard gauge. They would prefer to pattern their layouts after one or another of the odd sized prototype gauges, or perhaps model two gauges on the same layout. Such trackage, and both the prototype and model railroad too, is termed *narrow gauge*. Narrow gauge model railroading is a great favorite among hobbyists. The prototype railroads are mostly from another era, colorful, and unusual. Rather than the very early prototype roads that appeared in any number of strange gauges, the lines typically modeled are more contemporary. These are the more uniformly sized, and readily researchable high mountain railroads of the Rockies, logging and mining railroads with unusual equipment, the Maine Two-footers, and others of similar compelling flavor and character. This desire to model railroads of a different stripe than the standard gauge roads leads to some different wrinkles in the gauge picture.

To designate a gauge narrower than the standard one for any particular scale, begin with the scale designation, always written in capital letters. Then, add the small letter "n," followed by the prototype gauge in feet. For example, a road designated HOn2½ would be modeled in HO scale but the track would be narrow and scaled to a gauge of 2½ feet. But note—while the layout as a whole is modeled to HO scale, the locomotives and the rolling stock (passenger and freight cars) are not. This equipment in prototype was, and is, anywhere from a little bit to a whole lot smaller than its standard gauge cousins. So for modeling, some narrow gauge equipment is commercially available, some must be built from scratch, and some is cobbled up from standard sized kits and parts, or modified ready-to-run factory units.

In many instances, understanding proportion is not as difficult as it sounds, because more than two dozen fortuitous coincidences between scale and gauge help out, especially with the trackage. Of course, this makes the scale to gauge relationship that much more complicated, too. Accuracy sometimes suffers, as the scale is off by one to several percentage points. When properly done, such combinations are not off scale enough to interfere with the illusion of correctly proportionate sizes. The most important of these combinations of scale size and track gauge are listed in FIG. 1-5. Other combinations are possible, but take a lot of building and rebuilding. Much of this latter kind of model making is not for model railroaders, but for makers of railroad models, for there is a big difference.

SCALE—PROS AND CONS

The purpose of this book is to explore the details of building an indoor scale model railroad layout of small size, more or less typical of what can be readily put together in an average sized house or apartment. Small size implies that the entire layout might range from coffee table top or closet size to most of a basement or garage—say, 20-by-30 feet. In fact, most small pikes fall somewhere in between these two extremes, are built entirely by one hobbyist (perhaps with family help) rather than a group or club, and usually have a single theme or focal point. No one knows for sure, but probably most home layouts cover from 40 or 50 to about 200 square feet, often in an irregular configuration. This means that from a practical standpoint, only the small scales that are well known and in common use—O, S, HO, N, and Z—are best considered, especially for a beginner's first layout. Each of them has its own advantages and disadvantages.

O scale, currently the third most popular, is marvelous to work with because of its comparatively large size. The locos and rolling stock are hefty, sturdy, and easy to manipulate. They don't fall off the rails, or rattle apart easily. Structures, scenery, and trackage, plus all the appurtenant odds and ends, are similarly easy to work with, and in most instances, extreme delicacy is not a problem. You can work with ordinary, full sized carpenter's and mechanic's tools usually. You can detail everything to a far greater degree than in the smaller scales, and you can see what you're doing while you're at it. But size is also the biggest disadvantage. You need a lot of room to establish even a

Std Gauge	Std Ratio	Subs Gauge	Subs Ratio	Proto Gauge	Gauge Designation
O	1:48	OO	1:76	36"	On3
S	1:64	HO	1:87	42"	Sn3$\frac{1}{2}$
S	1:64	TT	1:120	30"	Sn2$\frac{1}{2}$
HO	1:87	N	1:160	30"	HOn2$\frac{1}{2}$
N	1:160	Z	1:220	42"	Nn3$\frac{1}{2}$

1-5   These are the most useful scale/gauge combinations for narrow gauge modeling.

modest layout in O scale. An 8-by-10 foot space would be a bare minimum, and that won't give you much to have fun with. Another problem is cost—steam locomotives can cost several hundred dollars, and rolling stock is also expensive. In addition, the range of available products is limited and variable. Only the largest hobby shops stock O scale equipment.

S scale is considered by those who work in it to be an ideal size. They feel that it is sufficiently smaller than O scale and sufficiently larger than HO scale to cancel the major disadvantages of each. Scale accuracy and detailing possibilities are very good, and somewhat less space is needed for a layout than for O scale. This is a good scale for creative modelers who enjoy fine craft type model making. The disadvantages are a limited range of commercially available products, a necessity for scratch building or cobbling up a lot of the layout elements, relatively high cost, and an almost total lack of stock at hobby shops. The size is still substantial; you will need a minimum space of 5-by-5, or 4-by-8 feet for a very tiny layout.

HO scale is the most popular one by far, and with good reason. A huge array of products is commercially available representing most phases and eras of railroading. The comparative costs for products and materials is the lowest of all the scales. The size is small enough that a lot of model railroading can be accomplished in a modest space, but big enough to allow good scale accuracy, detailing, and realism. Many fine little layouts have been built on a ping-pong table, a smooth faced door, or a 4- by 8-foot sheet of plywood. The equipment is reasonably easy to work with and on, though mostly downsized and model making tools are needed. A good selection of factory-made locos, rolling stock, structures, and other goodies for those who want instant results is available. Also, a vast array of kits of all kinds and skill levels for model makers can be found. Hobby shops stock HO products of all sorts in some depth. This scale probably has the best all–round quality level of products and is certainly the easiest of all in which to assemble even a large, complex, and sophisticated layout of great realism and accuracy. HO has been called the happy medium of all the scales, and rightly so. Disadvantages? Yes. To some, the scale just isn't large enough to exhibit the fine detail they want; the equipment is too small to see, handle, and work on comfortably; "everybody" models in it, so it isn't exclusive enough. Others feel that the size is still too big, and they can't get enough model railroad into the space they have available.

That last opinion is responsible for N scale becoming number two in popularity. The greatest advantage of this scale is that its small size allows you to build an amazing amount of model railroad in a small space. Even a 2-by-3 foot table top will hold a respectable, but not very complex, little layout. Although small, the equipment is surprisingly sturdy and not plagued with great delicacy, and the detailing is satisfactory. Possibilities for adding detail are good. Scale accuracy suffers to some extent, but is not usually objectionable. Realism is good, and improving. A wide range of products is readily available, and that range is increasing. Hobby shops are now stocking a modest number of products, and the rest is available through mail order. There are disadvantages. The small size limits detailing and scale accuracy, and does hinder realism somewhat. The cost of locomotives and rolling stock is relatively high, and there are very few kits and almost everything, especially locomotives, is *rtr* (ready-to-run, or completely factory built). The cost of structures and miscellaneous accessories is also fairly high, and most are in kit form. Availability and range of products is nowhere near as good for the N scale as with HO scale. The small size makes manipulating the locos and cars more difficult than with the larger scales, and putting kits together or scratch building models can be a challenge. Good manual dexterity, coordination, and eyesight are needed, along with a selection of model making tools in small to miniature sizes.

Z scale has the one great advantage of being so small that a remarkably complex layout can be sandwiched into a very small space. You can build one into a suitcase, or on top of a coffee table, and a half-sheet of plywood will hold a nice layout. And, the equipment is realistic enough to be enjoyable and make a worthwhile representation of a prototypical railroad. But there are several disadvantages. One is the size, of course—a Z locomotive will rest comfortably on your thumb! The size makes the scale hard to work with and details disappear. There are no locomotive or rolling stock kits—all that equipment, as well as most accessories, is factory made or must be scratch built (which is a challenge for a watch maker). Structures, however, are supplied in kit form and must be assembled. Product range is limited and availability is sketchy, and hobby shops carry only a small amount of stock. Cost is equal to or higher than N scale. Most of the products available are patterned after European prototypes, though more American items are beginning to appear.

HO AND N SCALES

HO and N scales deserve further consideration here for several reasons. They are the two most popular scales. They have the greatest variety of products and materials most readily available "off the shelf," and from a practical standpoint they are the two most workable of all the scales. Above all, they afford the most realistic model railroading in the smallest space. They are the two scales that best fill the bill for building a small scale model railroad layout.

In terms of commercially available equipment of all sorts, HO scale definitely has the most going for it. For the modeler, a myriad of kits of all kinds is readily available, tons of in-scale scratch building supplies and detail parts, and ample opportunity for *kit-bashing* (combining parts or all of two or more like or unlike kits to develop something entirely different). A fine assortment of steam locomotives, both kit and rtr is also available. All of the time periods from the early days onward are represented. An equally good variety of diesel engines, from their inception to the present day is covered. The range of freight cars is excellent, with dozens of road names and paint schemes. There is also a good selection of passenger cars. You can model any time period you wish.

You can also model various kinds of railroads, such as logging or mining, because equipment typical of such roads is available. You can run circus trains, military trains, unit coal trains, crack passenger trains. You can easily model numerous real railroads, like the Sante Fe or the "Pennsy" or the

Union Pacific, because many model locomotives and cars are patterned after them. Several kinds of trackwork are available, and there is a tremendous range of accessories such as controls, lighting, hardware, backdrops, track-side items, and such. Detailing a layout is a joy, because you can buy so many little odds and ends like kegs, barrels, telephone boxes, stepladders, hand trucks, sawhorses, wooden reels, platform scales, and fussy little parts to add to locomotives and cars.

You can readily model various geographical flavors, too, such as the typical West (old or new), the high mountains, the desert, an Eastern urban setting, the lush, green Southland, or an ocean dockside. All of the elements needed for such schemes can be found in HO scale. Or, you can model an industrial setting, a big switching yard, a standard gauge/narrow gauge transfer point, a steel mill, a mining and reduction works area, a big-city passenger yard and station. Just about anything you want can be modeled because the necessary ingredients are readily available, or can be readily assembled.

So where does that leave the second most popular scale, N? Second best? Hardly. There is no "best" scale, nor is any one scale "better" than any another. One will probably suit your purpose or pique your curiosity more than another, that's all. You can do just about anything in N scale that you can in HO, although that might take a little more work. There is a fine complement of rolling stock and an adequate variety of both steam and diesel locomotives being manufactured, and that situation continues to improve. You can choose plenty of structures, kit and otherwise, so you can build up just about anything in that line. There is an ample selection of accessories, and no problem with electrics and electronics for control, lighting, and sound effects. The quality level of nearly all products is excellent and comparable to those in HO scale.

The HO and the N scale have two big differences to consider. The first is that the scope of your layout—the amount and variety of trackage, structures, and focal points—can be considerably larger and more complex in a given space with N scale than with HO, while at the same time the realism is maintained. In fact, you can about double the size. Put another way, an HO layout that is designed for an 8-by-16 foot space—virtually a whole small room—will fit on a 4- by 8-foot sheet of plywood in N scale. Note that this is approximate, because some modifications might have to be made depending upon the track plan and kind of scenery, required track grades and clearances, and potential access problems, but that's the rough idea.

The other big difference is that because of the smaller size of everything in N scale, you lose some of the detail and scale accuracy that is present in HO scale. That doesn't always seem to matter, because with the smaller size the detailing becomes less important (or possible) and less visible. The result is that less time and effort is needed for super-detailing, leaving more available for creating a realistic appearance through illusion and proper proportioning, along with a few other tricks. And make no mistake, despite the small size there is ample opportunity for adding detail to an N scale layout.

Another point: If there is room on hand for an average, fairly large HO scale layout, like a spare two-car garage, the Layout in N scale could be a real dandy, capable of handling the biggest steamers and 40-car trains, with a number of focal points, lots of traffic, a busy high-capacity yard, and gobs of wide-open and expansive (or tall and impressive) scenery. N is an excellent scale for modeling British and European prototype railroads and equipment, as there is a wide variety of these model products being imported.

SELECTING A SCALE

It is an excellent idea to consider all the scales before you actually select one, and an equally excellent idea to continue to monitor the other major scales with an open mind even after you do make your pick. You can learn much by adapting ideas to your own purposes. Once you do make your selection, stay with it. The scattershot approach of doing a little bit in this scale and a little more in another just to see what they're like doesn't work worth a hoot, unless at heart you are just a builder of railroad models. Consider that just one scale can, with great ease, use up all your allotted model railroad hobby money, time, attention, skills, and energy for the rest of your life. Everything in the model railroading line that you accumulate, every structure you build, freight car you assemble, locomotive you acquire, scene you model, will over time just add to your enjoyment and mastery of this intriguing hobby, provided it's all part of a master plan.

It must also be said that there is a flip side to this coin. Plans do get altered or abandoned because of unforeseen circumstances. Lifestyles change, health or financial or family circumstances take a turn, fresh opportunities arise. For those or other or perhaps no reasons in particular, some model railroaders have assembled several layouts and probably will build more. Some model in two scales at once, have abandoned one scale and turned to another, and might try yet a third someday. All these folks, so far as is known, continue to be content.

No one can tell you, nor should they, what scale to model in. This hobby is an intensely personal and personalized one, extremely subjective in the way you plan, interpret, and assemble a layout. Only you can make that first decision about scale. It must be the one that best suits *your* purposes and requirements, and at the same time fits in with any external constraints that might exist—space, cash, time, whatever.

You might find the decision to be a simple one. If you want as much railroad as possible in the space you have, N scale is the answer, or maybe even Z. If your consuming interest is in running long trains through wide open landscape, you need N scale. Want to do a lot of scratch building with considerable detail and realism? Yes, it's S. If you've got to have an offbeat logging railroad, or want a really complete layout in modest size, and/or you're not much interested in scratch building or a lot of fooling around cobbling things together, or want quick results, go HO. If super detailing and eye-filling realism is your scene, O scale or even larger is your best bet. Whatever it might be, some compelling reason might lead you to unhesitatingly select the appropriate scale.

On the other hand, making the decision might be difficult, the myriad possibilities confusing. In that case, you will need to ponder. There is no point in rushing a decision just to say you made one. If you can, visit a large, well-stocked hobby shop, preferably one that stocks several scales and perhaps has a display layout as well. This will give you a better picture of what the equipment looks like. A visit or two to a model railroad club layout is another good idea; you might also be able to view some private layouts belonging to local club members. For that matter, you could join up. And by all means read the magazines that cover the model railroading hobby, and also prototype railroads and railroading. There are several, and you can find them on any large magazine rack. Sooner or later, after enough research and browsing through the literature, you'll be able to settle upon one scale.

Keep in mind that building a model railroad layout involves several different elements. Some hobbyists enjoy all of them more or less equally. Others are primarily interested in only one or two of the elements, and all else is merely something to accomplish in order to complement their specific interests and/or complete the layout. So if kit building/collecting locomotives or freight cars, or both, is your big love and the rest is just a showcase for them, HO would be a logical choice because of the huge variety available. If you yearn to sculpt a whole range of snowcapped mountains and only need a few trains to run through tunnels and over trestles just for effect, maybe you'll get the most enjoyment out of Z scale. Some modelers just want a bit of background, maybe even of the dioramic sort, for their super-detailed locomotives; HO will work for this, but S or O might be better. If electrical, electromechanical, and electronic gadgetry is your delight, you can have a field day with the material available and/or buildable in HO scale, and almost as much fun with N scale. Either of those scales will work nicely for long stretches of hand-laid trackage and custom-built turnouts, too. And so, in some cases the scale you choose can in large measure depend upon which, if any in particular, of the several facets of model railroading you prefer to concentrate upon.

Chapter **2**

Developing the concept

*R*egardless of the scale you select, the most important part of setting up a model railroad layout lies in developing a total concept for it *before* you begin work, and even before you start to draw up plans. This exercise can spell the difference between a collection of half-baked railroad models plunked down on wandering tracks in a ramshackle and nondescript setting, and an operational, realistic, well-crafted pike. The concept itself might determine which scale would be the best for your purposes. Concept development includes consideration of about a dozen different factors. All of them deserve some thought, and some of them a little research as well.

PICK A SPOT

The first thing you need to consider is where to build your model railroad. This is always one of the greatest stumbling blocks for would-be model railroaders, yet there are numerous possibilities. Even small apartments almost always have some space available, even if not as sizable and convenient as the modeler might prefer.

Various surveys over the years have shown that somewhat more than half of all home model railroads are set up in basements. Even in a small house, a basement usually includes a sizable area that can be devoted to the hobby. Although the space might be available and overall convenience anywhere from decent to excellent, there are potential problems. Recurrent or constant dampness is the most serious, and can be disastrous for a model railroad, as well as for the tools and supplies used to build it. Mildew and mold are companion difficulties, along with the expectable rust, corrosion, and general deterioration of practically everything.

Dust can also be a serious problem, especially in an old house. Decades of accumulated coal dust, perhaps asbestos fuzz from wrapped heating pipes, rodent droppings, ordinary soil, concrete and plaster particles, brick or stone dust, sawdust—who knows what all lurks there? There are hundreds of particulates small and large that can be hazardous to your layout's health, as well as your own. The presence of radon gas in a basement is another very real threat. There is seldom much if any natural lighting in a basement, and there is the chance of interference from other basement activities or functions, like heating equipment, laundry, or firewood storage.

All of these problems can be overcome by careful prior planning. Lots of cleaning and scrub downs and perhaps repair of leaky pipes or fuel storage tanks might be in order. Walls can be waterproofed, and an exterior foundation drainage system can even be installed (expensive, but worthwhile just in the interest of upgrading the house). The layout area can be completely enclosed with new partitions, basement walls can be covered, open first floor joists can be treated to a new ceiling. You can install dehumidifying equipment or air conditioning to control the environment. Arranging decent artificial lighting is no great chore. But whatever needs to be done should be undertaken and completed *before* work begins on the layout.

About one-quarter of all home model railroads are built in spare rooms. This is an excellent situation for a layout, which thrives best with exactly the same conditions and amenities as human occupants. Temperature and humidity are reasonable and controllable, dust is no more of a problem than usual. Heating, cooling, and ventilation present no special problems, and the layout is safe from abnormal conditions and can be locked up if that is desirable.

A few layouts are built in attics. In some circumstances this works out well, especially when the space is often not suitable for most other purposes. There are potential problems, though. Excessive heat can be destructive, as can wide temperature swings. Other difficulties might include dust and dirt, lack of or too much ventilation, inconvenient access, a shortage or absence of adequate electrical circuits, and insufficient working space or headroom. As with basements, attic spaces should be renovated as necessary before a layout is begun.

Another possibility is to leave the family buggy outdoors and take over the garage. If it is an attached two car type and you only want half, use the half next to the house and install a partition down the middle to separate the stalls. This makes access and the availability of heat and electricity a bit easier. This arrangement also is likely to have problems like dust, lack of adequate heat and/or electrical circuits, an unfinished condition with no insulation or interior sheathing, a drafty overhead door, and minimal lighting. Again, rework must be undertaken before a layout is started. You might rebuild a shed or other outbuilding to house your layout and a small work area. This often entails more work than converting an attached garage, especially in installing the electrical supply and heating/cooling equipment.

One approach to the space problem that assures you of getting just what you want is to put an addition on the house. Add on a hobby room, or add on space for some other purpose and take over existing space for the layout. Another idea is to move in a trailer. There are three kinds that would work— a recreational vehicle type of travel trailer, a mobile home, or a box trailer from a tractor trailer truck. These come in various sizes and are easy enough to buy, and not terribly expensive when old and road weary. Conversion to model railroading use is no big chore. Or if you want something really classy, find yourself a full-sized railroad box car or a caboose and renovate it. The one thing you have to check on first is the zoning where the proposed unit will be parked; it might not be allowable, or might be only if you fulfill certain requirements.

Many model railroaders are not fortunate enough to have such grand and wide open spaces as basements, spare rooms, additions, or boxcars available, so their pikes are tucked away in all sorts of ingenious spots. One of the more popular ones is under a bed. The layout is on castors and is scooted out when in use, back when not. A small pike can be set up in a disused closet or pantry. Another method is to replace your dining room table with a new one that serves the same purpose, but has a lift off or hinged top (or it can be glass for an interesting effect) that covers a complete, inset layout. The same thing can be done with a coffee table. With an oversized glass topped table and a Z scale layout, you can craft an intriguing piece of furniture.

Though less satisfactory, less convenient, and a bit more work, a fold-up arrangement can be employed. One way is to make a layout in two halves that fold together and stand upright, like a roll-away bed frame. A variation is a rotatable unit that contains a different layout on each side. A better arrangement is made like a fold-up ironing board or Murphy bed—you swing it down from the wall and out into the room to use it. Of course, in the storage mode all rolling stock must be removed, and all the components must be securely anchored.

One method sometimes overlooked is shelf-type layouts. The shelves can be anywhere from 3 or 4 inches wide to a couple of feet or more and attached to the walls at any convenient height. You can arrange them in tiers or cantilever them out into the room at certain points, or set them on varying grades (angles running up or down from the horizontal), or even connect different levels with spirals.

FIND THE RIGHT SIZE

As you search out a location for your model railroad, keep in mind that the layout cannot fill all of the available space unless that space is quite small. This depends upon the scale chosen and its working relationship to the space. You need to be able to reach everything on and probably under the layout (wiring and such), and you need to be able to move and work around it in order to build it in the first place and maintain it later. Don't paint yourself into a corner.

There's no theoretical maximum layout size for any scale, but there is a practical maximum. There are logical constraints for a home layout that will primarily be built and operated by one person. A common mistake among beginners is in starting a layout that is much too big in size, in track, wiring, controls, or scenery complexity, of cost in dollars or time, in difficulty of maintenance, or all of the above. Instead of a grandiose starting plan that will soon fail and impress no one, adopt a small plan that is expandable. Know that you will be able to afford the time and the money needed to complete it. Keep it small enough that you can see all parts of it from any spot around it for successful operating. Keep the size easy to maintain and work with, as even a small layout can be made incredibly complex.

There is a practical minimum size, too, for each scale. Rather than building a layout in the smallest possible size for a given scale (which wouldn't be much of a layout), go to a smaller scale for more railroading in the same space. The actual minimum size layout for any particular scale can be made complete and operational, but is so limited in scope it is likely to prove a disappointment soon enough. The exception to this is if you want a layout that is essentially a diorama, more of a scenic representation or showcase display such as one sees in a museum, rather than a conventional operating layout.

When assessing the potential size of your layout, keep in mind that the effective size does not necessarily equal the total available square footage of your chosen location. There are several possible reasons for that. First, you must be able to reach all parts of the layout well enough to work on the scenery, replace a derailed car, hook up some wiring, or whatever. The layout can measure no more than about 3 feet deep at any point when accessible only from the front, double that if accessible from the rear as well. This in turn means that in larger sizes, layouts have to be configured in assorted peninsulas and connecting sections, leaving walking/working room around them; this obviously takes up part of the allotted space in the layout location.

An alternative method (or it can be used in addition) is to create access holes at strategic points in the layout, either permanently open or covered with sections of removable scenery. This takes up proportionately more room as the scale grows smaller, and again decreases the amount of usable space. Yet another method fairly common to medium-size layouts is to make a rectangular framework that is perhaps 3 feet wide all around and maybe has a few outcrops here and there, with the entire middle area open as the walking/working space. Only about half the available space can be devoted to the layout itself.

On the other hand, a given layout area can also be expanded beyond what appears at first glance to be there. The tendency is to think of a layout spread over the available area in one plane. But by constructing long-run grades you can elevate parts of your trackwork to two or more merging levels, creating under and overpasses, trestle and bridge arrangements, and hidden trackage beneath. On a small layout, the same can be accomplished by spiraling tracks. Or, on a shelf or combination platform-shelf layout, you can construct the layout on two or more discrete levels, entirely separate from one another and even with different scenery and themes. All of these methods expand the railroad into a "third dimension" and increase the effective size of the layout. When space is at a premium, such arrangements can be worthwhile.

MAKE THE MOST OF THE SPACE

Making the most of the space that you have available is a tricky business. It requires some thought, and the use of some common sense and judgement. The object is to get as much model railroad into a given space as you can. But at the same time you have to strive for realism, trouble free operating, and ease of construction now and maintenance later.

One common mistake is to cram too much trackwork into the layout, using tight curve radii and sharp turnouts. This makes a crowded and odd-looking arrangement that just doesn't feel right and generates all kinds of operating difficulties. Too much scenery, or too many disparate scenery elements, is another common difficulty—the scenery overpowers the rest of the layout and looks unreal. Too many focal points can also destroy the illusion of realism. All of the planned elements of the layout must be in balance, or the overall appearance, and perhaps the operating quality as well, will be unsatisfactory.

For model railroaders who have limited space to begin with, making the most of what is available is important, and can mean the difference between having a layout or not. Part of this process involves using your imagination and ingenuity in selecting the layout location—you need the most convenient spot you can find that is workable, has the necessary amenities like heat, light, and power, and contains the greatest amount of accessible layout area. Then you can augment this by means of one or more of the space enhancing systems just mentioned.

Some unusual possibilities also might be present. For example, perhaps you can "tunnel" through a partition wall from a small space on one side to a second one on the other. This would enlarge the railroad, present a built-in chance for tunneling through a mountain, and give you the opportunity to incorporate two entirely different and visually separated scenic or focal arrangements, one on each side of the wall. Or, maybe you could run from one area to another by means of a narrow shelf line to clear some serious obstacle like the washing machine. You might occupy a corner with a small table top arrangement and take off along both walls with shelves. Get away from thinking in terms of plain squares or rectangles, too. Think instead of corner triangles, trapezoids, curvilinear and free-form flowing boundaries, combinations of shapes, or no particular shape at all. As long as there's some area of some sort, you can design a layout to suit.

PROTOTYPES AND REALISM

You can build a model railroad layout if you don't know or even care much about real railroads. All you have to do is follow a set of instructions for building some particular model railroad, rather like putting together a big kit whose parts you have to accumulate separately. It will be prototypical and realistic to whatever degree its designer made it, and no concern of yours.

But after all, model railroads are based upon the real thing, as they stem from prototypes. Most model railroaders find it difficult to divorce models entirely from prototypes. They want at least a reasonable degree of realism. Many want much more than that—to a high degree—and many more find themselves digging into railroad history and lore and finding it colorful and fascinating. Others study the ways in which modern railroads operate, their control systems, or their engineering. Most model railroaders embrace prototypical railroading at least to some extent, and that makes sense. You'd be unlikely to make all your model trees purple and the same height, lay orange roadways, and use simulated brick for house roofs. You'd copy the real things you find around you, and strive for some reasonably realistic appearance. When building your layout, you'll be using models and materials and even methods that are based largely on prototypes.

How much realism must a layout have? How closely should the models follow the prototypes? How much license can we take as we assemble a pike? There are no hard and fast rules. Total realism, total reproduction in miniature of every prototype detail, is impossible. As you'll discover as you get deeper into this hobby, there is much that is way out of scale, or glossed over, much that is rearranged and redimensioned to better suit practical manufacturing and modeling demands. The argument over just how precise and faithful to the real world all your modeling must be, or should be, will carry on until the final whistle blows. The degree of precision is immaterial. The scrutiny of minutiae can easily reach the point of absurdity. You cannot recreate the Union Pacific or the New York Central—what you seek is agreeable substance and good flavor in a miniature package.

A model railroad, to be successful, must be in all senses believable. To achieve that, its concept should be well and fully developed to your satisfaction. The layout should create an illusion of realism and be patterned after the real world. The scenes, the detailing, the settings, and the operating patterns, should be logical and harmonious and have some basis in fact, even if they are a little tenuous. It should be prototypical—but in the real world you can find precedence for all manner of strange and wondrous things. The degree of realism you require for your own satisfaction is something you'll have to settle upon for yourself. No one else can establish those bounds.

THE ROLE OF RESEARCH

The word "research" gives some folks the willies, but it's really not all that bad. Besides being necessarily informative, research can be fun. In order to pattern your model railroad after prototypical equipment, operation, scenery, and all the rest, you first need to learn about the prototypes. Thus, research. There's no other way. If you're not careful, you'll find yourself hooked. I strongly recommend that you dig into this phase before you start laying too many plans, because the chances are excellent that you will run across something, somewhere, that will give you an urge to model a particular era, railroad, industry, kind of operation, or geographic location.

Researching the model market will show what's available that will fit in with your plans, and also give you some fresh ideas. Visit a newstand and pick up the latest copies of the magazines dealing with model railroading. Peruse the advertisements and order up catalogs and brochures from all the dealers and manufacturers whose wares look interesting. At the same time, go through the articles and columns in the magazines as they are always loaded with product information, and you can see what other modelers are doing. Probably you will want to subscribe to one or more of these magazines, because they are invaluable sources of information of all kinds. They will be immensely helpful to you in numerous ways, and will spark a good many ideas. You will also see several how-to booklets advertised on various facets of model railroading, like wiring, building plastic models, and making scenery. You will find these to be worthwhile additions to your reference collection. Hang onto any published material you feel might be of help to you sometime. Clip out and file articles and stockpile books and magazines and catalogs. The information they contain can prove mighty helpful time after time and seldom becomes outdated.

Continue your research in the model area by visiting hobby shops. Bigger ones might have an operating layout that you can look over. All of them have products, supplies, tools, and literature that you can ponder. This activity will give you a much better feel for what the hobby involves and what it consists of than just reading about it or looking at pictures ever will. If you can, visit a model railroad club when they have an operating session. Also, consider joining the NMRA (National Model Railroading Association) as there are numerous benefits to be gained, including access to technical standards and information. This organization has local chapters, and you might also consider joining a local model railroading club. The exchange of information and ideas, not to mention the plain ol' fun you can have and friends you can make, makes this well worthwhile.

Prototype research is a different matter. If present-day railroading is your interest, observing the real thing in action is in order. Watch and photograph trains in yards and on highlines, visit stations, take train rides, watch freight cars being humped and trains made up, and investigate all the other aspects of modern railroading. You must be prudent, however. All railroad property is private, and all railroads are extremely sensitive to trespass—they don't condone it, and they don't hesitate to lower the boom on transgressors of any sort, whatever their excuses. They don't want folks poking around, because it can be very dangerous. Do your observing from safe and nonrailroad vantage points, or get permission. This is often possible, especially if a model railroad club is doing the asking.

Research that involves aspects of prototype railroading more than a few years old has to be done by consulting books, magazines, films, and similar sources. These sources abound, covering all kinds of railroading, hundreds of different railroad lines, and all parts of the world. Books currently in print can be found at, or ordered through, local bookstores, and many of them are advertised in the model railroading magazines. Several periodicals are devoted to prototype railroading, and these are very helpful. Your local library will have a lot of information, especially on those railroads that form a part of the history of your area or state. There are also "rail fan" clubs that are excellent sources of information, and rail excursions and photo opportunities are always fun and worthwhile. Once you get started in researching, you'll find that one thing leads to another and trails go off in all directions.

Research, for most hobbyists, becomes an important part of the hobby, though some consider it just to be a matter of satisfying their casual curiosity or filling in a few missing details. Once you've gathered enough background data, you can finish developing the concept for your layout. But gathering data will probably go on for as long as you're interested in railroading, especially if you are a history buff as well. "Railroadiana" is endlessly varied and fascinating.

PICK A TIME FRAME

One of the first matters to settle is the time setting you want to model. Prototype railroading, and hence model railroading, is broken into several periods. The exact dates vary according to which authority you consult, but the
periods merge gradually from one to the next and overlap a lot so that's not
crucial. The total span is 150 years or so, and there has been a host of changes
over that time. Your chore is to make sure that the railroad equipment, structures, details, and other elements of your layout are in keeping with your
chosen time period. American railroad eras, consolidated and condensed for
model railroading purposes, are as follows:

1825–1850, the beginnings. Cooper's *Tom Thumb* locomotive went to
work on the Baltimore & Ohio in 1830, the first locomotive headlights appeared in 1840, the first milk train was in use in 1841 by the Erie R.R., the
first 60 mph run was in 1848, and 9020 miles of railroad were in operation
by 1850. Very little commercial material is available for the hobbyist from
this period.

1851–1900, development toward standard railroading. First Mogul (2–
6–0) locomotive in 1863, the first Consolidation (2–8–0) in 1866, the first
Decapod (2–10–0) in 1867, the first Pacific (4–6–2) in 1893, and the first
Atlantic (4–4–2) in 1895. Many major advances were made during this period, such as air brakes, standardizing the track gauge, and automatic couplers. By 1900, 193,000 miles of railroad were in operation. The latter part of
this period is popular for modeling and a fair amount of equipment is available. Numerous mining, logging, and quarrying railroads were built during
this period, as well as many of the historic main-line railroads, in both standard and narrow gauges.

1901–1920, further improvements and standardization. First Prairie (2–
6–2) locomotive built in 1901, the first Santa Fe (2–10–2) in 1902, the first
domestic Mikado (2–8–2) in 1903, the first Mountain (4–8–2) in 1911, radio
communication first used in 1914, and rail mileage peaked at 254,000 in
1916. In modeling, this is a bit of an interim period, though plenty of equipment and material is available. But it seems to merge with the next era.

1921–1945, often called the "golden age of steam" or the "standard era."
First Berkshire (2–8–4) used in 1925, the first Hudson (4–6–4) and first
Northern (4–8–4) in 1927, the first diesel-powered streamliner passenger
trains appeared, the first Challenger (4–6–6–4) in 1936, the Pullman room-
ette sleeping cars appeared in 1937, the last Heisler steam locomotive was
built in 1941, the first Alco RS–1 diesel road switcher was used in 1941, the
first dome passenger car was deployed in 1945, and the last Shay locomotive
was built in 1945. This is a very popular period for modeling, with a wide
array of products available. A layout can concentrate on the best aspects of
the glory days of steam, or combine the phasing out of steam with the beginnings of the diesel era.

1946–1960, or about 1940–1955, the beginnings of the diesel and the
modern period. First Alco RS–2 and FA–1 diesels came off the line in 1946, the
last steam locomotives built by Baldwin and by Lima were delivered in 1949,
the Rio Grande Southern was abandoned in 1951, the last domestic steam

locomotive was built in the U. S. in 1953, the second generation diesels appeared in 1958, and the last regular steam passenger service ended in 1960. This is also a popular modeling period, with much equipment available. Layouts generally feature diesels of the period and little steam, and the more modern cars and equipment.

1955 or 1960 to the present, the modern age. Numerous models of diesel locomotives introduced through the entire period. Amtrak (1971) and Conrail (1976) emerged; many specialized freight cars appeared; the piggyback, container, and unit trains came into widespread use; and cabooses begin to disappear. This is perhaps the most popular period for model railroading, with a great array of products available and prototype information easy to come by.

When you select a time for your layout, it's best to settle upon a span of years, such as "around 1940–45," or "somewhere in the '20s," rather than a specific time like "May of 1961," period. This gives you more leeway and better assurance that the details you model will be true to the time frame. When you model a later period, you can use almost everything that would have appeared in an earlier period and which would still be around, within reason and the realm of common sense. Your 1945–1950 pike would have steam locos and could also have early diesels, a 1934 Ford dump truck would be a little unusual but explainable and a '47 Chevy convertible would be just fine. You would not have a stagecoach at the station, a very early model of automobile would be unlikely, and the main highways would not be made of dirt.

When you model any period other than the present, you have to be careful not to have anything on the layout that actually did not appear until a later date. It's easy to get tripped up, and there's always a purist around somewhere to spot the fault. Got an EMD SD7 on that 1945–1950 layout? Sorry, that came out in 1952. Some of your freight cars have lettering that says "rblt 7–55?" There's trouble. Is the paint scheme on that box car really the one the D&RGW used before 1950? Didn't that type of streetlight come into use around 1960? And so on.

Understand, that with some thought and imagination, you can justify, or at least rationalize, a lot of seemingly peculiar circumstances. If you are strictly modeling a prototype line and location, you have to remain faithful to the original. Otherwise, you can take some liberties. For example, there are still some 1930s–vintage vehicles rattling around in daily service. Some small railroads continued to use steam locomotives long after the big lines had gone wholly diesel. Theoretically, they still could be in use today. In fact, a number of excursion lines do use steam for tourist passenger use. Freight cars dating back to the turn of the century remained in service for 50 years or more—some might still be somewhere, or at least could be if you stretch the point a little and figure out an excuse for it.

The business of just what goes with what, and which details are correct in time-frame and which are not, can be confusing and sometimes you can't find a good solid answer. Research will help, and a plausible cover story will handle the rest, assuming you don't make a glaring error.

PICK A RAILROAD TYPE

There are three modeling and overall concept possibilities. You can follow, more or less faithfully, a prototype railroad, or a part of one. For example, a section of the Boston & Maine. Or you can use a prototype on part of the layout and an imaginary railroad on another part. For example, the Pine Tree Logging Co. line meeting the Union Pacific at a junction point. Or you can model in prototypical fashion an entirely fictitious railroad. For example, the Cinnamon Hill & Snowblind, a local coal, livestock, and general freight hauler.

In any of these three modes, you can model any of several different types of railroads. There are numerous prototype railroads both past and present in those types, that you can model prototypically or just use as a general guide. Definitions of the types vary somewhat, but in general they are:

- A *main line* or *heavy main line,* which is a principal, large railroad covering great stretches of country, like the Union Pacific or the Baltimore & Ohio.

- A *branch line,* which is a relatively short offshoot from a larger or main line railroad. Sometimes owned by and having the same name as the main line, they are sometimes different entirely. The branch often provided the same freight and passenger service as the rest of the line, but it also might have been built for a specific purpose, such as hauling coal. A branch line usually joins the main line at an *interchange yard.* Thus, the Creede branch of the Denver & Rio Grande Western runs from Alamosa to Creede, Colorado.

- A *bridge line,* which is a small railroad that connects two (or more) major railroads at interchange yards located in two cities a short distance apart. An example would be the Atlanta & West Point, linking the Southern in Atlanta with the Western Railway of Alabama in West Point.

- A *belt line,* which is a small line that runs around a metropolitan area and/or a crowded terminal area and expedites the exchange of freight cars between the major lines. The Denver Circle Rail Road set out to do this around Denver in 1880, but failed. There have been many other prototypes.

- A *terminal line,* which is a railroad devoted to switching cars, mostly freight but some passenger as well, between a number of main line roads in a large terminal area. One of the largest prototypes is the Terminal Railroad Association of St. Louis, while the Manufacturer's Junction Railway is an example of a small one.

- A *short line,* which is a relatively small, general purpose railroad hauling both passengers and mixed freight, usually generating and terminating its own traffic. There are many examples, such as the Bangor & Aroostook or the Silverton Northern. Probably every state in the country has or has had at least one.

- A *switching line,* which is like a terminal railroad only more so. It switches freight cars back and forth from point to point, typically between docks, piers, shipyards, and associated warehouses and other facilities. The Hoboken Shore Railroad is one such example. A variation is an *industrial switching line,* which centers upon a large group of industrial operations.

- An *industrial line,* which operates entirely within the physical confines of one industry, like a steel mill, shuffling equipment and materials around and about. The Coors Brewing Company Railroad is one prototype, the Colorado Fuel & Iron line is another.

- A *specialty line,* which can be a small, short railroad with no connection to any other, or a branch or short line connecting at only one point to another road. Specialty lines of many kinds abound throughout railroad history in all parts of the country. They were usually built specifically to transport a particular commodity from its source. In Colorado, for example, the Crystal River & San Juan hauled marble; the Rio Grande & Pagosa Springs hauled lumber; the Little Book Cliff hauled coal, the Great Western hauled sugar beets; the Noland Land & Transfer hauled sandstone; the Gilpin hauled gold and silver ore; and the Durango & Silverton hauled tourists (and still does).

These categories overlap, and are a bit fuzzy at the edges, and combinations and variations are both possible and acceptable. Modeling a main line may mean staying with one road name on motive power and passenger cars unless another road has trackage rights, so freight cars can be mixed. A branch line legitimately introduces at least one more road name at the interchange yard, a bridge line can sport at least two road names. Belt lines open lots of name-mixing possibilities. Terminal and switching lines mean one road name and any suitable names on freight cars. Industrial lines are largely in-house operations with one name, usually that of the industry. Branch and short lines can have their own names and meet with at least one other road. Specialty lines have their own names and might or might not connect with one or more other roads. These last three types are probably the most popular since they offer a great deal of flexibility and lend themselves well to modeling, especially if the entire line is to be fictitious, or if a layout has an imaginary railroad but needs an excuse for introducing some prototypical motive power. Connection of the road at some point with a main line or even another branch line is all that's needed. An example is the Sundance Mine Railway coming down the hill to the Ophir yard where it meets the Rio Grande Southern, and maybe the Silver Trail, Argo & Pacific as well.

PICK A LOCALE

In order to model the scenery and topography on your layout with realism, you need to select a specific geographic location. If you can choose one you're familiar with and/or can visit easily, so much the better. You'll have less trouble creating a believable replica. If that's not possible, you will have to depend upon photographs, preferably in color. That means research again, in order to learn about the local vegetation, geology, topography, or whatever is needed.

If you model a prototype road, you'll necessarily model the scenery and topography where the railroad is located, or the section that's of interest to you. Some kinds of specialty lines demand certain kinds of locations. A narrow gauge mining road, for example, would typically be set in the high mountains. A coal-hauling line, on the other hand, could be placed in any kind of countryside, from high mountains to desert's edge. A logging road obviously needs some forest to work with, and that could be mountainous country or rolling hills. A gravel hauler is usually found in a river valley. With an industrial road the ground would be more or less flat and the surroundings consist mostly of the trappings of the industry itself—perhaps not even a tree to be seen. A switching line running between numerous industries could be on several levels but would be modeled mostly with buildings, roads, and equipment.

If you model an imaginary line, you can choose whatever geographical and topographical setting you prefer and fit the concept of the railroad to that setting. If you're intent upon craggy mountains, work out what kind of railroad might fit in such a spot that you'd like to model. For example, you might choose the Colorado Midland through the Hagerman Tunnel. Or you can work out the other details first and suit the location to them. If you want lots of switching possibilities and you have some boat models, combine them with a waterfront shipping setup. For an example, use the Oakland, California waterfront arrangement. How you put it all together really doesn't matter much, just that the overall effect is realistic and believable. Keep in mind that the topography can work for you. Industrial, commercial, and urban settings reinforce the purpose of that type of railroad. Mountains give you something to tunnel through, set trestles across, and hide trackage under. Rolling hills or open plains leave everything in view, which can be either good or bad, and make the setting seem more expansive. Whatever area you choose, model it accurately—this will do more for the realistic impression the overall layout conveys than any other single element.

PICK A SEASON

Summer seems to be automatically chosen as the seasonal setting, and maybe that alone is good enough reason to pick another. Summer is indeed the easiest to model because most foliage and vegetation materials come in various shades of green, and bare-branched deciduous trees and shrubs are difficult to model. Most models of human figures are in warm-weather attire, too. Almost everything in the model world seems to be more in tune with summer than any other season.

The early to mid-fall season, however, is only marginally harder to model. This allows the opportunity for a lot of bright colors in the vegetation, and perks up the layout considerably. Some colored material is available, and painting or dying as necessary is not that difficult a chore. The colors, of course, should be prototypical of the location. Early fall is an interesting time of year to model if your layout setting is mountainous with lower elevation valleys. At the lowest elevation, late summer prevails and almost everything is dark green, with some light browns and golds in the shrubbery and grasses, maybe a sprinkling of yellows in the shrubs. As the elevation increases, the greens gradually diminish and are increasingly supplanted by reds, rust, yellows, and golds. This in turn gradually fades and becomes sere brown toward timberline, and the mountain peaks are already coated with snow.

The late fall to early winter period is seldom modeled, though there is no special reason that it could not be. It is a bit cheerless, though, and it's difficult to make bare-branched deciduous trees and shrubs look realistic; conifers present no problems. The ground should appear relatively barren, and this too is not easy to model with good effect. There is little color save for browns, grays, and black; everything is earth tone. Rivers and creeks in many areas are running low, maybe almost dry, irrigation canals and ditches are empty, and reservoirs are drawn down to low levels. Of course, much depends upon the geographic location, too—late fall in Florida looks a lot different than in Vermont.

Early spring is another period that is not often selected, but could be to good advantage. At this time the greens of the foliage are bright and delicate, tending toward the yellows, and the early flowering shrubs and trees, like the forsythia and crabapples, are in contrastingly brilliant full bloom. Streams and rivers are in full spate, and there is an opportunity here to model high spring snow-melt runoff, or perhaps spring flooding and washouts.

Full winter layouts are interesting but uncommon. This is partly because real looking snow and snow scenes are not as easy to model as they appear to be. There are some good techniques that make the job easier. Bare-branched deciduous trees and shrubs are needed to some extent, but usual practice is to plant a lot of conifers, which take very nicely to a "snow" cover and give excellent color contrast. Plows and other winter equipment can be modeled to good effect; figures might have to be repainted in some fashion to represent heavy outdoor clothing. Modeling ice and icicles is tricky but the results can be interesting and effective.

PICK A NAME

Not just any name will do. A lot of model railroaders have a lot of fun with this phase of the planning. If you are modeling prototypically, then of course you will use the name of the railroad you are modeling, along with whatever slogan, herald, and lettering style were in actual use by the road at the time. But if you are modeling a fictitious line, you've got to dream up a name for it.

The straightforward approach is probably the most common, using place-names of cities or towns served, or the states where the line supposedly runs, sometimes with a compass direction or an ocean thrown in. Thus, the Salt Lake & Western, the Syracuse, Albany & Atlantic, the Clarkville & Mayfield, or the Nebraska & Iowa. Some folks like a little more flair and might select some real but more unusual names. Like the Truth or Consequences & Tuba City, or the Tincup, Horse Tooth, & Wagon Wheel Gap, or the Nesowadnahunk, Mooselookmeguntic & Passadumkeag. Names that fit the character or activity of the region are often used, too, like the Silver Creek & Goldfield, or the Appleton and Peach Valley, or the Coaldale and Newcastle.

Some folks like puns or double meaning names, and you'll see a lot of them on model railroads, some of them on very well known layouts. Thus, the Search & Rescue, the Ouvre & Oute, the Upson Downes & Slovenly, the Alrite & Gudenov, and the Donner & Blitzen. Such layouts usually sport towns, industries, valleys, mountains, and practically everything else with funky names as well, like Allshot Auto Repair or Squeamish Town or Molehill Mountain.

You can also make your road name spell something out, especially if you include the R. R. or Ry. (standing for railroad or railway, often just RR and RY) that commonly follows road names, and that can suggest a slogan or herald as well. For example, the Bridgeton, Eden & Elmhurst would be the BE&E or the "Bee Line," with a bumblebee in a circle as a herald. The Holley, Union & Madison would be the HU&MRR, or the "Hummer Line," with a hummingbird as a herald. The Silver Notch, Ophir & Western (SNO&W) could have "The Snow Belt" as a slogan and a snowflake for a herald. The G&LORY (try fitting your own name) would be called "The Glory Road" and maybe have a waving American flag or a sunburst for a herald.

Some model railroaders like to have a road name the initials of which form an acronym for a definition, usually facetious or even scornful, of the road itself. This was common enough among real railroads. The Toronto, Hamilton & Buffalo, for example, was known as the "To Hell & Back." The Baltimore & Ohio was the "Beefsteak & Onions," the Nevada County Narrow Gauge the "Never Come, Never Go," and the Georgia & Florida was the "God-Forgotten." The Boston & Maine was the "Busted & Mined," the Dubuque & Dakota was the "Damned Doubtful," and the Waco, Beaumont, Trinity & Sabine was called, if you can believe it, the "Wobblety, Bobblety, Turnover & Stop." And that's hard to top.

One more point about names, with which you can play all kinds of games. It's a good idea to name everything of consequence on your layout. Why? Because, apart from being fun (if you enjoy that sort of thing), it makes the layout more real and gives credence to the whole affair. Name your main mountains, ridges, parks, valleys, gulches, washes, rivers and creeks. Put some numbers on your state highways and country roads, preferably on little signs. Erect some billboards, put nameboards on your industrial and commercial buildings, even the stores if you can. You're building a whole new little world.

PICK A REASON

A real railroad, and hence a model railroad, has to have a reason for its existence. It has to have a purpose, some circumstance that caused it to be built and allows it to earn sufficient revenues to continue operating. If you plan to model a prototype line, its reason for existence is your model's as well. In that case, you will probably want to do some research to uncover the history of the line up to the time period you are modeling. For a fictitious model road, you need some fictitious but plausible reasons.

Railroads make money in two ways; hauling freight, and in the earlier days, hauling passengers. Passenger service could still be a valid reason today, if you choose to develop something after the manner of the Durango & Silverton or the Toltec & Los Cumbres tourist excursion lines. As for freight, the possibilities are innumerable. Your line could handle all sorts of mixed freight, including machinery, livestock, vehicles or farm equipment, raw materials like ores or limestone or oil, agricultural products like wheat or corn, perhaps steel—whatever needs to be picked up and/or dropped off along the right of way.

Many lines hauled general freight as a matter of course—whatever was delivered to the freight stations or could be readily picked up at various industrial, agricultural, or commercial stops—but they made a large part of their revenues hauling one or two or three bulk commodities, often seasonally. Sheep and cattle might go out to summer range in spring, back to market or winter range in fall, for example. In the meantime, the line would haul some sandstone, coal, or perhaps wheat at harvest time. Or the principal revenue source would be iron ore, cement, or something else, supplemented by one or two other commodities, and helped out in between with a little general freight and maybe a passenger train or two, or even an occasional single passenger car and maybe a mail contract.

The switching, terminal, and belt lines made their money by providing a service for other railroads, operating under some sort of contract to be paid for shuffling cars around. Bridge lines operated much the same way, but might have some of their own freight-hauling revenue sources along the route. The specialty lines usually got most or all of their revenues from hauling one or sometimes two specific commodities. Chief among these are coal, precious metal ores, copper, iron and other ores, logs, stone of several sorts, and agricultural products. Industrial lines are not revenue producing, but rather a "cost-of-doing-business" item for the parent company.

PICK SOME POINTS OF INTEREST

Every model railroad layout has to have a number of points of interest. There are two kinds, the scenic features and the points the railroad serves. The former are the elements that afford visual interest and impact and add strong realism. The latter are the revenue producing stops for the railroad, and the elements that provide purpose for the action and afford the operating possibilities.

If you model a prototype line, the scenic features you select should best represent one or a select few of the most dramatic, or most interesting, or most obvious (most something-or-other, at least), of those on the section of the prototype that you are modeling. If the line is fictional and the setting of your own choosing, you have carte blanche within the constraints of what might actually exist in that setting. So you might have a spectacular waterfall, a huge gorge, overhanging cliffs, a pastoral valley, a towering snow capped crag, or a complete steel mill. A steel mill as scenery? Sure, or any other industry, as a compelling background focal point, a backdrop area, even the whole scene in an industrial setting.

The points to be served by a model following a prototype should be one or several of those that actually do or did exist. Most layouts, however, do take some liberties with exactly how and where they are located, their relative size, or other aspects, to make the modeling possibilities more manageable. On a fictional railroad, the points are those that provide the railroads reason for existence. Along with towns and both passenger and freight stations, these would be such items as quarries or mines of various kinds, logging camps and sawmills, stockyards or corrals, a meatpacking plant, scrapyards, all kinds of commercial enterprises, light and heavy industries, feed mills or grain silos, warehouses, tank farms—you name it.

Thoughtful selection of these elements and integrating them for maximum effect goes a long way toward making a layout an interesting one to work on and to operate.

PICK AN OPERATING MODE

Sooner or later you are going to actually operate trains on your layout. But now is the time to give some thought to what kind of trains, and how you'd most like to run them. Some model railroaders are only interested in prototypical operation and delve into the matter with zeal, running everything with precision and by timetables in a lifelike manner. But on a small layout with only one or two trains running at any one time and only one, maybe two operators, this is difficult. For many model railroaders, the operating is only part of the fun and just how that is done is not of great consequence.

Essentially there are three ways to run model trains. One is continuous, relatively high speed, mainline type of operation. There are few stops and minimum layovers, with not much switching. Double track or single lines with a lot of passing sidings are usual, on level terrain or with just a few mild grades. There might or might not be any short-train, slow, local freight/passenger operation on the layout. The second way is branch line type operation, mostly on single tracks with frequent stops and a lot of puttering around at industries, shuffling cars around, and some yardwork as well. Short freights, mixed consists, smaller and different kinds of motive power, and a wide assortment of rolling stock are common characteristics. The third way is strictly switching, with many spurs and sidings to numerous industries for a lot of car shuffling, and/or large yards for the same purpose. The larger the layout, the easier it is to combine all three ways, but a certain amount of each can be accomplished even on a small layout if the design is carefully thought out.

The kinds of trains you like best will make a difference in how you plan and operate your layout, too. For example, passenger trains come in three flavors. The *through* trains, the crack mainline, high speed, long distance ones, including the streamliners, make few and short stops with virtually no switching. The *accommodation* trains, which include mail cars, have fewer cars per train, make long stops, switch frequently, and make slower speed and shorter runs. And there are *local* trains, which are short haul, slow, stop a lot, switch a lot, and are usually only one to four cars long.

Likewise, there are several kinds of freight trains. The *drags* are long, slow moving, heavy, and usually made up mostly (but not entirely) of one kind of car. Hardly any switching takes place except some at terminals. The *unit* trains can be short or long, but have only one kind of car, usually hopper and usually intended for one purpose, like coal-hauling. Big main line engines do the work and there is no switching. The *general merchandise* freights are long haul, variable length, and fast, with big main line motive power and a full mix of car types. Little or no switching takes place except a little in large terminals. *Local* freights are short, made up of any kind of cars appropriate to the industries served, headed by a variety of locomotives, with frequent stops and a lot of switching and shuffling. The *mixed trains* are very short local freights with a passenger coach or combination tacked on.

For small home layouts, the locals and mixed trains are the ones most commonly run and are usually the most appropriate because of space constraints. But unit trains if not too long, and high speed express passenger streamliners can make effective appearances, too, if the trackwork is well designed.

MAKE A LITTLE HISTORY

If you're modeling a prototype railroad, the history of that road from inception to present day is real and documented. It exists. Dozens of books have been written about the big lines, like the Santa Fe and the Pennsy and the Union Pacific, and with enough research you can even uncover most of the details of even the little, obscure, old lines like the Fort Dodge & Fort Ridgeley or the Kansas City, Mexico & Orient. If your railroad is a fictitious one, it doesn't have a history. You'll have to dream one up. You don't really *have* to, but it's part of the fun. This helps make the whole scheme much more realistic to you, and also to whomever you're explaining the layout. If there's a story, it's much easier to keep all the elements of the layout straight and in good relationship, and it's amazing how many plausible reasons, rationalizations, and justifications you can thereby dream up and offer in defense of some of the strange things you might be modeling. The history becomes a vital part of the concept and of the layout itself. You can make this history as long and complex as you wish and it's a good idea to actually write it out for continued reference, so you don't forget and cross yourself up on details. But even a short tale will suffice. Something like this . . .

Lyman Mason was heartily sick of working on his father's small farm in western Kentucky, and when the opportunity arose it didn't take him long to head West. Silver and gold were there for the taking, so he heard, out in Colorado, and he wanted one or the other. Or both, and as much as he could get. Though the search was difficult and long, in the fall of 1882 he found what he sought.

Mason's claim, in the high mountains of the southwestern part of Colorado, was located on Mt. Emerald near the side of a narrow ravine, later named Stewpot Gulch, and proved to be rich beyond his greatest expectations in silver. There was nothing around when he arrived but wind gnarled trees, ice coated rocks, and a few Ute Indians. But by the time his mines, the Glacier, the Lucky Boy #1, and the Renegade, were all churning out silver ore at a great rate there were other mines in the area producing well. The Argent Mining District turned out to be unholy rich. A few miles away, down the gulch and over Buckshot Pass into the Hell Roaring Valley, the town of Paradox sprang up. A typical wide open, hell-bent-for-leather mining town at first, over the course of a few years it settled down into a respectable and growing community of varied commercial interests.

In order to get his ores to market in the early days, Mason had to have it hauled out by wagon, a slow, difficult, and expensive proposition. Not a man to accept matters as they stood, he determined that if he built a smelter in Paradox, and then built a railroad to haul to it not only the ore from his own mines but also from all the others in the district, he could greatly increase his profits. Within a short time, the Mason Mining Company railroad was in operation, carrying ores of several kinds down from the high country and hauling coal, machinery, and supplies back up to the mines. The plan was so successful that Mason and a couple of his cronies extended the rails further down Coyote Creek Valley to the growing town of Slickrock, and in 1888 the Slickrock & Paradox Railway was born.

But Mason fell into the same trap as many another Silver Baron. He allowed his arrogance and greed to overwhelm his good sense. With a seemingly captive freight market, plentiful and cheap labor, and unlimited prospects for the future, Mason rode roughshod in all directions. The S&P, now being called the "Slickfox & Profitbox," was charging outrageous freight rates while keeping expenditures at the lowest possible level. The line was being milked. Meanwhile, the Silver Crash of '93 loomed nearer and nearer.

When the Crash came, the market for silver evaporated. The silver mines were idled almost overnight, men were laid off, and machinery shut down. Revenues plummeted on the S&P, which by now was being called the "Slipshod and Perilous." The railroad continued to operate, due in large measure to the fact that it met the Denver & Rio Grande Western at the Slickrock terminal, where Union Pacific trains also came through. There was just enough combined freight and passenger business left to keep the line going. But Mason's personal fortunes were rapidly dwindling. In 1897 he and his partners sold the S&P to a group of eastern investors. On a raw, snowy November morning in 1899, a bitter and angry Lyman Mason passed on, leaving his wife, two daughters, and a son in much reduced circumstances.

The new owners of the Slickrock & Paradox had but one interest—to squeeze all the remaining juice out of this lemon and then throw the rind away. For several years the little railroad, now just called the "Slow and Puny," struggled along under a succession of managers, most of whom tried their best but were ignored by the head office when they pleaded for funds and equipment. The eastern syndicate finally decided there was nothing left to gain, and allowed the line to go into receivership in 1914.

Henry Bouchard, a leading Paradox hardware and machinery dealer, was dismayed at the thought of losing the valuable rail connection to Slickrock and the outside world. Several others in both towns felt the same. A new group was formed, and the S&P revived, slightly. One of the new group was Brackett Mason, Lyman's son. As the years passed, he and Bouchard became the driving force behind the railroad, eventually buying out the others.

Business grew, slowly and not at all surely, spurred a little bit at first by World War I, then more by the Roaring Twenties. Some silver continued to be shipped. Some of the old silver mines were rich in lead and zinc, which proved a profitable commodity. Several mines way over above Bear Park at the end of a branch siding were shipping gold ore. Logging became big business in the Coyote Creek drainage and surroundings. Down in the lower valley some folks were running hundreds of head of cattle, and on the other side of Cinnamon Ridge sheep ranching was big. Sugar beets came through from out in the western part of the county, sandstone, limestone, and some marble from another section.

The S&P weathered its storms successfully. Bouchard passed on, and Brackett Mason continued as the sole owner. Through the lean 'Thirties he conserved and made do, keeping the line together sometimes almost through sheer force of will. Through the World War II years his indomitable spirit was rewarded, and the line prospered as never before. Brackett's son Russell, old Lyman's grandson, served his country in the army and came home to help his father run the railroad. Following guidelines established through years of experience, the two Masons virtually rebuilt the entire railroad, starting in the late 1930s and continuing through the immediate post-WWII days. Everything useful was kept and refurbished, older rolling stock was rebuilt for new purposes, new equipment was added as necessary and as available. The S&P was one of the first short lines to start using diesel motive power. Their steamers were in top notch shape, freshly painted and clean. Their rolling stock, which included some pretty old and pretty odd specimens, was in excellent repair and kept freshly painted in the road colors of light blue and silver. Their trackage was in excellent repair, their revenues solid, and their future bright.

In this year of 1952, Russell Mason has just taken over the presidency of the line; Brackett remains as chairman of the board. A spur line has just been completed to a new coal mine several miles up the valley and a new EMD GP7 diesel switcher should be delivered anytime now. The continued success of the S&P, now called the "Surefooted and Practical," seems well assured.

Chapter **3**

Designing
the layout

*J*ust as there are several elements that make up the overall concept of a model railroad, so there are several you have to consider as you develop the layout design. The final design of the physical layout will be shaped by both conceptual and practical influences. Obviously the overall concept of the railroad you plan to model will play a major role. Two of the practical elements, the place you have available for the layout and its size and shape, have already been discussed. But there are others, some important, and some not so much but still worth thinking about.

PURPOSE

One thing you need to consider at the outset is the purpose of your layout and the use to which it will be put. There are numerous possibilities, and they influence layout design in different ways. You might, for example, plan to build and run the layout strictly for your own relaxation and amusement. Or it could be a mutual project between spouses, or father and son. Will it be used to entertain your and the neighbor's young children, or to instruct a couple of teenagers and give them something to do? Will you run the whole affair yourself, or have a friend or two to share operating the trains? You might want to start a club, using your layout as a focal point.

The "use" emphasis is important, too. Will you try to include diverse operation like running mountains and plains, or main line trains along with city streetcars? Be aware that this sort of arrangement usually has mediocre results for all elements and good or superior ones from none. Consider your interest areas, too. You might want an electrical/electronic marvel with all possible automatic bells and whistles, to the exclusion and potential detriment of, say, scenery. Your design will tend heavily toward devices, gadgets, and automation. Scenery might be your big interest, beautifully detailed, with only a couple of short trains to run through it. Your plans need to be carefully thought out to include the maximum amount of complex scenic elements.

There is the type of operating you like to do. Some prefer intricate switching maneuvers, as in a big yard. Others like complex operations running to schedules, maybe involving a multitude of industrial pickups in a point to point layout. You might be happy with continuous running loop-the-loops, or want double track, main line operation. One train at a time could be satisfactory, or you might want to run two at a time by yourself, or have several going which would require more engineers.

You may be torn between two or more conflicting purposes and uses, and you may want to incorporate bits and pieces of several possibilities, or be ready for whatever comes along. That's fine, because you should do whatever you feel most comfortable with. An emphasis on one layout element or another, like scenery, is common and natural. So is occasional use that was not part of the original plan, like a visiting engineer or two. But keep in the back of your mind that the most successful layouts, in all senses of the word, particularly small pikes, are almost invariably those with an undiluted single purpose and use.

TIME AND MONEY

Be realistic in your assessment of how much time and money you can spend on your layout. A common difficulty that besets beginners is to bite off more than they can chew, and that oversize chunk seems to be time even more frequently than money. Even a small layout will take a long time to complete—hundreds of hours if you wish—because so much can be put into one in the way of fine detailing. When taken to artistic, realistic, mechanical, and electrical extremes, those costs can be substantial. A large layout will cost proportionately more than a small one of equal quality and complexity, and take proportionately more time to complete. Likewise, a complex, sophisticated, and detailed layout will cost proportionately more in dollars and time than a plain and simple one of comparable size.

As you work out your design, keep in mind that if you plan more than you can possibly find time to do, or can possibly find the cash for even over a long period of time, you won't be very far into the project before the wheels will start to come off. You'll likely become discouraged, disgusted, disillusioned, and pretty soon an ex-ferroequinologist with a whole lot of cobwebby and dusty model railroad junk piled in a corner of the cellar. It's happened innumerable times.

BENCHWORK

Benchwork is the term given to the assembly that provides the support for the layout such as a table, bench, shelf, or whatever. It must be strong, rigid, and solid in every sense, but without being overly bulky and heavy. Constructing adequate benchwork can sometimes be difficult because of the compound requirements of both itself and the dictates of the proposed layout design. The layout, however, is the main consideration, not the benchwork. While benchwork may sometimes influence layout design, it should never dictate design.

There are several different styles of benchwork, with variations and combinations that are workable as well. Sometimes in order to achieve a satisfactory result a bit of ingenuity is called for. The nuts-and-bolts benchwork construction details are not of concern here, as that will be covered in the next chapter. Some general design factors do need early consideration.

The most important factors involve layout access (FIG. 3-1). You have to be able to reach every point on the trackwork with reasonable ease, so that you can right a derailed car or clean the rails, and do so without crunching part of the scenery or knocking over a structure at the front. To check your effective working reach, lean over the end of your dining room table and set a box car, wheels railed, on a length of track, and measure the distance. For most people that's going to be in the 32- to 40-inch range. The higher the layout the shorter that reach will be, and if the scenery rises and then dips, there's a problem, too. About 3 feet is a common working figure for unobstructed total width of the benchwork with access only from the front.

If accessible from both sides, the overall width could be 6 feet. If the layout must be designed deeper, then access must be provided by openings in the benchwork with the layout surrounding them. You can create peninsulas in some fashion, or make removable sections of scenery, or provide access holes up through the benchwork to reach hidden trackwork. This means that benchwork must be built to suit the layout design as much as possible. Although you might have to alter the layout design somewhat, do so as little as possible, especially if the design is affected adversely. In some cases the benchwork may be made sufficiently movable so that access can be gained that way. A layout 6 feet wide and 6 feet deep could be kept tucked in a room corner, for example, provided it could be moved out into the room when being operated or worked on.

Working and operating room around the layout is an important consideration, too. You need room to move around without bumping into the surroundings and running up against the edges of the layout, or knocking sce-

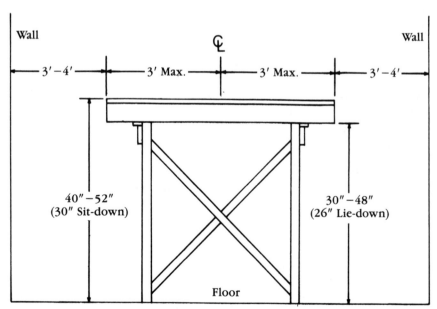

3-1   Although certainly not immutable, these general benchwork access dimensions seem to be the most workable in most circumstances.

nery over with your elbows. Again, for small layouts a free space of 3 feet at all points is usually sufficient. If there will be frequent visitors or two or three visiting engineers roaming around, or if walk-around control is a present or future consideration, make that at least 4 feet.

Access to the underside of the layout must also be considered. A lot of wiring goes on here, and switch machine installation, perhaps construction of some below-zero elevation scenery elements, and you may need passageway to under the scenery hidden trackage. In a small module, portable, or boxed layout, everything must be made so that the whole affair can be up-ended or turned over for this kind of work, and that in turn can be covered by a removable bottom panel. On permanent or semipermanent layouts, room enough to sit up beneath the main benchwork makes for the easiest working conditions, and that means zero elevation is generally about 48 inches above floor level. The lowest you can go and still have some decent working room is about 30 inches.

Remember that you are not confined to a table top kind of platform for your layout. Rather, the elevations are infinitely variable (within reason). You can build on several levels, slope to the floor, you can hang the works from the ceiling, create islands and jut-outs and cubbies, or run everything on shelves. You can even make movable and removable sections, gates, and duck-unders, but do that only if there's no other possible way to accomplish your purpose. Your layout can be permanent, movable, portable, oddly sized or modular, multimodular, roll out, roll about, fold up, and even swiveling. There's a way to do darn near anything.

TRACKWORK

Before you start the layout design, and especially the track plan (which is to model railroading what a floor plan is to a house), establish your basic trackwork standards. They need not be extensive, they should follow customary practice for trouble free operation, and you should adhere to them religiously when you make up the track plan and lay the track. The nuts and bolts of installing trackage will come later. For now, the guidelines need defining so you can judge your space allowances.

One area that needs thought, and sometimes compromise, is the *curve radius* of the track. The NMRA has established minimum radius standards for the popular scales, and over the years some radii figures have come into common usage (FIG. 3-2). Don't go below the minimum radius for your chosen scale, and keep all your curves to as great a radius as you can manage, even at the expense of other elements of the layout such as added scenery or structures. Large radii make for much smoother, more trouble free operation and greater realism. Large locomotives and heavyweight passenger cars will not negotiate minimum radii at all, and will overhang and look peculiar even on the smaller conventional curves. Make sure your intended motive power and rolling stock will actually operate on the curves you plan on having. Set your own minimum radius and stay with it, while at the same time making as many curves as possible as sweeping as you can make room for.

Scale	Min.	Sharp	Conventional	Broad
N	9	10−11	12−14	15 up
HO	18	19−23	24−29	30 up
S	23	24−32	33−44	45 up
O	36	37−47	48−59	60 up

3-2 These are common and workable track curve radius figures.

Where tracks run parallel to one another, they must be kept a certain minimum distance apart to avoid sideswipes. The distance between curved parallel tracks must be increased to compensate for car overhang at the corners as the cars round the curves. The sharper the curve, the greater the separation between tracks must be. Again, there are minimum standards and suggested clearances for all popular scales (FIG. 3-3). Select an appropriate number for your trackwork. Greater clearances than minimum are fine, and may be essential if you have some equipment with extraordinarily long overhang. Note that if you widen out too far the appearance will be peculiar, and unlike prototype double track lines.

A straight track is called a *tangent*. A curve that is shaped to exactly the same radius all the way around, as you would draw with a drafting compass, is called a *circular* or a *constant radius* curve. If you join a tangent to a circular curve, the point where one meets the other is an abrupt change of direction, a *hitch*. This will cause the cars of your train to lurch, possibly derail. The cure is to provide the curve at each end with a gradual transition from the tangent, called an *easement,* a short section of increasing radius curve, or spiral (FIG. 3-4). There are mathematical formulas for calculating various spirals for different radii, from the results of which templates can be made. But in practice, any easement that extends between tangent and radius a distance of about one quarter the radius dimension will work nicely. You can draw the easement free-hand and full scale, then make your own templates to suit. Don't bother trying to include easements on your plan drawings, though—they won't even show up.

Superelevation is a method of slightly lifting the outside rail on a curve above the inside one on high speed mainlines, to keep the cars on the tracks by tilting them against centrifugal force. You can do the same on your single and double track mainlines by tilting the roadbed just slightly. All other trackage, though, should remain flat, including low speed curves.

Scale	Tangent	Sharp	Conventional	Broad
N	1	$1^{3}/_{8}$	$1^{5}/_{16}$	$1^{1}/_{4}$
HO	$1^{13}/_{16}$	$2^{1}/_{2}$	$2^{1}/_{4}$	2
S	$2^{7}/_{16}$	$3^{1}/_{4}$	3	$2^{7}/_{8}$
O	$3^{1}/_{4}$	$4^{3}/_{4}$	4	$3^{7}/_{8}$

3-3 These are the suggested minimum track spacings; note that the sharper the curve radius, the greater the spacing.

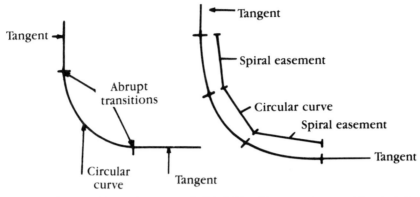

3-4   Tangents should ease into curves in this fashion (shown exaggerated for clarity).

Reverse curves, or *esses,* can cause all kinds of trouble, especially when run at speed. Derailments are inevitable if the curves are set together. Separate each curve, which should also be designed with easements, with a tangent at least as long as your longest car or locomotive (FIG. 3-5).

A *grade* results when a track runs up or down from zero elevation. Grade is expressed in percent, or the number of units of rise over 100 units of run (FIG. 3-6). A 2 percent grade would rise above zero to 2 inches over a

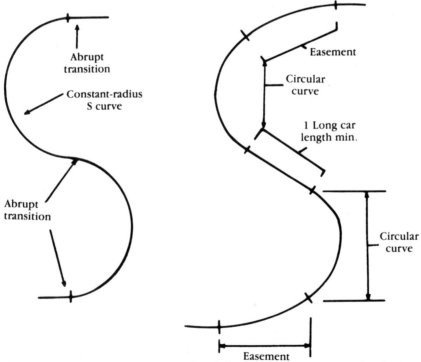

3-5   An "S" curve should have a car length (or greater) tangent separating the two halves, and the curves should be eased as well.

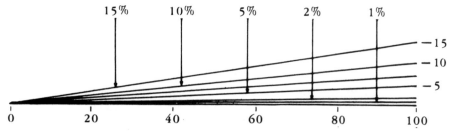

3-6   Grade is the number of units of rise divided by the number of units of run.

distance of 100 inches. For your planning purposes, the most convenient approach is to figure everything in *track units* of ⅛ inch; a 2 percent rise would be ⅜ inch over ¹⁰⅜ inch, or ¼ inch over 12½ inches. In modeling practice you can consider each nominal (it isn't exact), 1 percent of grade to equal 1 track unit per foot of run. A rise of 2 inches at 2 percent would take 8 feet of track (2 divided by ⅜ equals 2 divided by 0.25, equals 8). In usual prototype practice, maximum mainline grades are 2 percent, helper grades 3 percent, some industrial grades up to 5 percent, and yards are essentially flat. Many railroad grades were actually much steeper than that, but mostly in logging and mining roads and some early general service narrow gauge roads.

Keep your grades as low as possible, but don't hesitate to use them wherever they fit in and are in keeping. A grade as high as 8 percent on a mining line running very short trains and helper engines is not beyond reason. On any grade over about 3 percent, slack off on the grade as the track rounds a curve, then pick it up again if necessary. In spots where you want unattended, uncoupled rolling stock to stand still, keep level within ¼ percent maximum. At the transition point between level and the start of a grade—this is called a *vertical curve*—allow space for an easement. Do the same at the top of a grade. This will abate any possibility of derailment or unwanted uncoupling of cars.

Most model railroads today end up with some form of automatic uncoupling arrangement (more on this later), even though they may not start out with it. Install your uncoupling mechanisms only on straight, level track sections for best results, never on curves. Place them near the front or some other readily accessible place on the layout, never in some remote, hidden location. Allow plenty of maneuvering space to either end of the uncoupling area for backing and filling. A small layout will probably have only one or two uncoupling spots, a larger one might need several to increase operating possibilities.

Track switches are called *turnouts* to distinguish them from electrical switches. A complete discussion of them is not in order here, but you'll need some planning information now. *Straight* turnouts have one straight set of rails and one curving off at an angle. They are designated #4, #6, #8, and so on. The larger the number, the larger the radius of the curve and also the more physical space the turnout takes up on the layout. Use the largest turnouts you can for better operation. Use #6 as a minimum on main lines, and

#4 only in yards, on logging/mining lines, or similar tight, low speed spots. Curved turnouts are made with a curved main line and a more sharply curved leg; use these only where there is a definite need and a straight turnout won't work well.

Turnouts can be controlled manually, mechanically, or electrically. Because they can be troublesome at times, always place them where they are accessible, never in remote spots, inside tunnels, or behind scenery or backdrops. If there is a principal direction of train travel on any of your lines, try to design the trackage so that the tails of any turnouts face into this direction. This reduces the possibilities of derailments.

When you set two like turnouts tail to tail you make a tight reverse curve, and the smaller the turnout number the tighter the curve. It may not be negotiable for some equipment. Use this arrangement only where absolutely necessary, and in low speed areas like a yard. To diminish the difficulties of the arrangement, lay a section of straight track between the two that is about as long as your longest car or locomotive.

There are various special trackage units that look fancy and do fulfill certain purposes nicely under certain conditions. They include three-way wye switches, crossings of several sorts, lap switches, and single and double slip switches. Use them as you need them, such as when space is at a serious premium, but only in circumstances where standard turnouts and track realignments will not serve a like or similar purpose. The fancy trackwork is expensive, and more importantly it much increases the chances for derailments, electrical problems, operating slowdowns, and added maintenance.

Many layouts feature overpasses/underpasses of various kinds. Select minimum grade separation figures to allow ample clearance (FIG. 3-7), and use them throughout your design. Overhead clearances can be set in a number of ways, but one safe method is to measure from the rail top to the lowest underside point of whatever is overhead. When both the track and the overhead structure are level, the minimum clearance is one figure. When the track is on a grade, and perhaps meets the overpass at a vertical angle, that figure must be somewhat greater. The easiest course is to select a dimension that will allow your tallest equipment to pass freely in any circumstances and use that number for everything.

There is another clearance figure that is sometimes ignored, and that is the distance from an outside track line to the edge of the benchwork. If the area is flat and there is no edge restraint, allow a "shoulder" roughly three times the width of the track to catch a derailed car. Alternatively, you can

Scale	Min.	Rec.
	(in inches)	
N	$1^{21}/_{32}$	$2^1/_8$
HO	3	$3^1/_2$
S	$4^1/_8$	$4^5/_8$
O	$5^1/_2$	6

3-7 These minimum grade separation dimensions allow ample clearance under most circumstances.

build the scenery up along the edge so that it is higher than the track, or secure a railing of some sort to the edge of the benchwork. In any event, there should be enough space to allow a natural looking track banking, ballast, drainage ditch, and a bit of landscape between the outer rail and the edge of the layout.

ELECTRICS AND CONTROLS

The electrical wiring and the control system has less influence on a small layout than a very large one, but nonetheless deserves some thought during the planning stages. Electrical circuitry is almost infinitely flexible, so whatever track plan, lighting arrangement, automation, and operating gadgetry you'd like to install can be worked out, especially with the aid of various electronic components and circuits. You can even computerize the entire operation.

From a practical standpoint, it's helpful to have some idea ahead of time what you would like to use and how far you would like to carry the electrical/electronic element of the layout. A small powerpack and a pair of leads will run a single train around even long and complex trackage. You can also go to great lengths, making the layout a showcase for your electrical system. Either way, a certain amount of space and access will be needed for the equipment, and you'll need to factor that in.

Some electronics gadgetry is carried in the locomotives or rolling stock, but that will not affect the layout plans. For the electrical circuits that feed the trackage, you will need to be able to route several hidden conductors (electrical, not train) to various points along the rails, and quite a few if you set up sections and blocks. Some layouts are wired with a common rail (more on that later), in which case space is needed for a heavy common conductor that will make a loop around the layout, underneath. You will also need access to run wires to accessories like track signals and crossing gates. For lighting in structures, again you will need hidden access for wires, plus a means to connect them to lamps within the structures. This means lift-up structures or lift-off roofs, or pigtailed light sockets, or insert lamps.

Track turnouts can be set manually from above, or mechanically or electrically, usually from below but sometimes above. The latter two methods mean space for rods, cranks, and levers, or for switch machines, plus clear routes under the layout or through the scenery for cables, strings, or wires. For above-layout switch machines you'll probably want to devise some means to disguise them. Once you get past just a few wires running here and there, you might want to have room enough somewhere to install a long series of terminal blocks with labels, for convenience and for easier troubleshooting (never think for an instant that you'll escape facing that chore). You will also need to reserve some room for one or more control panels and associated wiring. Exact needs depend upon layout size and the control system you adopt (refer to Chapter 6 for more details). Typically, control panels are attached to some part of the front of the benchwork. They don't usually take space away from the layout itself, but rather extend into the working and walking area around the layout.

BASIC SCENERY

You need to start thinking about the basic scenery of your layout right at the earliest stages of the planning, and never stop until it's all built. The overall concept of the railroad, the trackwork and the structures, some of the benchwork, some of the wiring, all are affected by the scenery. The planned structures and trackwork of course in turn affect the scenery. Scenery usually needs a supporting framework, that must be attached to the benchwork and subroadbed, and it takes up a lot of room. It must be built just so and look just right, but yet it cannot interfere with the other elements of the layout.

As you plan and design, consider the overall impact of the scenery. On a small layout, build only one kind of scenery (mountains, plains, urban, industrial, etc.), as a mix is likely to be a mixed-up mess. On larger layouts there is room to blend from one kind of scenery to another. You can, however, separate even a small layout into sections of entirely different character by installing a tall dividing backdrop that physically and visually splits the layout into two parts, or by making some similar arrangement. In some cases, three or more sections are possible.

One of the first items to pin down is the location and size of all bodies of water such as creeks, rivers, ponds, waterfront, swamps, marshes. These may be partially or even entirely below zero elevation, requiring some specific construction procedures in the benchwork or the scenery subbase. Likewise, make allowances and flexible plans for (theoretical) water drainage of all kinds. All trackage should have drainage ditches alongside, with under-track culverts here and there, ditches, and puddling areas. Consider where heavy rainfall, or spring snowmelt, might run off on your particular scenery, and create dry washes, gullies, ravines, erosion courses, whatever suits your kind of topography and geology.

It is a rare layout that doesn't have a corner that needs to be disguised somehow as the world isn't right-angled. One popular method is to build a hillside, or a tall mountain, into a corner. A series of industrial buildings, a big water tank, a false track going into a tunnel in a cliff face, elevated track on a trestle curving through the corner, an urban facade, even a painted backdrop, are all possible hide-'ems.

You also have to determine the location of your overpasses and underpasses, trestles, bridges, viaducts, and tunnel portals. All but the portals need to be supported by piers and abutments and all may also have wings and retaining walls as part of their makeup. Those components must be accurately positioned and melded in with the scenery, and properly aligned with the track roadbed as well.

One item that adds greatly to the appearance and realism of a layout is a backdrop. There are many ways to arrange one and an infinite number of scenes, but the object is to blend your modeled foreground into a one-dimensional background. A rectangular layout against a wall might have a backdrop at the back and both sides. This could consist of painted panels, a runner of heavy printed paper, even a color photo mural. Shallow building facades made in perspective have been used. As mentioned earlier, backdrops can also be employed as dividers. If you have an artistic bent, you can try your hand at painting your own backdrops. If not, you will have to match a commercially available backdrop to your scenery. Either way, your layout design should include the necessary space and support for whatever kind of backdrop you prefer to use.

An amazing number of tricks with scenery can be played with mirrors of various sizes installed at strategic points on the layout. This takes some thought and some study, and some experimenting as well. If creating illusions in this way appeals to you, now is the time to look into the matter with an eye toward including a few tricks in your layout design.

As you work up your design, consider what specific construction sequence might be necessary, and what order of steps are most beneficial. Much depends upon the size and complexity of the design, but certain things always have to be done ahead of others. Bridge abutments go in before the bridges, but after the watercourse is set, but before it is finished, and usually before the water is modeled . . . It is good to start building and finishing the scenery at the back or least accessible parts of the layout and work your way forward. That way, completed elements at the front won't get leaned on and crushed, splattered with plaster or paint, or demolished entirely.

FREIGHT/PASSENGER FACILITIES

Some layouts are comprised entirely of a specific environment such as a single industry or an industrial switching complex or something equally all-encompassing. Most run full freight trains of some ilk to and from various destinations, imagined or otherwise, and unlike modern prototype railroads, model layouts frequently offer full passenger service. In such cases, realism and interest are both served by including in your design at least some of the facilities common to freight and/or passenger service. There are a number of possibilities, and most need preplanning.

A freight yard is one of the most common and popular layout installations. It can be as small as a single *run-around* track where cars can be left, or a couple of double sidings. A sizable *ladder* or series of sidings offers more flexibility and interest (FIG. 3-8). Large prototype yards include tracks

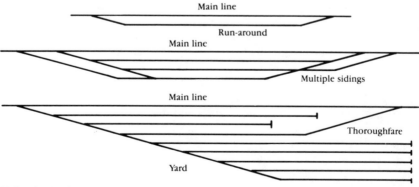

3-8 A simple run-around siding, multiple sidings off a main line, or a yard with a thoroughfare off the main all offer increasing degrees of operating interest and flexibility.

with specific purposes (FIG. 3-9). For example, a *receiving* track is at least a minimum of a train length long, where incoming cars are left. The cars go to *classification* tracks where they are separated according to destination. Local freight cars are set on *local order* tracks. A run-around track allows the switcher to move about from track to track. The *departure* track is for making up outgoing trains. Additional tracks may be needed for storage.

Service tracks also lend realism and interest to a layout. One such is a *weighing* track, where loaded cars can be weighed for billing purposes. *Caboose* tracks, usually double ended for convenience, are for caboose storage. Parallel *transfer* tracks are needed if you model in two gauges and want to shift freight car loads from one to the other. If you are running a lot of reefers, an *icing* track and facility can generate some operating opportunities.

Engine and shop facilities (FIG. 3-10) are popular, and attributable to both freight and passenger service. They do differ somewhat between steam and diesel needs. An engine house is a good adjunct and they were typically one, two, or three stall and don't require a turntable. A full fledged roundhouse does, and the two together take up a lot of room. Several short tracks are needed for such facilities as a sand tower or bin, coaling station, diesel fuel tank and pump, water tank or spout, ash dump, inspection pit, and perhaps a wash rack. Other possibilities include a boiler plant, shop buildings, storage sheds, service platforms, yard office, a wrecker storage stub, and a work train storage track.

Other items to consider are special *holding* tracks, as for coal, ore, or wheat cars, or *TOFC* tracks for loading and unloading. Many yards contain one or more *freight house* tracks for servicing LCL box cars, and *team* tracks where bulk materials like gravel or scrap metal can be handled directly to and from trucks and flat or gondola cars. Freight platforms and/or stations were common at every stopping point.

Central to passenger facilities are the stations. Most small layouts include at least one, that might be a separate one close to a freight station, or a combination freight/passenger station. Sizes vary as even small towns sometimes had fairly large stations. Separate through-type stations often had adjoining platforms no longer than the building itself, but sometimes they extended for a substantial distance to either side, and on both sides of the track. Stub stations, located at the end of the line, were usually small but there are many large prototype examples as well. Either type handled mail and express. There is much flexibility here, and even a small layout can have at least two passenger stations if that service is to be featured.

Facilities could include a separate yard or yard section just for passenger cars, called a *coach* yard; these were often stub tracks set in ladder fashion. Large facilities also had separate express and mail sheds on their own tracks. There were sometimes separate short tracks for light repairs, and shops for heavier, more extensive repair work. Car washing equipment was common, and often arranged so that an entire train could pass through and continue on. Some, though, were one or two car hose-equipped platforms on a stub track.

On layouts where freight service is emphasized and passenger service is limited, as in a typical late steam-era branch line operation, no special passenger facilities are usually installed.

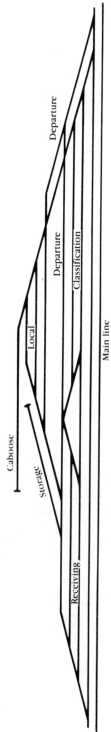

3-9 If a yard is large enough, some of the tracks can be designated for special purposes.

3-10 This is one way to arrange a steam engine service yard area; the possibilities are endless.

LIGHTING

Lighting is one of the most important and also one of the most often skimped-on aspects of a model railroad layout. Good lighting can make the difference between a superior pike and just another average layout. As such, it deserves some thought.

The first consideration is the lighting that is part of the layout itself. Here is a chance to add more realism and some fine night time atmosphere. The lighting should emulate, in miniature, that of the real world of that time, in the way of street lamps, stop lights, crossing lights, locomotive headlights, automobile lights, even a campfire or bonfire. You can put lights in houses, stores, factories, atop radio towers and water tanks. You can stand a farmer with a lantern in his barnyard, a conductor with a lantern in the station. With the present-day miniature bulbs and electronic circuits, there isn't much you can't simulate.

The next consideration is the light you rig up to work by, that oftentimes is abysmal and the direct cause of mistakes, poor workmanship, peculiar color tones, and a good many headaches. At the modeling bench or design work table, use high-powered task lighting close to your work, preferably a mix of incandescent and fluorescent lighting such as draftsmen use. Any good drafting lamp will give you that, though not inexpensively. When working on the layout, you need equally strong light directed at the area where you are working and preferably shadow-free. Do not use a mechanic's incandescent bulb trouble lamp, because you'll fry or melt or crunch something for sure. Your best bet is plenty of general room lighting, supplemented by strong bulbs in adjustable, clamp-on reflectors that you can park almost anywhere, including on a tripod if necessary.

Finally, the general lighting for a completed (or well along) layout needs much thought—a bare bulb hanging from a cord tacked to the ceiling won't get the job done. The installation should be a part of the overall layout design, and the installation made as layout construction proceeds. Proper lighting will afford good visibility around the layout, bring up detail, create the shadow effects you need for depth perception, and bring out the subtleties of color necessary for an aura of naturalness. It will impart a time sense (by the sun, it's mid-afternoon) and a direction sense (by the shadows, the train is heading west, folks on this side of the street are in the sun, but in the shade over there), and greatly enhance the overall illusion of realism. All this and more, if you do the job right.

There's no simple answer; much depends upon the size and configuration of your layout, and particularly your scenery. Select a time of day. Not high noon, but preferably early to mid-afternoon or mid-to-late afternoon, depending upon the season, and assume a sunny day. Try to match the sunlight as it would actually fall at that time of day and season on the landscape you've modeled. Visualize the light angles, the way the shadows would lie, the relative light intensities at various points. One way to do this is by experimenting with a powerful floodlamp in a reflector that you can move around here and there.

Then work out your lighting arrangement. If the layout is permanent, so can be the lighting installation. In small, movable layouts, make it part of the layout framework. Use a series of ordinary 25, 40, and 60-watt bulbs mounted above the layout but out of sight, as behind a valance or baffle. Set the lamps so that the light pools from each bulb overlap to create a continuous wash of light. The shadows should be fairly dark but not black, and sharp-edged, not fuzzed or doubled or tripled, and they should look realistic. Fashion adjustable tin can reflectors, baffles, or shades for the lamps to direct the light as necessary. Most of the light will probably shine down and back from near the front of the layout, but secondary and backlighting behind baffles positioned partway back may enhance the overall effects.

Permanent installations should be wired according to the National Electrical Code, and the work done by a qualified electrician if need be. On portable and movable arrangements, the wiring is best done in what is classed as a "temporary" hookup. This means porcelain sockets on plastic junction boxes, or clamp-on sockets, lamp cord wiring to outlet strips as necessary, with the whole affair ultimately plugged into a nearby standard wall outlet. Keep cords to a minimum, well dressed and out of the way, with each circuit limited to about 1000 watts or somewhat less than the capacity of the cord or outlet strip being used, whichever is smaller. Install a dimmer and you can control the light output. Motorize the dimmer and you can simulate scale night and day.

DUST AND CLIMATE CONTROL

The biggest maintenance problem most model railroaders face is dust. Moisture follows close behind, and in some circumstances may loom even larger. If you can work out some ways to keep your layout dust-free and rust-free, whatever effort you have to make will be well worthwhile.

Dust is unsightly, irritating, requires a lot of cleanup time, is very difficult to remove from delicate structures and landscaping, and causes operating problems. If aerosol grease, cigarette smoke particles, and assorted other particulates are part of the mix, the problems are compounded. Dust never is completely escapable.

One control measure is to build the layout in a separate room, or enclose the layout within its own walls, perhaps sheets of plywood. Keep fabrics out of the area such as curtains, rugs, whatever, and strive for relatively hard, smooth surfaces everywhere, such as semigloss paint or varnish. The overhead area above a layout should be covered and preferably painted, never open joists or uncovered insulation that will sift dirt down whenever someone walks across the floor above. Do not use highpowered fans in the layout area, or permit open windows; always keep access doors closed. Forced-air heating or airconditioning can be a dust disaster unless the air flow is scrupulously filtered. Don't do any work in the layout area (after the layout is built) that would create dust, like cutting ceiling tile or sanding woodwork. Obviously you can't always manage all these "don'ts," but you can attempt to minimize the potential problems.

Moisture, dampness, high humidity, all can wreak havoc with a layout, and controlling it is difficult. When dampness occurs from moisture seeping through a concrete cellar wall, that can (and definitely should) be cured before a layout is built, by waterproofing inside, outside as well if necessary or possible, and installing a proper foundation drainage system. Using commercially available dessicants to protect specific delicate equipment that might easily corrode or rust is possible, but does not answer a layout-wide problem. Enclosing the layout in its own room will help. Double-glaze the windows and weatherstrip outside doors. Good air conditioning with efficient air filtration can also help, and a dehumidifier of sufficient capacity to handle the entire immediate area is probably the best bet. In addition, sufficient heat should be kept in the area to prevent the formation of condensates and keep everything reasonably warm to aid evaporation as well.

TRACK PLANS

The track plan is the heart of your model railroad design, around which you build the rest of your layout. Development of the plan deserves whatever time and thought is necessary (that may be a whole lot), until you are completely happy with the result. Upon this plan depends much of the appearance, realism, and operating pleasure of the pike, and thus your own personal satisfaction.

There are four basic track configurations; point-to-point, point-to-loop, loop-to-loop, and oval (FIG. 3-11). When you unravel a complex track plan into a straight line schematic, those are the combinations that appear. By adding to and combining any or all of these basics, you can develop an infinite number of variations. Along with them you must introduce turnouts, spur tracks, sidings, and crossovers as necessary to work out operating diversity and to service the focal points of your layout.

There are four ways to develop your track plan. One is to draw up the entire plan yourself, suiting it to a fictional model railroad master plan. This requires some research, study, and basic trackwork experience, as well as pertinent trackage data, to do so successfully. Laying out a complex track plan can be tricky (but fun—try it). Though time consuming and sometimes frus-

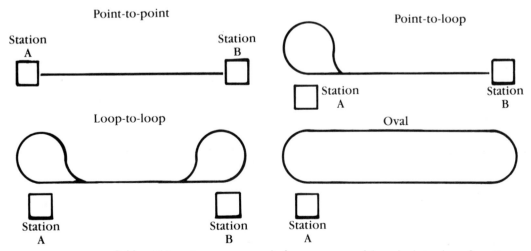

3-11 All layouts are composed of one or more of these basic track configurations.

trating, this method has the advantage of resulting in a unique and tailor-made plan, that can be very satisfying.

Another approach is to select a certain section of a prototype railroad and scale it down to fit your layout. This can't be done exactly, or anywhere near exactly, and the prototype trackage has to be folded, compressed, hidden in spots, and otherwise jiggered about to fit your layout but retain the visual and operational essence of the prototype. This is not an easy job either, but is a challenge. To see how it's done, study a number of the "railroads you can model" articles that appear frequently in model railroading magazines.

A third approach, and by far the easiest, is to search through the several booklets available, along with as many back issues of model railroading magazines you can lay your hands on, for a track plan that fills your needs. There are hundreds of them in all shapes and sizes, many complete with scenery, structure, and general theme outlines. Curve radii, electrical feeder attachment points, and block separations are often noted. Any plan can be used for any scale simply by refiguring the overall dimensions. Any plan designed for a different scale than yours, though, you must redraw to scale because many of the lesser dimensions will not be proportionate. Don't attempt to make a direct transfer to another scale. The advantages to this approach are twofold; a great savings of time and effort, and assurance that the plan will indeed work because it's already been built and tested by somebody.

Chances are you won't find a published track plan that will entirely fill the bill. That leads to the fourth and perhaps most common approach to track planning. Find a published plan and modify it, or combine parts of several plans. You can make the higher elevations of a plan lower and vice versa, mirror image a plan, flip-flop all or part, shift a loop from down there to up here, relocate a yard or graft one on from a different plan, combine a couple of yards, add or subtract spurs and sidings and run-arounds, introduce undulations in tangents, change curve radii, and generally do whatever it takes to suit your fancy.

As you formulate your track plan, keep in mind the various physical constraints of not only the trackage itself, but also the other elements of the layout that will have an effect on it. This means such items as accessibility, too-tight radii, inadequate clearances, and similar standards. Be aware of the most common mistake that beginners make in laying out track plans, that of cramming as many feet of track into the layout as possible. This inevitably creates all manner of difficulties. Complex operating possibilities do not necessarily equate with a track plan that looks like spilled spaghetti. Keep the plan reasonably simple and spread out, except for yards and compact industrial areas and such, and allow ample space for structures, scenery, and detailing. (An exception would be certain mountain scenes where everything is jammed together in precarious niches). A couple of other common errors to avoid are running tracks along and exactly parallel with the straight edges of the layout, and not leaving any provision at all for some future growth. It is a fine idea to position at least one and preferably two or three sidings or stubs for expansion later to a new layout section, simply by joining more track to them.

The specifics of your plan will depend to some extent upon the kind of track you plan to use. Plans for rigid, short, snap-together track sections must be drawn to suit the available, fixed curve radii and the various combinations of section lengths and standard turnouts. Plans featuring flexible track and its associated turnouts and other trackage components, on the other hand, you can draw (and later install) with considerably more freedom. This is especially true of curve radii, lengths of tangents, and the placement of turnouts, all of which are essentially unrestricted. However, it is usually possible to match up some of the products of some manufacturers of both snap and flexible track (all of which vary from time to time) so that you can use both on the same layout to good effect, if you wish.

The plan that you ultimately devise should include trackage that will foster the kind of operating modes you prefer and give you ample flexibility in running trains. A shelf-mounted, point-to-point industrial switching layout obviously must have plenty of stubs and switches and a main line between points. But less obvious sometimes, and capable of getting lost in the shuffle, are such items as full train-length passing sidings, workable ladder tracks in yards, reversing loops to allow running in the opposite direction, a run-around track at a yard or station, double-ended station sidings, alternate routes for out-and-backs, or sufficient run-around loops. Be sure you can run your trains to wherever you want them with whatever maneuvers you prefer, and then get them back again preferably in some different fashion. This is usually possible on all but the smallest of layouts.

MAKING THE PRELIMINARY DESIGN

The first step in making the preliminary design is to gather up all your notes and get them in order. You'll need to refer to them often to check the standards you have established earlier, such as for grades and clearances, and to remind yourself of various ideas you want to test and specifics you want to include. Dimensions of various components will prove important, too, as you refine the plans and work toward the final design.

Because everything else follows from the track plan, that's the next step. If you choose a published plan, make a small tracing of it to start with, whether or not you plan to modify it at all. If you follow a prototype, make a rough sketch of the track section and principal elements, such as a town, station, trestle, river crossing, or whatever. For a fictional layout, start with a blank sheet of paper.

On a piece of plain paper, lightly rule off grid lines in both directions and of uniform spacing—½ or 1 inch should be fine. Make a dozen or more copies of this sheet with the copier set so that the grid lines are faintly visible. Keep the master in case you need more copies. Let the size of the grid squares equal a dimension of your layout, such as ½ inch equals 1 foot; this will be your drawing scale for the moment.

Start working out the details of your track plan. At the outset, this is a matter of transferring a published plan, or sketching in a prototype plan, or setting out your first fictional idea, just to see how it all fits into your proposed layout space. There is no set of handy instructions for this informal process. Keep working the plan like a block of modeling clay, stretching some here, squeezing some there, shifting directions, altering radii. Keep the operating possibilities, along with all the other technical odds and ends like clearances, in mind throughout. As the track line up progresses, add in some of the most important features in their approximate locations, such as trestles, bridges, and tunnels. Unless the track plan is small and simple, you will probably go through a whole lot of rough sketches before you develop one that might be satisfactory (FIG. 3-12).

Once you develop a plan that looks good, expand the scale and be a little more exacting. The ideal arrangement now is a complete set of drafting equipment to work with. Failing that, you can get along with a 2-foot carpenter's square, or a 3-foot steel or aluminum ruler/straightedge, a large plastic drafting triangle, a good soft eraser that works cleanly, a drafting pencil or several ordinary wood pencils or a mechanical pencil using 0.5 mm. leads, a sharpener as needed, and a supply of large sheets of paper. The 17 by 22-inch size is usually adequate, larger is better, and you can find it at art and/ or drafting supply outlets. You can also purchase track planning and layout templates for your scale. The largest available are scaled at 1 inch to 1 foot, which would allow you to draw up a layout about 15 by 20 feet on 17 by 22-inch paper.

Select an appropriate drawing scale for the sheet/layout size; 3 inches equals 1 foot is a good one for a small layout in N scale, or use whatever your

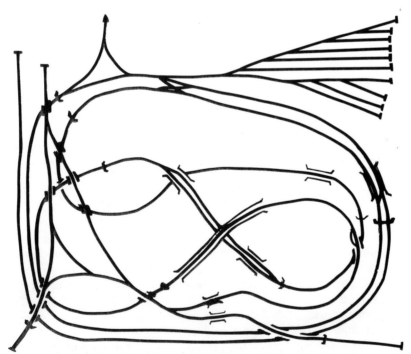

3-12 This is a typical rough sketch of a track plan that appears to be workable and interesting enough to polish up into final, larger-sized and scaled form.

templates are designed for. Lay out a scaled perimeter outline of your layout, then crosshatch it into a lightly-lined scaled grid for reference points. Following your final track plan sketch, enlarge it on the big sheet. This time, scale the radii accurately, include the approximate turnout space requirements, scale out the distance between double tracks, introduce the slight curves and bends that add character to absolute tangents, and generally draw out the entire plan in as much detail as seems reasonable. Don't bother with tiny details like transition easements. Do remember that the single line you are drawing to represent a pair of rails is actually the centerline of the track. Then study the whole affair to see what changes might be in order, especially with regard to clearances, space crowding, too-short sidings or stubs, a lack of reversing track or run-arounds or whatever, or any previously hidden trackage difficulties.

With the trackage in place, you can work out the elevations, grades, and vertical clearances. Select your zero elevation point. This is commonly a freight yard, a particular station, or some similar element near or at the front of the layout. Mark it with a 0.0 in a circle, next to the track. Pick a track line that must rise, and put a good sized dot beside the line right at the point where the rise will begin. If the track must achieve a certain height above zero elevation, or above another track line (as for an overpass), by the time it reaches a certain point, place a dot at that point. In a circle, note the required height in inches above zero elevation. Then measure the distance between the two dots. One easy way to do this is with a little measuring device for calculating mileage on road maps, equipped with a dial face and a tiny wheel to run along the route; it measures linear inches. (The device is called an *opisometer* or map meter, and is available from Brookstone, 5 Vose Farm Rd., P.O. Box 803, Peterboro, NH 03460–0803. It's a super gadget.)

Convert this measurement into track units, equal to ⅛ inch each. Inside a small box penciled in at the first dot, put a 0. In a second box at the second dot, note the distance in number of track units between the two. Convert the required elevation (the rise) to track units, and divide that by the measured number of track units along the rails (the run) and your answer will be the grade in exact percentage. Example: The required rise is 2.5 inches or 20 track units (8 times 2.5) and the run from dot to dot is 392 track units. Dividing the rise by the run shows a 5.1-percent grade. If the grade is steeper than your allowable standard, you'll have to change the track plan in that area in order to lessen it. Figure 3–13 shows a typical set of plan notations.

If you want to find out how long a section of track must be to achieve a particular elevation at a given nominal grade percentage, divide the elevation in track units by the desired percentage written as eighths and your answer will be in nominal feet. Example: You need 2 inches of elevation (rise) at a 3-percent maximum nominal grade, so ¹⁶⁄₈ divided by ⅜ equals 2 divided by 0.375 equals 5.34 feet of track (run) nominal. You could disregard the decimal point, too, and consider the answer as 534 track units, which converts to 5.5625 feet actual, or 5 feet 6 and ¾ inches. Vertical clearances, overall elevation gain or loss requirements for track, switchback lengths, bridge and trestle heights over rails, and similar matters can all be calculated the same way, by referencing track units to zero elevation.

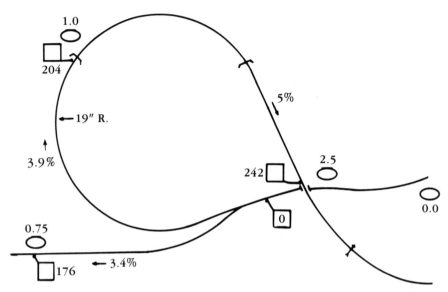

3-13 These notations are typical of the ones you will want to include on your plans, for reference as you build the layout. Note that numbers are typically placed inside the boxes and circles.

When you are satisfied with the track plan itself, sketch in some of the layout features. Locate tunnel portals, bridge piers, river and creek courses, and similar items. Then run some light contour lines to see how it all fits together. Draw in the principal structures, especially those along the right of way or in yards and service areas, like a roundhouse or engine shed, water tank, station, and factory or warehouse. These dimensions should be of structures you have, or plan to get. It's a good idea to have the most important ones on hand, lest they disappear from the marketplace (which happens frequently) before you can get them. By this time you should be getting a pretty good mental picture of what the layout will look like when full sized. Shift and shuffle the different layout elements on your drawing until you have what appears to be a satisfactory, workable arrangement that is to your liking. Then hang the design on the wall and let it age for a while.

MAKING THE FINAL DESIGN

There really is no such thing as a final design for a model railroad layout. There's no way to refine everything to the last nut and bolt and fraction of an inch, so it's important to keep an open mind and a flexible response pattern to whatever doesn't seem to work out just right. As an example, the specific dimensions of turnouts made by different companies vary, and may change from time to time. Another example: The product you planned to use has disappeared and its replacement is different. So the plan you probably will end up with is not a final design but a final *drawing,* that should serve as a well detailed *guide* to layout construction. You'll make minor changes by the dozens, count on that.

To develop your final drawing, or your working plan if you prefer, reconsider everything on your preliminary plan. If you've had some new ideas, or some second thoughts, or perhaps decided on a different structure or two, plug in all the necessary alterations. If need be, transfer everything to a fresh, clean sheet of paper with new, clear notations. The track plan should be especially well defined by this time, along with the positioning of major scenic elements, all the trackage components (portals, abutments, etc.), and the principal structures (FIG. 3-14). Now you can add whatever finishing touches you wish to. Depending upon the nature of the scenery, this is a good time to add contour lines as a guide in building up mountains, ledges, or other relief features. Creeks and rivers can be better defined too, and you might want to note trackside details like signals, or lay out roadways, irrigation ditches, or power lines.

One aspect of the layout design yet remains to be developed. The trackage of all but the tiniest layouts is divided into blocks, and sometimes into electrical sections as well. This arrangement has to be committed to a track drawing that contains notations of just where on the lines there should be insulating gaps in the rails to interrupt the electrical flow, and also at what points the electrical feeder wires are to be connected to the rails. This subject will be fully discussed in Chapter 6, Wiring the Layout. The details can be noted on the final design drawing you have just finished, especially if neither is complex. Many modelers prefer to make a copy of just the scaled track plan and enter all of the electrical information on it to serve as a complete wiring plan.

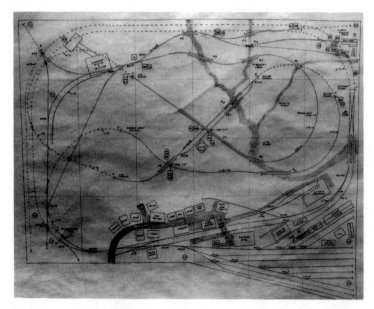

3-14 This is a typical scaled, almost-final version of a track plan complete with notes on clearances, elevations, turnout numbers, bridge and tunnel schedules, and other details.

STRUCTURES

In theory, the structures on a layout should not influence the design, but rather be subordinate to the design and complementary to the concept. In practice, matters usually don't work out that nicely. You will find plenty of structures available, both ready made and kit form, but often they do not fill the bill. A few are crude, badly designed and/or poorly manufactured from inferior materials. Some are toy-like and incorporate seriously out of scale dimensions and features. Many are patterned after European prototypes. Many more will not be typical of the time period you wish to model, and many more than that will not be suitable for other reasons. So a relatively small selection may be available for installation on any given layout, and even some of those will come and go in the marketplace.

When you set about designing your layout, it is well to decide which particular structures will work and which you like, and make provision for them in your plans. Actually purchasing them is a wise idea, even if some time will pass before you can put them to work. At least then you can use accurate dimensions from structures on hand and not have to worry about their disappearing before you're ready to buy them. This very problem, along with a relative lack of choices, is what impels many modelers to kit bash some of their structures, or build them from scratch.

Trackside or right-of-way structures like stations, section houses, yard-master's shanties, and similar buildings that are a part of the railroad organization need the closest attention during layout planning. They are an integral part of the modeled railroad and by design must be positioned in certain places. An engine shed, for example, has to be set over a stub track, typically near a yard or a set of service sidings, and a yardmaster's shanty should be placed in a freight yard. So, track and space provisions must be made for them, and clearances allowed as required. Likewise, there are a few nonrailroad structures like warehouses or factories that are served by tracks, and they must also be planned for.

With other structures there is more leeway. Commercial buildings, houses, gas stations, churches, farm buildings, and structures that are typically more or less isolated like scrapyards or sawmills can be shifted here and there, deleted, or substituted for as necessity dictates. In the design stages, it is probably sufficient in most cases just to know that you want a row of stores here, perhaps a farm over there, and a small industry near the creek bank. Even though noted on the design drawings, the final placement or even the existence of structures can be very flexible.

Chapter **4**

Building the benchwork

Benchwork is the term given to the structural assembly that supports the entire model railroad layout. There are several approaches to benchwork construction, and several types of benchwork that are suitable for various kinds and sizes of layout. The assembly should be strong, rigid, and well constructed, especially for large layouts and the bigger scales. You don't have to be either a cabinetmaker or a civil engineer to build sturdy and functional benchwork for your layout.

TABLE TOP BENCHWORK

Table top benchwork is just what the name implies—a flat surface like the top of a table to serve as a platform for the layout. This is a simple solution, but there are drawbacks. The wood surface acts as a sounding board and transmits the clatter of running trains as most unrealistic and often very loud noise. The regular shape can be difficult to work with and to disguise, and restrictive to track planning. Installing elevated trackage is difficult, and building anything below the solid top is even harder, maybe impossible. Just about all work, often including wiring, must be done from above. There are advantages, too. Low cost, simplicity, little or no construction needed in many cases, and the ease and rapidity of getting ready to build the layout head the list. A big plus for beginners, the track plan can be laid out directly on the flat surface right at the outset to see how it will work, and shuffled around easily to try out different arrangements.

This kind of benchwork can actually be a table top. Many a layout has been set up on an old pingpong table. Any kind of table can serve. If the top is warped or in bad shape, it can be covered with a piece of ½-inch plywood. If the legs are wobbly (definitely not good) they can be braced and shored up.

An alternative is to use, or build, just a table top or flat platform that can be set on a table when in use and stood in a closet when not. One common ploy is to use a door. Hollow core flush (smooth surfaced) doors are inexpensive, lightweight, and easy to handle. Your best bet is to buy a used one at a second-hand construction materials outlet, and check it carefully to make sure it is not warped. A flush solid-core door is better if you can find one, though it is much heavier. You can also use a paneled door, by covering one side with ⅜-inch plywood with the upper face grade either A or B. A small layout, say 2 by 2 or 3 feet, can even be built on a 2-inch thick slab of foamed plastic rigid insulation like Styrofoam.

Another possibility is a sheet of plywood. If you use ¾-inch thickness it will remain fairly stable in small sizes, like 2 by 3 feet. A full sheet is likely to develop some warp. To get around this, build a frame. Determine the perimeter size of the top, and make the frame to fit flush with the edges of the top, or ½ inch or so smaller all around to avoid tricky fitting along the flush edges. Use 1-×-4 No. 2 kiln-dried pine, with the cross pieces set approximately every 24 inches. The recommended thickness for the plywood top is ¾-inch, but you can use ⅝ or even ½-inch if you wish, and expect reasonable results. The plywood should have one face of grade A or B, with the other C or D, in an interior sheet grade. Put the frame members together with 2-inch drywall or deck screws and aliphatic resin (yellow) glue. Secure the top to the frame with glue and 1½-inch screws, countersunk flush. Drill clear holes for the screws through all pieces being attached, but no holes in the pieces being attached to. This basic arrangement can be used for table-top benchwork larger and of a different configuration than a plain 4-×-8-foot layout, simply by adjusting the components to suit. The arrangement shown in FIG. 4-1 is a good one because it eliminates the square corners; the points can be

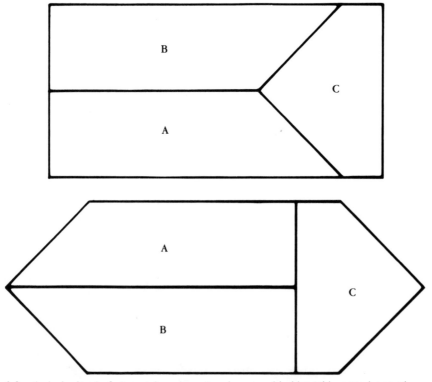

4-1   A single sheet of plywood can be cut and reassembled into this more interesting layout shape.

lopped off. You can set this kind of benchwork on sawhorses, or build leg sets to support it.

COOKIE-CUTTER BENCHWORK

The cookie-cutter style of benchwork (FIG. 4-2) is not overly popular but is used now and again, especially for small, portable or semiportable layouts. It has the advantage of the table top style, plus a couple more. You can elevate the trackwork with relative ease and with smooth transitions, and you can cut openings for lower level scenery such as a pond. The disadvantages are that careful preplanning is needed to avoid cutting into the framework under the top, as well as the fasteners, and making the cutouts takes equally careful planning and once done cannot be undone. Also, the cutting itself is a chore, and installing trackwork below the level of the top is not really feasible.

To build this kind of benchwork, follow the same pattern as just described for the framed table top variety. Begin by attaching the flat top to a perimeter frame. Leave the cross pieces out for the moment. Lay out the track on the top and shuffle it about until you have exactly the plan you want, including turnouts. Check the curve radii, and most importantly, be sure of your vertical clearances. Trace the trackwork onto the table top, remove the track, and go back around the plan making solid, well defined lines to cut along. Keep the width at least as wide as that of the roadbed or subroadbed you plan on using (see Chapter 5). Then make the cuts. To position and secure the cut strips, block under them with scraps of wood, glued and screwed in place.

GRID BENCHWORK

Grid benchwork, also called open top benchwork, is essentially the framed table top type without the top. The layout is supported mostly on risers of various kinds that are attached to the grid, or open frame, that in turn may be set upon sawhorses or a table if small but usually is fitted with leg sets. Whenever the layout is large enough to warrant it, especially if irregular in shape, this is the benchwork type to use. The great advantage is that the

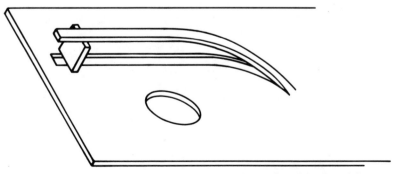

4-2 The cookie-cutter type of benchwork allows elevated trackwork and depressed scenery on a table top style. The hole is for a pond.

trackwork elevations are fully variable (within reason) and there are no re-strictions caused by a flat, uniform, hard, horizontal surface. The main dis-advantage is that the trackwork cannot be laid out and tried first, but must be well preplanned. The subroadbed is attached to risers, which offers the great-est flexibility of any arrangement (this is covered in Chapter 5). It also has the disadvantage of being more difficult to build, but balancing that is the fact that cabinetwork precision of assembly is not necessary. It does require less wood for a given area of layout, but the materials should be top grade and are therefore relatively expensive. Another advantage is that this kind of con-struction lends itself to building so that some of the leg sets can be removed and sections disconnected from one another so that the layout can be moved if necessary.

Butt Type Construction

The butt type of construction is best suited to smaller layout sizes consisting of one to just a few fairly small rectangular sections, or a broad shelf arrange-ment. In a *regular* grid design (FIG. 4-3) it is much the same as the framework beneath a framed table top bench. The perimeter frame is strengthened and stiffened with a series of cross pieces screwed and glued together. Spacing between the cross pieces is typically 16, 20, or 24 inches on centers. Closer spacing makes a more rigid frame but usually is unnecessary and can restrict roadbed construction. Wider spacing may make the assembly too limber and subject to easy warping or racking. If the width is greater than about 3 feet, further strength can be gained by running a third lengthwise member down the center, egg crate fashion. In the *offset* grid design (FIG. 4-4) the sizes of

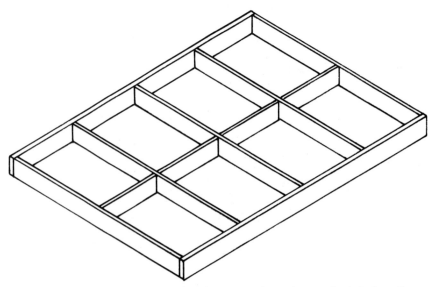

4-3 In regular grid butt construction the pattern is made up of relatively uniform rectangles.

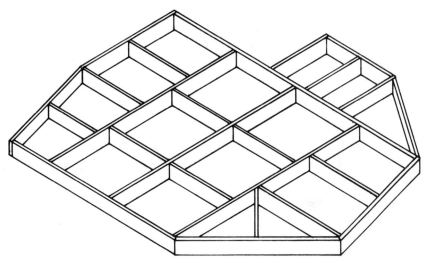

4-4 Offset grid butt construction has a non-uniform pattern that follows the demands of an irregular overall layout configuration.

the grid rectangles vary and they are positioned according to the dictates of the overall layout plan, as to what elements extend below zero grade elevation, how large, what shape, and where. Construction details are the same for either type, and either can be used under any layout design.

You can use kiln-dried No. 2 pine 1-×-4s for both constructions. Hand-pick the lengths if possible, and select those that are as straight and free from knots as you can find. Make the end cuts clean and square for the strongest joints, and secure the pieces with glue and 2-inch drywall or deck screws, two at each joint. For greater rigidity, cut some gussets and corner blocks from scrap pieces and secure them at all outside corners and at other random points if you wish. As a help in keeping them out of the way of layout elements, mount the gussets in lower corners rather than upper. As an alternative, or along with, you can fit as many joints as you wish with full-height glue blocks. This will add a considerable amount of strength and rigidity.

Girder type construction

Girder type construction (FIG. 4-5) is probably the most commonly used benchwork today. It is easy to build, lightweight but strong, adaptable to any layout perimeter configuration, and workable for any layout design except for portable, fold-up, narrow shelf, or very small arrangements. Because of its slender proportions, it must be well braced and built from good materials. The cutting, joinery, and fractional dimensions, however, are not crucial to a successful construction, so long as the connections all are solid.

The most sensible material to use is pine, either western or eastern white. It is easy to work, readily available almost anywhere, and in most areas is the lowest-cost wood. It does have a couple of problems—it shrinks, and it warps. You can't keep it from doing either, but there are some ways to

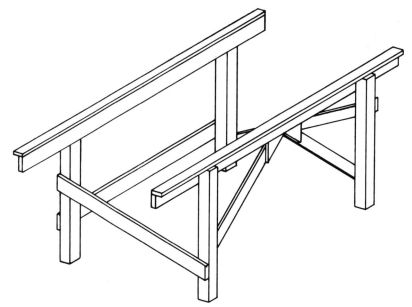

4-5   This is a typical girder benchwork construction, probably the most common arrangement for layouts larger than 4 by 8 feet and used under smaller ones as well.

minimize the resulting difficulties. For stringers and cross pieces, instead of No. 2 pine select only the grade called *clear,* which has no knots and is straight-grained. It is considerably more expensive than No. 2, but less apt to cause you problems. You may have difficulty in finding pine 1- × -2s for girder tops and braces. You can substitute spruce or fir strapping stock, but I don't recommend it. Instead, rip 1- × -2s from 1- × -4 stock on a table saw, or have it done for you at a cabinet shop. Or just use 1- × -4 stock for everything, a more satisfactory solution in most cases. If a hardwood like lauan is available at a matching price, as is sometimes the case, use that instead as it's more stable.

Usually ordinary 2- × -2 stock is specified for legs, but again, pine may not be available. Common lumberyard 2- × -2 stock is ripped 2- × -4, and is rough and probably spruce or hem fir. Construction grade will bow, warp, shrink, and give you fits. If you can, opt for a high grade of pine 2- × -4 or-6 that you can rip, or virtually any other material that is of high quality, dry, and at least relatively stable. A leg construction alternative is to ell a pair of 1- × -4s and add a couple of gussets (FIG. 4-6). Corner and glue blocks can be of any scrap material, and gussets are best cut from minimum ⅜-inch plywood; scraps are fine, in any grade. For hardware, use drywall or deck screws everywhere, instead of nails. Drive them through clear holes in the upper piece, no holes in the lower unless you are close to an edge or end and there is danger of splitting. Exception: Driving into hardwood or plywood will require pilot holes in the underneath pieces, or you'll twist the screw heads off. For glue, woodworking yellow glue (aliphatic resin) like Franklin Titebond Wood Glue® is fine. You might find tubes of panel or construction

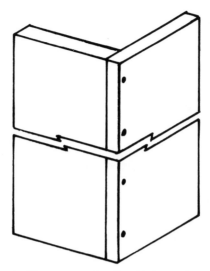

4-6 An elled leg construction like this is sturdy and stable.

adhesive that you apply with a caulking gun more convenient. Bead it on, spread it thin with a putty knife or wood scrap. It's tough stuff.

There are two approaches to girder construction (FIG. 4-7). The most common is called L-girder, where the lengthwise girders are comprised of a 1- × -4 upright and a 1- × -2 top set flat, flush along one edge and protruding at the other in an ell shape. The other is T-girder, where the top of the girder is a 1- × -4 centered along the upright. This is a stronger version, less susceptible to warping, more resistant to lateral forces, and offers more contact area for the cross pieces, or joists, mounted atop the girders.

To build an L-girder benchwork, start by making up the girders. Only two are required for each layout section, equal in length to the width of the layout. Assemble them with glue and 1½-inch drywall screws spaced about 1 foot apart. Then make up the leg sets as shown in FIG. 4-8. You will need two sets for every girder section up to about 12 feet long. This assumes an

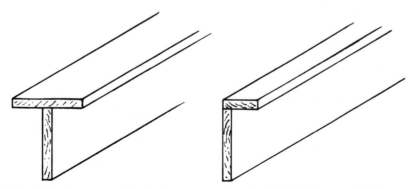

4-7 "L"-girder construction is the most common, but "T" girders are a bit stronger and stiffer and afford more joist attachment and bearing area.

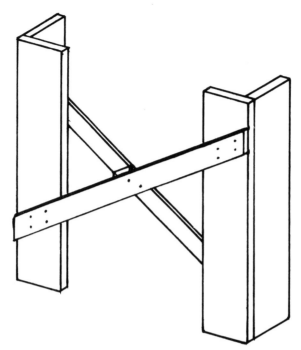

4-8   This construction makes a solid, sturdy leg set.

average-to-light layout weight. If yours will have masses of plaster, heavy motive power and rolling stock, and natural rock loaded on it (at about 160 pounds per cubic foot), use more leg sets. Adjust the height to your chosen zero-elevation layout height from the floor, taking into account the height of the cross pieces. Optimum layout zero level for you might be anywhere from about 36 to about 50 inches, depending upon your height, but the 42-to-46-inch range is common. The width between legs, front face to rear face, should be at least 1 foot less than the narrowest part of the layout. This allows you to have at least a 6-inch cross piece overhang at front and rear. Exception: When the layout is very narrow at some point(s), you will have to shave those figures down.

Stand the leg sets up and clamp the girders to them. You can temporarily tack or nail a cross piece or two on to keep the proper width while you work. Glue and screw the front and rear angle braces in place. Make sure the legs are exactly at right angles to the girders. The brace angle should be about 45 degrees. Install plywood gusset plates as shown in FIG. 4-9, using 1-inch screws into the braces and 1½-inch into the legs. Secure the girders to the legs with 2-inch drywall screws. To increase sturdiness, you can install a stretcher at the rear from leg to leg. Either 1-x-2s or 1-x-4s will serve. You could do the same at the front, but it likely will be forever in the way.

The joist, or cross piece material, is pine, either No. 2 or clear grade. Hint: If possible, store this stock in the layout area for several weeks before

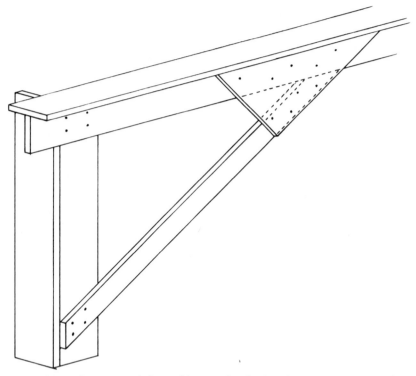

4-9 Plywood gussets and diagonal braces give the benchwork its needed rigidity.

you use it. By then it will shrink and warp about as much as it's going to, and you can pick and choose the useful lengths and have no fear that warpage will later throw your roadbed out of alignment. At the outset, attach a joist above each leg set with glue and 2-inch screws. Drive one 2-inch screw up through the flange of the L-girder into the edge of the joist at each intersection. Drive two into T-girders. Attach added joists as you need them, wherever you need them, with their length and placement made to suit. They need not be regular and uniform. They should be angled and of varied length as required. Do not glue these joists, so you can shift them later if you decide to alter some trackage or other layout elements as you build them.

When more than one section of benchwork is needed, it can be joined with no trouble. In many cases some auxiliary girders may be needed. Attach them securely to the principal girders with glue and screws, using brackets or glue blocks as necessary. Outrigger girders might be needed where the layout bulges to an abnormally wide spot. These can be held by a third leg added to a set, and anchored by joists, or can be part of a wider-than-normal two-leg set. Girders can also be employed to fill across corners by anchoring them to existing girders. Wherever added stiffness is needed, you can add an extra angle brace or two. With a little ingenuity you can adapt this basic arrangement to suit almost any configuration and size of layout.

BENCHWORK VARIATIONS

It's normal to think of a model railroad layout being made in a rectangular shape, like on a stock sheet of plywood or perhaps in an ell shape, and with everything built upward from that level. Perhaps more are done that way than in any other. But being tuned only to that form and blind to any other means a lot of lost opportunities. An awareness of some of the more important benchwork variations might spark some ideas on how you can make better and more impressive use of your layout space. It can be said that many of these constructions are not recommended for beginners. Maybe so. But in fact, many beginners have built them. By the time you get around to building some of them, you may not be a beginner anymore. Besides, the only thing you learn by sitting on your hands is how to sit on your hands.

Multilevel benchwork

Having the tracks rise a few inches above the zero elevation level on a layout so that overpasses, viaducts, or trestles can be installed is fairly routine. What is not as common, but is an interesting layout arrangement if carefully planned, are two or more levels of layout on multilevel benchwork. There are several possibilities here.

One is a freestanding layout, table-fashion. The lower level has a complete layout on it, operating at, say, 30 to 36 inches above the floor. The second level has another complete layout on it, separate from the first and set perhaps at about 56 inches high. Either or both could be split lengthwise by a center divider backdrop, different on each side, so there could be two different railroads running, and at least four different scenes (FIG. 4-10).

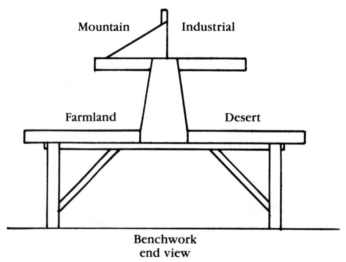

Mountain   Industrial

Farmland   Desert

Benchwork
end view

4-10 With this setup (seen in end view) you can have two separate layouts with two to four scenic settings.

Another possibility is a two-level arrangement—it could also be three—containing a single layout with a central operating and scenic theme. Or, it could change gradually from one kind of road and type of scenery to another. This layout could be set against a wall or in a corner. The upper level should be around half the depth of the lower one, so that all of the lower one can be easily seen (FIG. 4-11). Transition from one to the other can be made by elevating the grade gradually over a length of trackage. If there is not room enough for this, an alternative is to build an upward spiral of track, within a mountain or ledge or similar scenic feature. Want to go for three levels? Build another one at the opposite end of the second level.

Where there is no room for a conventional layout there can be for a continuous slender ribbon type of arrangement. Even if very narrow, maybe a double track and a couple of inches of scenery front and back, two or more vignettes could be stacked bookshelf fashion and separate. If there is room to install long shelves, steep switchbacks could be arranged from one to the next to simulate a mountain narrow-gauge road servicing a series of silver mines. If the shelf could be built all the way around a room, there would probably be length enough to join the levels by grade elevation. Relatively wide shelves would of course afford more flexibility and operating possibilities.

There are often ways to stack levels of a layout to compensate for the lack of open space, and/or to construct an impressive operational or static display.

Peninsulas

A *peninsula* is an oft-forgotten construction that can be added to good effect on almost any size or shape of layout. It consists of a jut-out from the main part of the layout at any workable point into any otherwise unused open space. The peninsula might be small, just big enough to hold an engine shed and a stub track or a three stub yard. Or it might be long but only a few inches wide, maybe with a bulge at the open end to hold a turning loop. Or it could be as large as the rest of the layout.

If the peninsula is small and does not protrude far, the benchwork for it can be joists cantilevered out from the main benchwork. A long, skinny affair is more difficult because the construction is fundamentally unstable and prone to getting bumped into. A single L-girder with a framed flange is one method, anchored securely at the main benchwork. The best arrangement is to anchor the outboard end to a 2- × -4 or 4- × -4 post that extends from floor to ceiling and is itself well secured. A large peninsula is best constructed in a normal benchwork design and attached to the main benchwork in the usual way.

Hanging benchwork

When there isn't enough space to build a layout in the conventional ways, by standing it on the floor or tacking it to a wall, what then? Hang it from the ceiling, that's what. This has been successfully done a number of times, and mostly in basements or garages where there was free access to the open

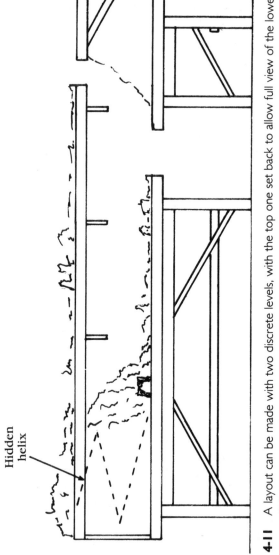

Hidden helix

4-11   A layout can be made with two discrete levels, with the top one set back to allow full view of the lower one.

framework of the building. Such a system can be equally well constructed in a finished interior room or area, provided only that the existing ceiling is high enough. The system works well, but must be carefully engineered and strongly built and fitted with a rugged and foolproof lifting arrangement.

The overall construction must be such that there is minimal deflection, distortion, and racking, because the layout remains in suspension most if not all of the time. Various systems have been devised for raising and lowering the layout, including ropes or cables and pulleys, screw jacks, and suspended hoists. Operation can be manual or powered by an electric motor with gear drive or winch. In the absence of any other suitable layout location, this possibility is worth investigating.

Depressed benchwork

There is an almost automatic tendency to build the entire layout upward from the level of the table or joist tops. But you can gain greater realism, greater variety, and greater flexibility of scenery construction if you also build downward. With proper planning and construction, even some of the trackage can be laid below zero elevation. Usually, only scenic effects, often of a dramatic nature, are so constructed on small layouts.

When the area required for such construction is small, usually all that is needed is ordinary scenery framework slung beneath and attached to the table top edges or the L-girder joists (FIG. 4-12). This is especially easy when the scenic element parallels the joists and drops down between them. But when a larger area is needed, and/or the area extends perpendicularly beyond a pair of joists, then modified benchwork construction is required.

Just how the modifications are made depends upon their size and shape, but the general idea is to set additional cross pieces to support track risers or scenery framework. They can be attached to drops from nearby joists,

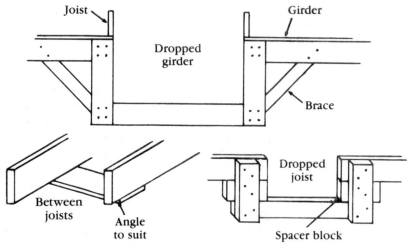

4-12 The benchwork frame members can be modified or added to in various ways when depressed scenery or trackage is called for.

from girders, or set upon or suspended from stringers that run from leg to leg. In some cases, where the depressed section is wide and extends essentially from front to back of the benchwork, it might be best to build extra leg sets to provide support for low level girders. These in turn can support a series of joists. In effect, this is another benchwork section built shorter than the others and connected to them.

Angled joists

In most benchwork all the joists or other cross pieces lie in the same horizontal plane with their top edges level and even. But if there are high mountain peaks, a ledge or cliff, or a mesa to be built, adding supplementary angled joists could be advantageous. Such scenery is typically built toward the rear of a layout, so installing angled joists (FIG. 4-13) is easy. They can be run directly from the front-to-back horizontal joists to a rear riser of appropriate height for a peak, or they can be squared off at the top for a mesa or bench. With a little added support, you can fashion a double bench.

For some dramatic scenic effects, you can slant the joists downward from some interior point on the layout, starting from zero elevation and ending at minus X inches (FIG. 4-14). This requires preplanning, probably setting the front girder back farther than it would normally be, or perhaps fashioning a dogleg front girder arrangement. Then slant the joists down from an attachment point on the front girder or horizontal joist ends to a cantilevered lower support stringer. Another possibility is to run slanted joists from a set-back front girder or from horizontal joist ends all the way to the floor.

These constructions can be made continuous across a small layout, or only in certain places or sections on a larger one, just by modifying the framework to suit. The transitions from conventional to modified benchwork are the most difficult points, but usually can be well disguised with scenery. Trackage can be run across and alongside these slanted areas simply by installing appropriate upright risers and attaching the roadbed to them, just as is done with conventional horizontal joists.

BENCHWORK STYLES

General benchwork types and construction practices, as illustrated by unspecified and essentially generic examples, have been covered so far. But in

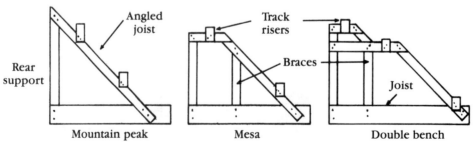

4-13 Angled joists sometimes make mountain scenery building, as well as subroadbed construction, a bit easier.

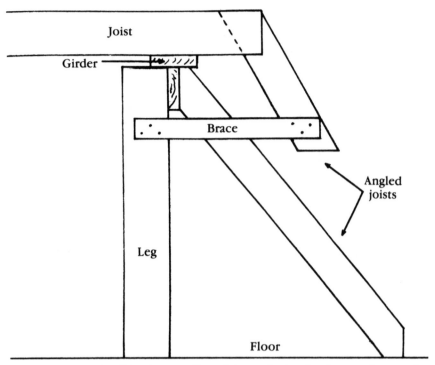

4-14 For dramatic cliff and gorge effects, joists and other framing members can be slanted downward toward or to the floor for easier scenery building.

fact there are several different styles of benchwork, or perhaps more accurately, benchwork to suit different classes of layout. Certain construction needs are required by each, beyond or apart from what has already been discussed.

Permanent benchwork

In the normal course of model railroad affairs, *permanent benchwork* usually means an arrangement that can't be readily taken apart and transported elsewhere, at least without dismantling the layout too. This can be a freestanding affair like a conventional table-type layout or an L-girder island arrangement. More accurately, it means benchwork of any design that is actually secured to the building walls and anchored to the floor. This makes the most satisfactory all around installation.

The best way to do this is to first attach one or more plates or cleats to the wall(s) of the building. 1- × -4 stock is usually adequate, but 2- × -4s could be used just as well. Attach them horizontally to the wall studs with ¼-inch lag screws at an appropriate height. If the benchwork is fitted with legs at the outer edges, secure the legs to the cleats with more lag screws, fitted with flat steel washers beneath each one, and add spacers as required. If the benchwork is girder-type, fit attachment cleats between pairs of joists at appropriate points. Secure the cleats to a wall plate with a series of lag screws and flat washers. Figure 4–15 shows the details. To anchor legs to the floor,

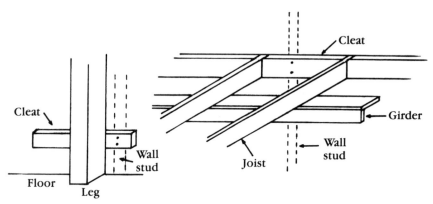

4-15   The most rigid, vibration-free benchwork installation involves anchoring it to the building walls or floor, or both.

first make sure that the benchwork is exactly in its final location, then adjust the height of the legs as necessary until all is level. Attach a steel corner bracket—3- or 4-inch size is ample—to each leg, facing forward on rear legs, rearward on front ones. Anchor the brackets to the floor.

Semipermanent benchwork

Semipermanent benchwork can be disassembled into pieces or sections small enough that the layout can be transported elsewhere, probably with some disruption and considerable effort. There are variations depending upon the size and shape of the layout, but the overall design should allow removal of the leg sets, then separation of sections at bolted joints. Each section must be small and light enough that it can be carried and will fit through doorways on edge if necessary. Some layouts, where moving is a "maybe sometime" chance, are constructed so that at one or more points the solid framework, scenery, and tracks can be actually sawn into sections (FIG. 4-16) and then trimmed up and reassembled later.

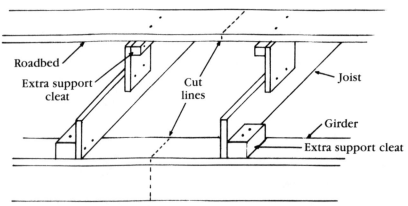

4-16   This is one way to construct reinforced benchwork points that can be sawn through without unduly weakening the sections, allowing the layout to be cut apart for relocating purposes.

Movable sections

In the context of this book, a movable layout or layout section is one that can be shifted about as a complete unit without much difficulty or preparation. For example, a small freestanding layout, if the benchwork is sufficiently rigid, could be picked up by two people and moved into the middle of the room for use, then replaced against a wall for storage. Movable layout sections might be designed to store side by side along a wall, and be pulled out and joined together for operating.

You can make a movable layout without much trouble. A single unit layout, even if fairly large, needs only to be sufficiently stiff to be picked up by two or four people at ends or corners without any appreciable sagging or racking. You can accomplish this on a small layout just by mounting carry handles to the benchwork. On larger ones you could add one or two extra girders, make the girders with 1-×-6 or even 1-×-8 webs, or add combination stiffeners and carry bars to the benchwork. These are rigid, lengthwise members attached to the underside of the layout and protruding at each end. For small to medium-sized layouts, 2-×-4s are ample and inexpensive, and you can fashion the ends into wheelbarrow-type handles.

Movable layout sections need to have stiff benchwork. A butt grid frame for each section with a deep perimeter frame, such as 1-×-6, or an L-girder style with deep girders, will do the job. If you can, make the sections small enough that they can be handled by two people. As few tracks as possible should cross from one section to another, to minimize alignment problems. Where sections join there must be a means of aligning them accurately, such as locating pins or a docking frame (FIG. 4-17). There should also be a means of cinching the units together effectively once they are aligned. A series of bolts is one method. Just tighten them up while keeping the sections mated and matched. Another possibility, especially useful in joining two flat surfaces edge to edge, is to use hardware like Tite Joint fasteners.

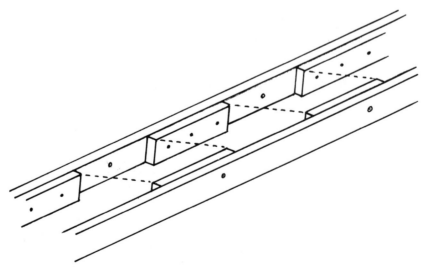

4-17 Locating pins or a docking-type frame, or both, allow layout sections to be perfectly remated and aligned.

Movable layouts or layout sections can also be mounted on casters. This requires some care in the mounting, and the benchwork legs must be well steadied in all directions with solidly anchored diagonal braces. Use top quality industrial casters in large size, like the ones often used on heavy power tools, that are capable of handling 300 or 400 pounds each. The load capacity of heavy-duty casters doesn't matter, but the relative stability they afford does. Each caster should be fitted with a positive lock. You probably will have to fashion a small platform at the end of each leg in order to mount the casters, and this arrangement should be solidly attached.

Portable benchwork

This might better be called portable casework, because conventional benchwork really plays little part in a portable layout. To be truly portable, the layout must be completely enclosed and encased when buttoned up for transporting. Everything has to be internally secured and packed away where it can't be harmed.

As an example, consider a complete layout inside a large, solid sided suitcase. The benchwork consists of a sheet of ½-inch plywood atop a frame of 1-×-2s on edge. The frame has a detachable bottom of sheet aluminum. This sits on props at suitcase mid-depth, with storage underneath for motive power, control unit, and rolling stock. The layout locks into place within the case, and the foam-filled top, when lowered, affords clearance for most of the scenery and locks a few selected structures into place.

This general scheme can be followed to construct casework for any layout design up to the point where the case becomes too heavy and unwieldy to transport. Some cases are designed to open in half and lay flat to present a 4-by-8-foot layout, and that is about as large as you can conveniently get. Some arrangements include legs that fold against the case, others are meant to be placed on a table or horses or just set on the floor. Lightweight cases can be fitted with a single suitcase-type handle or heavier carrying handles at the ends, like a trunk (that can itself house a portable layout), while heavier ones are equipped with bottom casters so they can be rolled along on a tether. It would be easy enough to fit one to a two-wheeled utility dolly.

The keys to a successful portable layout are rugged construction with tough materials, rattle-proof protective storage for equipment and accessories (if carried with), and vibration-proof connections (electrical and otherwise), scenery, structures, and trackage.

Modular benchwork

There are two kinds of modular benchwork. One occurs when any particular model railroader builds a series of similar layout sections that can be readily stored away when not in use, then rolled out and plugged together for a work or operating session. The design is to the modeler's specifications and whims and the modules, even if all alike in size or benchwork design, don't necessarily match up with anyone else's.

The other kind has a different makeup and a different purpose. The N Trak modules, which are N scale, 4, 6, or 8 feet long, 2 feet wide, and 40 inches high, are probably the best known. These modules must be built to a certain rigid set of specifications, including benchwork, trackwork, and electrical system. A module is not a complete layout, but a vignette that can be attached to any other modules anywhere and plugged into the operating system. Their owners can, and frequently do, get together and set up complete operating pikes of substantial size. A modeler can build his own complete layout by making up several scenically and thematically compatible modules and operating them at home. Nationally universal modules are a great way for a modeler without enough space for a conventional layout to join the fun.

You can get complete details on the N Trak system from the organization at 2424 Alturas Rd., Atascadero, CA 93422; the NMRA will know of any address change. There is also a possibility of a similar modular system soon appearing in HO scale, and by the time you read this it may be a reality.

Fold-up benchwork

Fold-up benchwork is just that—a box-framed platform or butt-type grid with a bottom panel that folds up against the wall (FIG. 4-18). A typical construction

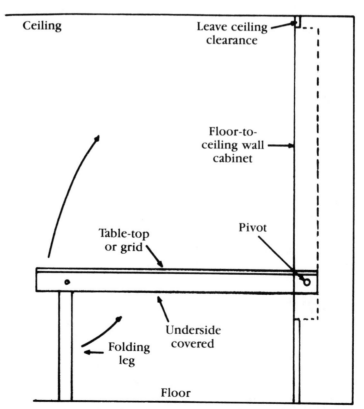

4-18 This basic foldup benchwork construction can be modified in numerous ways and made in many shapes and sizes.

folds into a cabinet rather like a shallow armoire, or into a specially constructed niche in the wall like a shallow closet. Access in the open position is from three sides, with the fourth anchored to wall or cabinet, so size is restricted to about 5-by-7-feet maximum to keep everything reachable.

Basic construction involves building a box of sufficient depth to contain wiring underneath (make the bottom panel removable) and the desired height of scenery and structures above zero elevation. This box must fold into the wall or cabinet with the hinge assembly typically being about 3 feet from the floor (but that height can be less if you wish). A mating cabinet, that can be attached to the wall or freestanding, must also be constructed. Depending upon its location in the house, this may have to have a furniture-grade finish and appearance. Or, a shallow closet could be built into an interior wall, protruding and finished on the opposite side of the wall. The bottom of the benchwork serves as the door to either the closet or the armoire. The area beneath the unit can be fitted with shelves, with or without cabinet doors, and used to store motive power and rolling stock. All in all, this is a substantial project for an amateur carpenter with some experience. However, you can let the job out to a home remodeling contractor or a cabinetmaker if you draw up the plans and set the specifications.

Frame the benchwork with top-grade pine 1-inch nominal boards. The perimeter frame, however, is best built of ¾-inch A-B plywood, gusseted and glue-blocked at the corners and fastened at every joint with screws. This whole assembly must be strong and stiff. Plywood ½ inch thick is suitable for the bottom panel, and can be decorative hardwood plywood if a furniture effect is needed. Trimwork can be pine or hardwood as required. The case could be painted plywood, finished hardwood, or whatever else might be suitable to match the surrounding decor. A leg assembly can be made up to fold down out of the benchwork, or you can use a separate leg set built like a sawhorse on which the end of the benchwork can rest when in the down position.

You can rig up a satisfactory hinging and latching arrangement with readily available hardware. Heavy-duty piano hinges or two or three large ball bearing butt hinges would work. Barrel bolts or any one of a number of different kinds of latches could be utilized to secure the unit in the storage position. Another possibility is a full set of murphy bed hardware, available from woodworking/hardware specialty supply outlets. Expensive, but rugged and foolproof.

Shelf benchwork

The benchwork for a shelf type of layout (FIG. 4-19) is not difficult to construct. Because it is stable and unlikely to warp or shrink to any great extent, plywood is definitely recommended here. A minimum thickness of ½ inch is needed, and ¾ inch if more than 1 foot wide. For the sake of appearance, the outer edge of the shelf structure should be kept as thin as possible, so the plywood can be attached to 1- × -2 pine as a framed platform. For greater rigidity, substitute 1- × -4 stock for the edges. Use the rear frame member to mount the shelf to the wall studs; ¼-inch lag screws about 2½ inches long

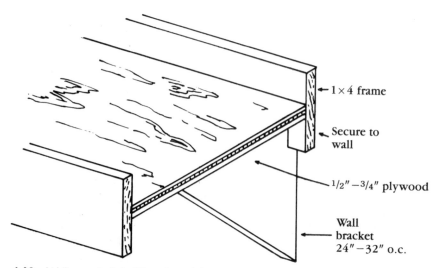

←1 × 4 frame

←Secure to wall

←¹⁄₂″ −³⁄₄″ plywood

← Wall bracket 24″ − 32″ o.c.

4-19 Wall mounted shelf benchwork is easy to build and install, and allows construction of a layout in an area where floor space may not be available.

are satisfactory. If the wall is concrete or block, use lag shields or masonry nails.

Anchoring the rear frame alone is not enough—more support is needed. Diagonal bracing is one answer, and the braces can be simple 1- × -2 lengths set on a 45 degree angle and anchored to the wall, or a fancier bracket attached the same way. Another alternative is to mount sturdy, braced angle brackets, that can be plain galvanized utility brackets or the fancier decorator-type brackets. Unbraced brackets are not recommended, especially for the large scales, as they can allow too much deflection at the outer edge and tend to pick up vibrations from running trains. Vertical legs spaced here and there and extending directly downward from the shelf edges to the floor are not a good idea, because they will sooner or later get kicked and cause damage. Slant them back at least partway to the wall.

DUST PROTECTION

Apart from oxidation of the rail tops that causes electric discontinuity and operating difficulties, the accumulation of dust is probably the most irritating problem with any layout. That thin layer of fuzz gets onto and into everything. Cleanup is difficult, sometimes impossible, always time-consuming and hard on delicate scenery and detailing. As discussed earlier, it is important to build your layout in an environment that is as clean and dust and dirt-free as possible, but you can't get away from ordinary house dust. It's always present to some degree. One way to minimize the problem is to make a protective cover for the layout. This is often not practical for a large, sprawling pike, but is almost always possible on small layouts. Usually you must start building it as the benchwork is constructed. Trying to add on later is difficult.

In simplest form the cover isn't much different than a canopy bed. Assume a small, rectangular, freestanding layout. Mount a post at each corner, and drape fabric over the post tops and down the sides, making a tent over the layout. When operating the layout, flip the front and sides up onto the top. Fabric covers can be fitted in all manner of sizes and shape variations. All you need to do is provide some sort of framework to hang the material on. That might be metal rods, dowels, wood rounds, shower curtain rods, closet rods, drapery rods, whatever. The fabric should be one that doesn't itself create dust, as any fuzzy or nappy material will. Sheeting, ripstop nylon, or something similar would work. You can just drape the material, or attach it with shower curtain or drapery rings, or set grommets in the material and slip them onto framework hooks. Plastic sheeting is not recommended, as it has a habit of accumulating static electricity charges and is a great dust attracter, and difficult to clean.

You can also protect the layout with solid materials. By building a suitable number of uprights into the benchwork as you go along, you can provide support for a solid ceiling over the layout, perhaps ¼-inch plywood. Depending on the pike's location, the room ceiling might serve equally well. Enclosed sides or rear, as when against a wall, could be fitted with a solid panel back, that could double as a backdrop, or backdrop support. Open sides and the front might be fitted with solid, removable panels, perhaps just hung on nails or fitted over L-hooks. Instead of opaque wood panels, you might use some clear plastic panels, say at the sides where access isn't normally needed. Or, you could install ball bearing slider track and fit the front with sliding plate glass panels.

One way or another you can make your layout mostly dustproof, and the effort is worthwhile. The key is to plan ahead and make the framework for the protective cover an integral part of the benchwork.

Chapter **5**

Building the
trackwork

The trackwork on your model railroad layout consists of three principal parts: subroadbed, roadbed, and tracks. The three together form the heart of a model railroad, and in the construction of this assembly lies the key to a successful layout. Excellence of installation is crucial. Do the job well and your trains will operate perhaps not faultlessly, but with hardly a hitch attributable to the trackage. Otherwise, well . . . .

CHOICES

There are a number of choices you'll have to make with regard to your trackwork, preferably well before you begin building it. Most of the different possibilities will be addressed throughout this chapter. But to begin with, there are several different kinds of track to consider. They have one thing in common—they all require a subroadbed. Beyond that, requirements vary.

Sectional track (snap-track)

The most complete trackage package consists of factory-made sections comprised of roadbed, ties, rails, and ballast, all finished and ready to lay. The sections are of specific lengths and curvatures that vary with different manufacturers, and there is a small selection of matching turnouts. Lay the pieces down, plug them together, and you're about done. The Kato Unitrack is a typical product.

Another type of sectional track consists of only the rails attached to ties. You must provide a roadbed, arrange the track sections and snap them together, then spread ballast. A typical product is the Atlas line, with a good array of turnouts and accessories.

Flexible track (flex-track)

Flexible track consists of lengths of rail attached to ties, usually about 30 to 36 inches long depending upon the manufacturer. The lengths can be curved and recurved to any desired practical radius, including slight bends and easements that are not possible with sectional track, and trimmed or fitted as necessary. There is a good array of choices in this type track, with many turnouts and other accessories offered. It is a very flexible system in all respects. A roadbed is required, as is ballasting. The Atlas product is very popular and readily available, the Peco and Shinohara lines are considered top quality, and there are others as well.

Hand-laid track

There are several options in hand-laid track. You can build a roadbed, attach individual ties to it, then mount the individual rails upon the ties with tiny spikes. Or, you can attach ties and rails to factory-made roadbed. Or, you can attach rails to factory-made roadbed with integral ties. Construction can be made compatible with certain commercial makes of turnouts and other accessories. Some modelers also build their own turnouts from scratch. Campbell, Rail Craft, and Tru-Scale are respected makers of these products. Hand-laying is not usually recommended for beginning modelers, and the techniques will not be discussed here.

INSTALLING THE SUBROADBED

Oftentimes the top surface of table-top benchwork is made to serve as the subroadbed. This can cause difficulties later with the scenery construction, especially in providing prototypical drainage arrangements. In most constructions, it is best if the subroadbed surface is ½ inch or more above the table surface, or, in grid-type benchwork, above the joist tops.

In grid-type benchwork, the subroadbed is mounted upon risers attached to the joists. The risers can be made of ½-inch-thick plywood or any nominal 1-inch-thick plain wood stock. Cut the pieces a bit wider than the necessary subroadbed width, with the length equal to the joist width plus the required elevation at the riser location. The elevation should be closely figured and must be accurate when the installation is complete. If you haven't already done so, install the required joists on the benchwork This is sometimes left until the trackwork is underway, so their positions can be adjusted for optimum support.

Locate the riser position. This is most often done by a combination of measuring and placing the already cut subroadbed strips in place to judge by. Clamp the riser to the joist, adjusting the height meanwhile. Make sure it is exactly at right angles to the joist. If a bit of superelevation is needed here, make sure the tilt is in the right direction, and not too severe. Attach the riser to the joist (FIG. 5-1) with four screws. Don't glue it, as you may want to remove or adjust it sometime. Attach all the other risers the same way.

On a flat tabletop surface, you can support the zero-elevation subroadbed on small blocks of wood screwed to the tabletop. If the required thickness of the blocks (subroadbed height) gets beyond about 1½ inches, attach a cleat flat to the tabletop and a riser to the cleat (FIG. 5-2).

The distance between risers necessary for a sturdy installation depends upon the kind and thickness of the subroadbed material, and the weight of the trains that will run over it. There is no handy rule of thumb, except that the roadway must be stiff and solid. If you push down fairly hard with your thumb at a midpoint between two risers, you shouldn't be able to detect any deflection.

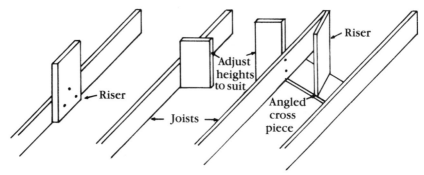

5-1   Wherever the trackage rises above zero elevation, the subroadbed is supported by a series of risers positioned appropriately and attached to the benchwork joists, like this.

The subroadbed material most favored is plywood. A ⅜-inch thickness works all right in most cases, unless the risers must be far apart, then ½-inch plywood is better. Flexibility is sometimes desirable for making upgrade/downgrade transitions. Some modelers use a single layer of ¼-inch-thick plywood, some set one layer, then glue another to it. And some use layered hardboard.

For the tangents, use straight strips a bit wider than the roadbed. Lay the curves out with trammels or some other accurate device, leaving a bit of extra width to take care of easements. The longer you can make all of the sub-roadbed pieces, the better, as there will be fewer joints. Make as many of those joints as possible in the tangents rather than the curves. Make all joints directly over a riser, of course, and add a cleat to one or both sides of the riser to give yourself plenty of attachment bearing surface (FIG. 5-3). The sub-roadbed for yard areas usually consists of a one-piece sheet of plywood of suitable size. Prototype yards are usually quite flat without much provision for trackside drainage ditches and such. These pieces, as well as wider-than-normal sections such as at a wye or siding, can be mounted on cleats attached to pairs of risers, forming bridges of sorts. The shapes and sizes of sub-roadbed sections at congested trackage points is just a matter of what seems logical.

5-2   Risers are used to support elevated trackage on tabletop layouts; use cleat attachment when the risers are taller than simple blocks about 1½ inches high.

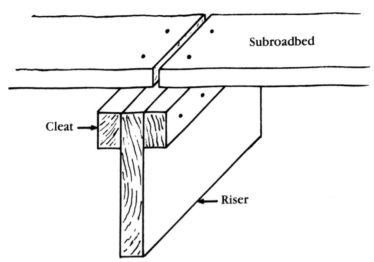

5-3 Joints in the subroadbed should always be well supported; a single or double cleat affords ample attachment and bearing surface.

Secure the subroadbed strips to the risers with screws; there is no need for glue. Where there are changes in elevation, some modelers like to cut the tops of the risers to a matching angle so the subroadbed joins flat. This is effective but a bit tricky, and is most easily done with a bandsaw, table saw, or disc sander where you can tilt the table to the required angle and fashion a true, flat end on the riser. The subroadbed is continuous at tunnels, but stops at predetermined points for bridges, overpasses, viaducts, and trestles, leaving a precalculated open span.

When all the subroadbed sections are in place, go over the whole layout and carefully check the elevations. Make sure all joints are exactly even. If not, sand or file or fill as necessary until they are. All vertical curves should be very gradual, with no abrupt transitions. Fill with a material like Durham's Rock Hard Water Putty and sand as necessary to get smooth, even curvatures (FIG. 5-4). Check all superelevations to make sure they are not too tilted. Look for loose or wobbly sections, pieces you forgot to secure, or any misalignments of any kind. This is the foundation, and it has to be right.

LAYING THE ROADBED

If the subroadbed is well done, laying the roadbed will be easy. If you are using the all-in-one type of sectional track, you'll skip this step. Special roadbed considerations are needed for hand-laid track. That system is not common to small, first-time home layouts and it won't be covered here.

Plain snap-track and flex-track is most often laid on cork roadbed (FIG. 5-5). This comes in precut strips sized accurately for your scale. Start by drawing accurate centerlines of the track right on the subroadbed. Separate the cork roadbed at the slit down the center. That leaves two pieces with one squared and one beveled edge each. Turn them with the bevel facing out and

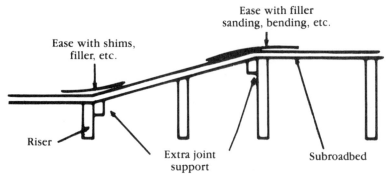

5-4 The roadbed transitions at top and bottom of vertical curves must be eased substantially by filling, shimming, bending the material, and sanding.

angled down. Glue one half down with the squared edge running along the centerline and pin it in place. Woodworkers' yellow glue or premixed heavy-duty wall covering adhesive applied with a brush or roller works well. Butt the second strip against the first. Pin down the lifted points in radii. Match in as necessary with strips and with flat sections at turnouts, crossings, and the like. In yards or other multitrack areas, lay flat cork sheets. Make sure all the cork is properly aligned and lies absolutely flat, with no air bubbles underneath or ripples along the curves.

5-5 Cork is the most commonly used roadbed material and is easy to install.

There are alternatives to using cork. Homa-Bed is roadbed manufactured from Homasote, available in strips and sections for all scales, formed with beveled edges and curvable within specified limits. Vinylbed is a soft, flexible, tough roadbed available in strips and sections for all scales. It too has beveled edges, and can be mounted on matching Subvinylbed for extra elevation and soundproofing (ordinary subroadbed is still required). Foam roadbed is another possibility, and these products are made to accept certain brands of flex-track. There is a flexible mastic roadbed that sticks to a clean, dry, subroadbed. Flex-track is anchored to it by simply pressing it down and sticking it, and ballast can be applied the same way, with the excess being taken up by a vacuum. All of these materials work well, are applied to the subroadbed in much the same way as cork, deaden sound about the same, can be used with either snap-track or flex-track, and the latter four cost about the same when finished. Plain cork is the least expensive by a considerable margin.

DRAINAGE AND SCENERY CONSIDERATIONS

As you construct the roadway, keep in mind that you need to allow certain clearances along the line for other elements of the layout. The need to keep the trackwork above the table or joist tops was mentioned earlier, so as to provide space for the trackside drainage ditches common to all prototype trackage, except for yards and possibly some minor branchline sidings. Mainlines typically are elevated quite a bit above the immediate surroundings, branchlines from a bit less to a lot less so. In addition, you may want to build in culverts that pass beneath the track as drainage aids.

All landscape sheds water downslope, so wherever you have tilted scenery, especially if mountainous, there should be logical watercourses for rain and snow runoff. This also calls for culverts, some of which may be good-sized, and substantial drainage ditches. Where trackwork runs along close to steep hillsides and particularly rocky cliffs, there should be a wide space between the tracks and the cliff—this is where loose rock falls harmlessly in real-life circumstances, to be cleared periodically by work crews.

You also need room for various trackside items, such as signals, relay boxes, set-asides for track-workers' gear, section houses, cattle guards, signposts, and a host of other odds and ends. All of this detailing increases the realism of the layout, but a lot of it always seems to come to mind as afterthoughts, rather than in the early preplanning stages, hence the need to make the space allowances just on general principles. The scenery may play an important part, too. You have to have some place to attach some of the scenery framework, such as screening or cardboard strips. You need space to work in and room enough to make the attachments. In short, crowding along the roadway can cause problems later, while leaving ample space will not. If some particular point looks too open to you, chances are you'll have no difficulty in finding something to fill it.

BRIDGE, TRESTLE, AND PORTAL PREPARATION

Where a bridge or trestle is to go in, the subroadbed and roadbed stops. The size of the gap has to be nicely figured. One way is to make a continuous installation, then go back and cut out the gap. The problem here is that the vibration and stresses of sawing are likely to weaken and/or damage some of the nearby trackwork. A better way is to build to the bridge or trestle ends. In all cases it is best if you have the bridges, trestles, piers, viaducts, and abutments already on hand. If you can't, at least have the accurate dimensions.

First, consider a single-span bridge. It needs support only at the two ends. The cut ends of the subroadbed at the gap need to be supported for good stiffness. This means installing risers at each end of the gap, which is likely to require an auxiliary crosspiece between two joists. A length of 1-×-2 is sufficient, a strip of ¾-inch plywood is better. If the strip must be so long that it is limber, make it a T-girder. If the bridge runs parallel with the joists, or close to it, install cleats between the joists at an appropriate height and spaced to allow support at the bridge ends.

Now the bridge must be fitted into place, and just how that is done depends upon the construction and dimensions of the bridge and the abutments. The bottom line is that the rails must cross the roadbed-bridge-roadbed joints without a hump or a hitch, in exactly the same plane. You may be able to place the bridge ends on the subroadbed, perhaps with a bit of shimming. Or the bridge ends might have to be placed directly on the abutments. The abutments should be glued to the risers, and Hobsco GOO works well for this. Either way the bridge ends must be solidly supported. Figure 5–6 shows the details.

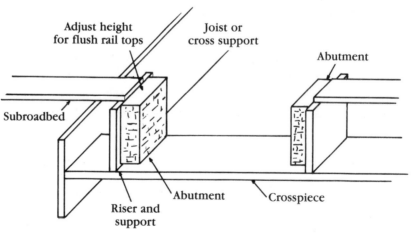

5-6 The roadbed gap for a single-span bridge must be closely figured, and the bridge ends well supported and set flush.

Now consider a two- or multiple-span bridge, where piers support the midpoints. Something is needed in turn to support the piers. Install one or more shim blocks at the appropriate spots on the crosspiece between the joists, with the height calculated to just support the bridge span ends (perhaps a bit less, but no more). Then, as necessary, you can shim beneath the shim blocks with cardboard or heavy paper to get just the right final height. In the case of a bridge parallel with the joists, run a crosspiece between the cleats. Secure the necessary shim blocks to the crosspiece. Figure 5–7 shows typical details.

A trestle installation is a bit different. If all the bents (vertical members, or legs) rest upon essentially flat ground, install a support board or plywood strip at an appropriate height between two joists if the trestle is at right angles. For a parallel trestle, install a pair of cleats between two joists, and a support board across the cleats. If the trestle bents are to rest on uneven ground and are of varied length, start by mounting a support board to fit beneath the tallest bent. Arrange support blocks of appropriate height on the board under the other bents (FIG. 5-8). The abutments and trestle ends are set in the same manner as those for bridges.

Tunnel portals are installed with a different procedure. Each portal is a separate piece, basically trimwork to surround the tunnel entrance. It should be glued to a wood framework directly behind it, and be supported from below. Attach a support cleat to the subroadbed, a joist, or both, that extends outward on both sides of the tunnel opening. Attach a 1-×-2 (or smaller) frame to this, sized to the portal shape so that it does not encroach upon the opening and is not appreciably larger than the portal piece. This frame will also serve as an anchoring point for the surrounding scenery framework. Shim the portal as necessary to set it at the proper height relative to the roadbed, and glue it in place. Make certain of the proper clearances all around the opening. See FIG. 5-9 for details.

In all such installations the scenery will eventually be worked around the structure ends, abutments, piers, and bents so that no raw edges, portions of supports, cracks, or seams will show. Everything will be hidden and invisible, so your support materials and constructions need not be up to showcase quality level. They do need to be solid, sturdy, and stable.

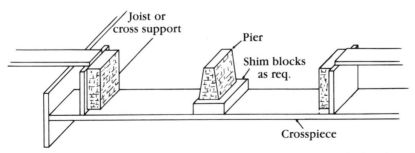

5-7   Multiple-span bridges necessitate adding an extra crosspiece to the benchwork to form support for the bridge piers.

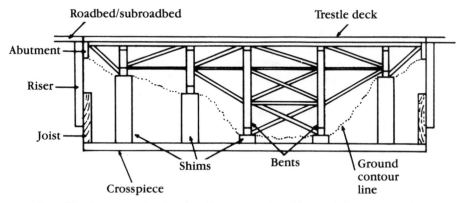

5-8 Trestle support involves installing a crosspiece low enough to support the tallest bents and placing suitable shim blocks beneath all the bents.

INSTALLING HIDDEN TRACKAGE

Hidden trackage effectively creates the illusion of a larger layout and adds to operating realism. This trackage should be completely installed and tested before any permanent scenery is built over it, even if enough access is available from below or behind to allow making minor adjustments or picking up derailed cars. It's just much easier that way.

Unless absolutely unavoidable and crucial to layout operation, don't install turnouts and never position crossovers or other fancy trackwork in hidden locations. Stay with unbroken tangents and curves with as gentle radii as possible. It's not a bad idea to make the subroadbed wider here than in ac-

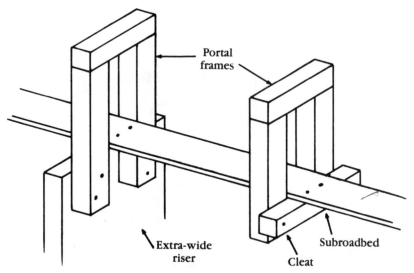

5-9 A frame for a tunnel portal can be attached to the subroadbed or the benchwork, and serves as an anchoring point for the surrounding scenery as well.

cessible spots. You might also want to erect a series of "crash barriers" along the subroadbed edges. Any thin, flexible material will work, such as ⅛-inch hardboard or even thick cardboard. The barriers need extend up beyond the subroadbed surface only far enough to restrain any car that might derail, and keep it from crashing to the floor. If too high, visibility and access will be limited.

The secret of trouble-free hidden trackage is simple. Use extra patience and care when you install the roadway to make sure that both vertical and horizontal curves are both easy and eased, there are no rough spots or abrupt transitions of any kind, and the roadway and all its supports are solid and sturdy.

RAIL CODES AND KINDS

Model railroad track is frequently advertised as, and frequently referred to as, Code this or Code that, which confuses a lot of beginners. The explanation is simple, and has to do with the height of the rails. In FIG. 5-10 is a sketch of a typical prototype railroad rail in cross section. Many different sizes have been used, but the approximate shape of the rail stays the same. The height, width of the base, and width of the head in particular are variable; the rail is designated in terms of pounds of weight per yard of length. The heavier the rail, the greater the dimensions. A small, narrow-gauge branchline, for example, might expectably use 40-pound rail, which is quite small. A modern mainline, on the other hand, might use 120-pound or larger rail.

The code system was developed to designate different sizes of model rail (TABLE 5–1). The number designates the height of the rail, from underside

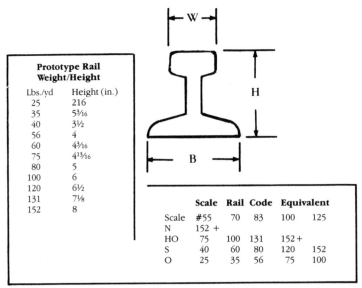

Prototype Rail Weight/Height

Lbs./yd	Height (in.)
25	2¹⁶
35	5³⁄₁₆
40	3½
56	4
60	4³⁄₁₆
75	4¹³⁄₁₆
80	5
100	6
120	6½
131	7⅛
152	8

Scale	Rail	Code	Equivalent	
Scale	#55	70	83	100	125
N	152 +				
HO	75	100	131	152 +	
S	40	60	80	120	152
O	25	35	56	75	100

5-10 The height of model railroad track rail is designated by a code number which can be related to prototype rail size.

of base to top of head, measured in hundredths of an inch. Thus, Code 55 rail measures 0.055 inches high, Code 70 measures 0.070 inches high, and so on. The Code number can be correlated to any scale by formula, converting it to a prototypical likeness. So, Code 70 rail in N scale, which is in common use, is actually out of scale because it represents a prototype rail much heavier than has ever been used. But in HO scale, it would be the approximate equivalent of 100-pound rail, suitable for modeling average mainline rail. In O scale, it would represent 35-pound rail, maybe good enough for a rickety old freight yard.

Most modelers select a particular Code and stick with it, as there is not a wide choice available anyway. Some, however, prefer to use a large size for mainline, smaller for branchline service, and smaller yet for yards. With proper shimming and fitting, the different sizes can be joined at track sections and turnouts so that there are no operating problems.

As to the kind of model rail available, there are two in common use today. One is brass, the other is nickel-silver. Nearly all new track and plain rail sold today is of the latter kind. Though it does not conduct electricity quite as well as brass, neither does it oxidize as badly and so there are far fewer problems with electrical contact between locomotives and the rail heads. A variation is preweathered rail, which is nickel-silver rail that has been treated chemically to blacken it for a more realistic appearance than the bright and shiny standard product.

TURNOUTS AND CROSSINGS

Turnouts, or track switches, of various sorts permit routing a train from one track to another. They are the biggest single cause of locomotive and car derailments, electrical discontinuity and shorts, and associated problems. They are nonetheless essential. No matter what their type, they should be placed in accessible locations. If they must be hidden under scenery, the scenery section should be removable for easy access.

There are several parts in a turnout, and the nomenclature is confusing for beginners. It's important to know the terms and understand how a turnout operates, though, because they are a subject for frequent discussion and a crucial element of the trackage. And, there are a lot of variations and possible modifications. Figure 5–11 shows the basics.

There are two general types of turnouts available for model railroading. One is the fixed-radius type, made primarily for use with sectional track but also compatible with some brands of flex-track. These turnouts take up relatively less space than the other kind and have a turn-off leg curved to the same fixed radius as is offered in the same brand of curved track sections. The other type is the numbered turnout, longer but considerably more realistic in appearance and intended for use with flex-track. This is the type of turnout most modelers install.

Numbered turnouts are designated as #4, #6, and so on. The lower the number, the more abrupt the branch angle and the shorter the turnout unit. The number is a frog number and refers to the amount of divergence between the frog and the crossing rail, which relates to the angle between the

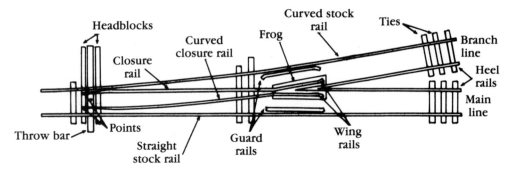

5-11 The basic makeup and nomenclature of a standard turnout.

heel rails and thus the angle of the branching track. The branching track of a #4 turnout turns out at a sharp 14 degrees, while a #8 turnout branches at a much gentler 7 degrees (approximately). As a variation, some brands of turnouts do not have a number, but rather an angle designation. For example, Arnold offers 15-degree turnouts, or roughly #4. Figure 5–12 shows some common equivalents. Note that most commercial model turnouts are not exactly prototypical and they do vary. The designations also include the branch direction, such as #6LH (left hand).

There are several turnout configurations (FIG. 5-13). The simplest and most widely used (and most reliable) is the straight turnout, with a straight main line and a curved branch. A ladder is just a series of straight turnouts, usually three or four, all angled the same way, connected together, and ready to install in a freight yard. A curved turnout has a curved main line and a curved branch. A wye turnout has the lines curving away from each other, usually an equal amount. A three-way turnout has a straight center track, another curving away to the right, and a third to the left. A single crossover is a back-to-back pair of turnouts allowing transfer in one direction from one

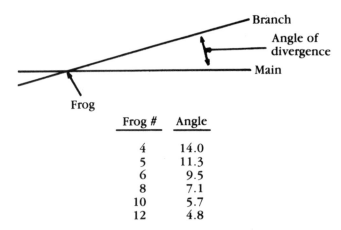

Frog #	Angle
4	14.0
5	11.3
6	9.5
8	7.1
10	5.7
12	4.8

5-12 Equivalent branch angles and number designations of turnouts.

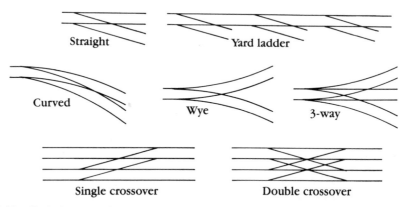

5-13   Typical commonly used turnout configurations commercially available in model track.

line to a second, parallel line. A double crossover is four turnouts in back-to-back pairs that cross in the center, allowing transfer in either direction.

While crossovers are installed between parallel lines, crossings and slip switches are used with two divergent lines (FIG. 5-14). Simple crossings do not allow transfer from one line to the other; the two merely cross. Crossings are designated according to the angle between the two lines—30-degree, 45-degree, 90-degree, and so on. Slip switches have switches inside the crossing and do allow transfer from one line to the other. A single slip allows transfer in one direction, a double slip in both.

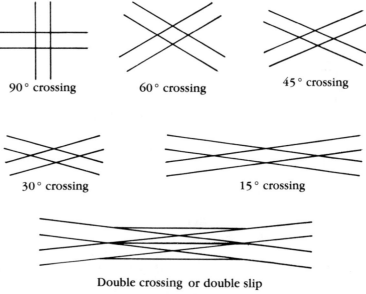

5-14   Typical crossing and slip switch patterns.

A caution is in order here. The fancy turnouts and crossings are appealing. *But.* Straights, ladders, wyes, and simple crossings are quite reliable. Beyond that, the more complex the unit, the more problematical it becomes. The harder it is to install and maintain, the trickier is the electrical circuitry, and the more expensive it is. As a rule of thumb, arrange your track plan— revise it if necessary—so that you use as few of the more sophisticated units as possible, and then only when unavoidable to carry out your plan and operating scheme.

LAYING TRACK

Newcomers to this hobby have a tendency to slap track down and nail it tight, willy-nilly, without paying attention to the fine points. Most modelers only do that once, because the usual result is a hatful of problems. Track laying is not difficult, but you do have to exercise some care and patience. Most of the track laid on home layouts these days is flex-track. When properly done, it is reliable and realistic-looking, and it is extremely versatile. Many beginners also use snap-track as a matter of convenience and speed.

For flex-track, start by marking a guideline on your roadbed. (This is impossible on mastic roadbed, unnecessary on foam with the factory-impressed tie slots.) You can use the seam in the center of cork roadbed, or draw a centerline if there is no seam. If the flex-track has no predrilled nail holes in the tie centers, draw a guideline where the outer (or inner) ends of the ties will lie. Include guidelines for the turnouts and crossings, too.

Next, set the turnouts temporarily in place to make sure they will actually fit the way you want them to. You might have to make some minor revisions to the roadway if not. There is nothing to say you can't trim turnout rails back, or rebend the curvatures slightly if necessary to make them fit into place better. Just do it cleanly, and don't disturb the frogs and points. Set some lengths of track in place to see if you really have what you visualized earlier.

If you're a beginner at this, pick as a starting point a couple of turnouts with lengthy runs of straight track attached—leave the more congested, difficult parts until later on when you've gotten a feel for laying track. Check the turnouts to make sure they operate properly and smoothly, and there are no defects, bad ties, plastic flashings, or other problems. Check the rails with a gauge and adjust as necessary. Slip rail joiners halfway onto the rail ends, using needle-nose pliers. These may be metal or plastic, according to your plan and depending upon the electrical circuits to be set up later (see Chapter 6). Make sure both sides of each joiner are fitted evenly over the rail base, and that the joiner didn't kink in the middle as you slid it onto the rail. Either mishap will cause a serious hump in the track. You will have to cut the plastic ties away in most cases in order to fit the joiners, so save the ties.

Set the turnouts, align them, and secure them with a few small track or wire nails (not brads, which don't have heads) through the small holes provided in the ties, using a small hammer and a nailset. The heads should just barely contact the tie tops. If you drive them down too far you can rack the ties and force the rails into misalignment.

Next, connect lengths of track to the turnouts, pushing the rail ends securely into the joiners. Be careful not to disrupt the turnout's position or loosen it up. Align the track on the guideline, and drive nails through the holes provided, about halfway in. If there are no holes you'll have to drill some in the tie centers, about every 4 inches, with a pin vise and suitable drill bit. Sight along the rails to see if they are straight, or if the arc you've laid out is smooth and not hitchy. When you're satisfied, drive the nails home, and take care not to set them too tight. Before snugging the track down at the joints, be sure to slip some ties back into the gaps left at the rail joiners. Shape the ties to fit as necessary and slide them into place loose—the bonded ballast will hold them in place later. Make sure they don't fit too tightly, which will drive the rails upward and create a bump.

One way to lay track is to set all of the turnouts and special switches first and go on from there. Another is to lay all the curved track first. The point in either method is to fit the more easily laid straight sections to all the more difficult portions. This also allows you to see just how well your trackage is going to fit in place, and to make adjustments in the straightaways if necessary. So lay the radii first and turnouts next, or vice versa. Then go on to the tangents.

When bending the curves, start several inches downstream of the easement. Mold the curve slowly and gently, every couple of inches along the rails. Unless the curve is gentle, don't try to bend it all at once. Make two or three passes, until the rails stay positioned by themselves in the desired curve. Eyeball the curve and check that it is smooth and uniform with no kinks or jogs. It is essential that the radius be constant, or that it diminishes/increases steadily. Check the whole length with a gauge for track width. Then attach the track firmly to the roadbed and check it again.

As you make the curve, the inner rail at the free end will extend beyond the outer one because the outer arc is longer. In order to fit the next section you will have to trim the inner rail back. Some modelers prefer to trim so that the joints are not directly opposite one another, but this is a matter of preference. You can trim by sawing with a razor saw or even a fine-tooth hacksaw blade stub, but this is difficult, inaccurate, and can damage the track (or whatever else is nearby if you slip). A hand-held hobbyist motor tool fitted with an abrasive cut-off blade will do a good job with little effort (safety goggles are a must). But the most efficient, easiest, and quickest method is to cut the rail with a special rail nipper if Code 100 or less in size, and a rail cutter if larger than that. Make an accurate measurement and mark the rail—a Sanford Sharpie® permanent marker with an extra-fine point is great for this and many other modeling chores—set the nipper blades exactly, and nip. Then dress the rail ends flat with a file and mate it to the next section.

Once the turnouts and curves are all set, fill in the gaps with straight sections and those with very gentle cosmetic curves, all of which must be fitted to suit. The fit at closing joints, where a run of track between two previously laid sections is completed, is the critical point. If you make the last cuts too short, leaving the gap between the rails greater than the thickness of an index card, you will have to try again. Nip a tiny bit long, and use your file to pare the rail ends down gradually until you get a nice fit.

Metal rail joiners are not reliable electrical connectors. In order to ensure electrical continuity at those rail joints where it is required, you will have to solder them. (Remember that some joints may be purposely gapped.) Dress the ends of the rails square and flat with a small file before fitting the joiners. For most joints, butt the rails together. With a hot, hot, small-tipped soldering iron, flow rosin-core solder into the seam around the joiner. The instant the solder rushes into all the cracks and spreads like water, remove the iron. If you do this rapidly, not enough heat will reach the plastic ties to melt them. For insurance you can attach a heat sink to each side of the joint to draw away the heat. There are soldering tools for this purpose, or you can lay a block of aluminum on the rails or attach a couple of small modelmaker's clamps. Do a few practice runs on some scrap track, and you'll see how easy this really is.

Do the joints on straightaways a little differently. Butt the rails with an index card or a slip of thick paper between them. Form a small length of number 24 wire as a jumper and lay it against the rail base on the *outside* of the rail, where there is no chance of a wheel flange hitting it. Solder the jumper in place with dabs of solder at each end, but do not solder the joiner or the rail ends (FIG. 5-15). This leaves a gap for expansion that will prevent any possibility of rail buckling.

Joints on curves should be kept to as few as can reasonably be arranged as this is no place for open gaps. The problem is that unless the rails are solid, they tend to form a kink that can be a sure derailer. Before laying the track, install the metal rail joiners and butt the rail ends tight, with the two (or more) track sections laid out straight rather than curved. Solder the joint thoroughly, allowing solder to get into the rail butt joints as well as the joiner seams. Now you have a single long length of track that will curve uniformly and not kink.

Laying sectional track is an easier job. All you have to do is snap the sections and turnouts together, starting at any convenient point. Anchor the sections by whatever means the manufacturer recommends, usually a few short nails per section or turnout. Take care not to pinch the track down or misalign it by fastening it too tightly. The sections must be fully snapped together and you cannot force them into alignment or onto a different course

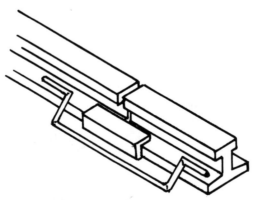

5-15   A jumper soldered to the rail, leaving the rail joiner and the gap unsoldered.

than they naturally take, as the rails will kink or buckle and cause derailments. Any adjustments must be made to the roadbed alignment, not the track. In some cases, however, you can use flex-track in combination with the snap-track. This allows you to fill odd-length gaps, introduce nonstandard radii, add easements to fixed radii sections, or lay gentle cosmetic curves. The flex is laid as just discussed.

WEATHERING

In this instance, weathering consists of coloring the rails and ties in various ways to disguise the factory-fresh, shiny brass or nickel-silver and uniformly colored plastic or wood ties. Not all modelers choose to weather their trackage, but the process does make for a more realistic appearance. By blending into the scenery better and appearing more natural, out-of-scale rail like the commonly used N scale Code 70 looks less obtrusive and more in keeping.

You can weather track before it is laid or after. However, because so much cutting and fitting and adjusting is required, preweathered track needs a whole lot of touch-up later on and some of the original effort is wasted. Most modelers prefer to weather after laying the trackage but before ballasting. An alternative is to apply a uniform base coloring to everything prior to installation, then do the finish weathering after. Yet another possibility is to purchase factory-weathered rail or track, which is a uniform, dull charcoal gray, and go from there.

Prototype track exhibits a surprising mix of colors, mostly all earth tones in a mottled effect. If possible, inspect some real trackage yourself to get a first-hand idea of the appearance (use binoculars so you can stay off railroad property). The coloration varies with the nature of the surrounding countryside, use factors, age, local weather conditions, and sometimes the kinds of loads that the line predominently hauls, like coal. Ties range from dark creosote blackish-brown (new ties) through lighter reddish browns into brownish grays and finally, for old, old ties, weathered silvery-gray. There are always dark stains here and there—grease and whatnot. Steadily used rail is shiny on top, seldom-used rail is rusty black. New rail is brownish-black depending upon how much rust has started up. The older the rail, the rustier, from blackish-brown through several rusty shades to almost orangey-brown.

Weather the ties first. Brush or spray on a suitable base color like Pactra Dark Earth or Earth Brown by Polly S. After that dries, dress with heavy and scattered washes of other colors like Pactra Light Earth, Polly S Brown, perhaps some Polly S Gull Gray, and maybe some daubs of Polly S Grimy Black. The approach is much the same for the rails. Apply a base color first, such as Floquil Grimy Black or Weathered Black or a mix of Polly S Panzer Gray and Grimy Black. Or, you can use Blacken-It, which is an oxidizing chemical rather than a paint, and is electrically conductive (unlike paint). Then wash on colors that are compatible with the natural surroundings, like some Floquil Antique White (chalk, limestone), Polly S Venetian Dull Red (red earth), a mix of Polly S Brown and Gull Gray, or other suitable earth tones. Dust and Mud also work well, and Polly S Black makes excellent coal dust. Finally, depending upon the age and use of the rail, touch up with Rust and mixes of orange-red-browns to simulate rusty conditions. Shiny grease or oil patches can be made by applying Floquil Glaze or Polly S Gloss Finish over a blotch or spill of Grimy Black, perhaps with a swirl of Light Earth or even a tinge of Olive Drab mixed in.

Don't hesitate to experiment and try to match coloration that looks right to you, or that you have observed first-hand. With a little experience you'll be able to create a prototypical, realistic appearance with little trouble. Be sure to keep the paint out of the turnout points and operating mechanisms, or it will give you fits later.

BALLASTING

Ballast is crushed rock or gravel, usually of a kind that is readily available in the vicinity of the railroad. Cinders are sometimes mixed in. On a prototype railroad it has several functions. It supports and restrains the ties, allows relatively easy leveling and alignment adjustments, spreads the weight of the train over the earth railbed and keeps the track from sinking in, and permits water to drain freely away from the ties. On a well maintained line it keeps weeds from growing in the right-of-way, which helps to prevent grass fires. On old, little-used, rundown trackage, however, what little ballast was spread (and that may have been stretched with cinders, ash, and sand) has almost disappeared, the ties have sunk into the earth, and the weeds have taken over. There is trackage in every imaginable stage of condition between these extremes.

On a model railroad, the ballast is partly cosmetic. It covers the roadbed for a prototypical appearance, but it does help lock the trackage in place. On a top-grade main-line track it is thick, uniform, clean, and well shaped to the grade. On a little old short-line siding it is sparse, shallow, patchy, weedy, full of dirt and cinders and oil stains. As with the prototypes there is every gradation in between. Ballast comes in an assortment of coarseness grades for each scale, and in several colors. Select a size and color suitable for your layout. Or you may want a large size for main-line trackage, a smaller one for yards and sidings. The colors are quite uniform, so mixing two similar colors makes for a more realistic appearance. You might even sprinkle in a third color here and there. A little experimentation is a good idea.

To ballast the track, drizzle the material in windrows between the rails, then along outside each rail, from a tablespoon or a paper cup, just a few inches at a time. Spread the ballast out with your finger or a palette knife, then finish working it around with an artist's soft paintbrush until you have it the way you want it. The ballast should also run down the shoulders of the roadbed on a well maintained line, but in yards there are no shoulders and on many sidings they are minimal (FIG. 5-16). To make uniform slopes, stand a piece of cardboard straight up about ¼ inch or so from the tie ends and fill the space from there to the rail with ballast. Pick the cardboard straight up and the ballast will find its own angle of repose and slide to a slope. Use a narrow strip of cardboard to scrape the remaining hillock of ballast outward

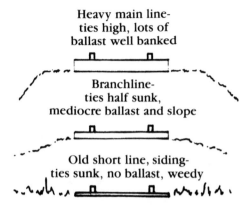

Heavy main line-
ties high, lots of
ballast well banked

Branchline-
ties half sunk,
mediocre ballast and slope

Old short line, siding-
ties sunk, no ballast, weedy

5-16   The ballast configuration and the amount used varies (prototypically) with the kind of trackage involved, its age, and how well it is maintained.

so it follows the rest down the shoulder, and finish up however you wish with a brush.

As soon as you have a short stretch of rail ballasted, it's time to bond it before it is disturbed. Clean up any stray ballast and check to make sure no grit is in the points and moving parts of turnouts. Make a wetting agent by filling a pump spray bottle with a pint of water and 6 drops of any liquid detergent or better, Kodak Photo-Flo (from a photo supply store). In another container, mix 1 part white or yellow woodworking glue with 4 parts water. Or instead, and better, mix 1 part acrylic matte medium (from an art supply store) with 1 part water. This is the bonding agent.

Pump the spritzer into a paper towel a couple of times to get a fine mist going, then mist a couple of feet of the ballast with the wetting agent. Make sure it is well dampened, but don't put on too much, and take care not to disturb the lie of the ballast or make marks in it. Next, using an eyedropper, or a pipette (a length of drinking straw with your index finger over the top will do), drop 4 or 5 drops of the bonding agent between the ties and 4 or 5 more outside each rail at about 5-tie intervals. The bonding agent will follow the wetting agent into every crevice and lock all the granules together. That's all there is to it—go on with the next 2-foot stretch. Let the ballast dry for about 24 hours and go back over it with a small, stiff brush or similar tool and poke at the ballast in places. If you find some loose spots where the bond didn't take or that you missed, doctor them up and you're done.

CHECKOUT

As soon as the track is all laid and before going any further with the layout, it's a good idea to make a complete check of all the trackage. If any repairs or adjustments need to be made, this is an easy time to do it because there isn't anything else in the way and there is not yet any power to the rails.

Check all the moving parts of all the turnouts, and make sure that there is no ballast, paint, or other scrap caught up in the works. Operate the points manually to make sure they travel properly and most importantly, close tightly. Check each one with a track gauge. Run a fingertip over each rail joint; the ends should be dead even, no bump. File rail heads smooth and flush if necessary. There should be no humps from bent rail joiners or cockeyed ties, either. Run your track gauge around all the curves and along all the tangents and test for out-of-gauge rails.

Take one of your lightest, most free-running cars and set it on the rails. Scoot it free with a snappy push across all the turnouts and crossings in all directions. If it derails more than once in the same place, you've likely got a problem that needs attention. Watch the car to see if it bumps or sways excessively as it passes through turnouts, which can indicate other problems. Send it along the tracks at various points and watch for sway or peculiar motions that might indicate difficulties. Verify all vertical and horizontal clearances. When everything checks out, you've completed the most demanding part of the layout.

Chapter **6**

Wiring the Layout

Some model railroaders find the electrical, electromechanical, and electronic elements of the hobby to be the most fascinating part. They accept the challenge to their ingenuity with delight and relish the intricacies of the circuitry—the more the better. But for most beginners this is a big stumbling block to be regarded with dismay, if not suspicion. Many experienced modelers consider this the least rewarding, most confusing and complex aspect of building a layout. The subject can be perplexing, it can be intricate and a bit mysterious, and it is altogether much too large to cover here.

The fundamentals are covered here in sufficient depth to allow you to understand the basic circuitry and wire your layout for conventional operation. You should recognize, though, that there is far more to the subject and you can create some marvelous effects electrically and electronically if you care to investigate further.

TOOLS AND SUPPLIES

There are a few tools that you'll need for wiring your layout. A wire stripper is essential for removing insulation from wire ends. The one hand automatic type is best. A pair of needlenose pliers and a pair of miniature diagonal cutters are equally necessary. You will probably want a pair of full-sized diagonals as well—get the bullnosed variety. If you will use crimp-on terminals (some do, some don't) you'll need a crimper, or you can also solder terminals on. A selection of screwdrivers is required for working terminal and mounting screws. You will probably want to have a ¼-inch electric drill handy and a few fractional sized bits, and you will also need a pin vise and some small bits, like a #60.

Many connections must be soldered, so you will need a small soldering iron or pencil for small connections, and possibly a larger iron or gun for large, high-mass connections. The solder you use must be rosin cored and the eutectic type is best. Select a small diameter of the sort used in electronics work. For desoldering if you make a mistake or want to change a connection, get a small spool of wire braid, like Soder-Wick, made for this purpose. And finally, a good circuit tester is a must. There are many kinds that you can cobble up on the home workbench, but I strongly recommend that you purchase an inexpensive multi-tester, or VOM (volt-ohmmeter). This versatile instrument will let you test continuity on a live or dead circuit, measure current, resistance, and voltage both AC and DC, and make a variety of tests. Get a unit with an accuracy rating of 5 percent and a sensitivity of 1,000 ohms per volt, a scale for up to 3 amperes minimum, a low resistance scale of 0–10 ohms, and a burnout-proof meter. The digital readout type is easiest to read but is more expensive and has a hard time reading current draw of operating motors, while the analog (dial face) type is cheaper but harder to read.

ELEMENTARY ELECTRICITY FOR MODEL RAILROADS

First, a few fundamental facts and terms. Electricity is energy, a force. Electric *current* is a flow of electrons, measured in *amperes.* The pressure, or *electromotive force (EMF),* that moves the electrons along is called *voltage.* Electricity travels through some substances extremely well (gold, copper, aluminum); these are called *conductors.* It does not travel through others (glass, plastic, porcelain), and these are called *nonconductors* or *electrical insulators.*

In order to harness electricity for useful work it is routed through wires, typically fashioned of copper or sometimes aluminum. On a model railroad, the metal track rails are also used. In both cases the current-carrying lines are conductors, and their shape doesn't matter. As the electricity travels along the conductors it meets with a certain *resistance,* and this is measured in *ohms.* Resistance varies with the conductor material and size. *Electric power* is the work that the current is doing at any given moment, and is measured in *watts.*

The relationships of these four factors are expressed by Ohm's Law, which is $E = I \times R$, where E is volts (electromotive force), I is amperes (current), and R is ohms (resistance), and the formula for power, with the symbol W expressing watts. Figure 6-1 shows these relationships.

Electricity travels in a path or loop, going out on one side from the *source* to something to be operated and back again on the other side. The

Voltage	Resistance
$E = IR$	$R = E/I$
$E = W/I$	$R = E^2/W$
$E = WR$	$R = W/I^2$

Current	Power
$I = E/R$	$W = EI$
$I = W/I$	$W = I^2R$
$I = W/R$	$W = E^2/R$

E = Volts, R = Ohms, I = Amperes, W = Watts

6-1 Ohm's Law and power formulas.

loop is a *circuit,* the lines out and back are often called *legs,* and the something to be operated is the *load.* Like the conductors, the load also has resistance. The source might be a battery, or your wall socket and ultimately a power plant somewhere. The legs are variously called *plus* and *minus, hot* and *neutral,* or *positive* and *negative,* depending upon the circumstances. If a leg should fall off a load terminal or break somewhere, you have an *open circuit,* no current flowing. The leg, and the circuit, is said to have *no continuity.* If that loose leg should chance to fall onto and make contact with the other leg, you have a *short circuit,* maximum possible current flowing briefly. There must always be a load in the circuit when it is *closed* or *energized.* These circuits are shown in FIG. 6-2.

A circuit is *complete* when all of its elements are in place and it is operational with no faults. It is *incomplete* when an element is missing or nonfunctional. A complete circuit has continuity. Any segment of the circuit that is intact from test point to test point also has continuity. So, any circuit can be tested in sections for continuity. An incomplete circuit does not have continuity, but most of its sections do. This can be checked with source voltage applied—a *live circuit*—by inserting a load like a lamp or buzzer at various points, or on a *dead circuit* (no source voltage) with a self powered tester. Continuity checking is probably the most important and useful test routine on a model railroad, and you'll do lots of it.

There are three kinds of circuits, according to how the loads are connected (FIG. 6-3). When the two legs are connected to the two sides of a load, this is a simple circuit and there is no other way to make the connections except to swap the legs. When two or more loads are connected across the legs, it is a *parallel circuit,* and the loads all receive the same voltage but the current draw through each load depends upon its resistance. When two or

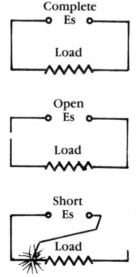

6-2 Complete (closed, continuous), open (incomplete), and short circuit paths.

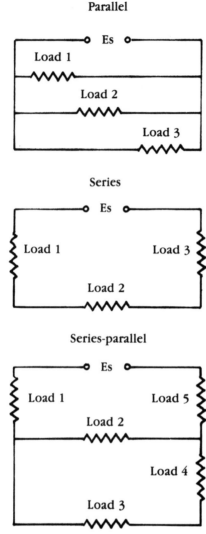

6-3 Parallel, series, and series-parallel circuits.

more loads are connected end to end along the legs, this is a *series circuit*, and the current is the same throughout the circuit but each load absorbs a certain portion of the voltage, depending upon its resistance. If there are loads connected both in parallel and in series with the legs, it is a *series-parallel circuit*.

Copper conductors all have a rated current-carrying capacity, depending upon their *gauge* or *number* (diameter) and the ambient operating temperature, that includes a built-in safety factor. Exceed this capacity and the conductor will overheat and eventually burn out. Also, after a certain length is reached, a conductor of a given size is increasingly less able to carry its rated current because of the increased resistance, leading to voltage drop, overheating, and eventual breakdown. Where increased current is needed the wire size must be increased, and long conductors must be oversized for a given current requirement.

Electricity comes in two types, alternating current (AC) and direct current (DC), symbolized in FIG. 6-4. Your household supply is AC, providing 115 and 230 volts nominal of electricity that alternates from plus to minus 60 times per second (60-cycle power). Your car uses DC from a storage battery rated at 12 volts, where the current flows continuously from plus to minus. A complete, energized or live circuit has the required voltage present and a certain stable resistance. Current does not flow until a demand is placed upon the source by the load, by virtue of a switch being closed, a thermostat actuating, or some similar circuit-closing action.

MODEL LOCOMOTIVE CIRCUITRY

Your model locomotives are fitted with tiny electric motors. They may be *open-frame* with the internal parts visible, or can-type, which are sealed into a tiny metal cylinder. Either way, the motor shaft rotates as a result of a magnetic field created as current flows through the motor brushes and armature coils. The electrical energy is converted to mechanical energy, and the motor shaft turns a series of gears to transfer motion and power to the locomotive wheels.

In operation, electricity in one rail travels into certain of the locomotive wheels, called the *pickup wheels*. The wheels on the opposite ends of those axles are insulated from the axles to prevent a short circuit. The current passes along a *pickup wiper* that contacts the wheels, flows through one motor brush into the commutator and on through the armature coils, and back through the opposite brush. This brush is connected to another pickup wiper

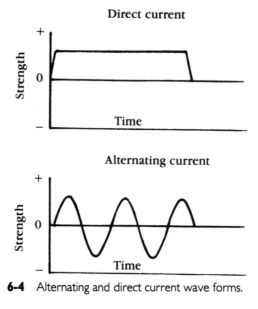

6-4   Alternating and direct current wave forms.

on the opposite side of the locomotive, which feeds the current to the locomotive pickup wheels on that side of the locomotive, which are in contact
with the opposite rail. Because these wheels are insulated from the opposite
ones the current flows unhindered out along the rail and back to the source.
The details of just how this is accomplished varies somewhat from model to
model, but the basics remain the same, as shown in FIG. 6-5.

POWER SUPPLIES

A model railroad layout is operated with electricity from one or more elec-
trical/electronic assemblies called power supplies. Most of those commercially available include a means to control the locomotive speed and direction, and are called *power packs* or *throttles*. In addition, they provide current
for accessories like lamps and switch machines. Many layouts use only power
packs for all such purposes, but if there are numerous switch machines they
may be powered by a special supply. The same is often true of extensive
lighting and/or other electrical apparatus.

A typical power pack consists of a transformer that steps 115-volt household current down to 24 volts or less, a rectifier to convert the AC output to
DC, a filtering section to provide pure DC, a locomotive control means, a
polarity reversing switch, and several output terminals for different purposes,
sometimes both AC and DC. Some units include an ammeter and a voltmeter
for operating and diagnostic purposes.

Locomotive speed is controlled by varying the voltage to the motor, from
stop at zero volts to full speed at 12 volts or less. The direction is changed by
reversing the polarity of the current (the plus leg becomes the minus and
vice versa), which makes the motor turn in the opposite direction. This is
accomplished with a simple switch in the output circuit. The traditional
method of speed control is by means of feeding full wave DC to a wire-
wound rheostat. This is a manually operated variable resistance unit, placed
in series with the motor. Unrealistic jackrabbit starts from a dead stop are
common to this method, and a worn rheostat produces hitchy operation.

A better arrangement is called *pulse power*. This can be introduced by
flipping a switch to cut a rectifier diode out of the circuit and produce half
wave DC, which consists of steady, staccato bursts of voltage. This allows fine
low-speed control but tends to cause overheating of the motor and noisy

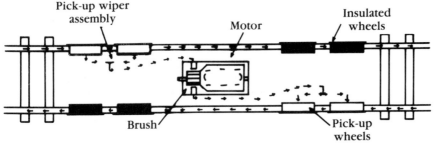

6-5 The basic path of electrical current through a model locomotive.

operation. The way to cure that problem is to use pulse power to start, then flip the switch back to full wave DC for running. There are other means to do this as well. Pulse power is available on many modern power packs.

Most power packs today, except for a few inexpensive models, have done away with rheostats and feature throttles made up of various solid-state components. If you are planning to purchase a new unit, this is the type to opt for. Note too that some power packs offer a means to control two locomotives individually on separate circuits.

TRAIN CONTROL

There are numerous ways to control trains on a model railroad, some of them quite sophisticated, some even computerized. But for conventional control, there are two main methods. One is called *section* or *tower* control. The layout is divided up into sections, each run by a separate operator, power supply, and control means. As a train proceeds along the track it is passed from section to section and operator to operator. This is a good system for large and especially modular layouts. The other, more common and satisfactory system is called *engineer* or *cab* control, where one person operates the same train all around the layout.

With a conventional power system feeding the layout, a single throttle, the cab, controls a single train over the whole layout. The cab is located at a fixed central point on the layout where the operator can see everything. If the trackwork is divided into electrical sections, the cab is switched from section to section as the train moves along. To operate a second locomotive you need a second cab. This can be a speed control attached to the first power pack but is usually a dual-throttle power pack or a second complete power pack. You also must divide the trackwork into a minimum of three electrical sections—more about that in a bit. Then two operators can control two trains and coordinate their travels. If you are quick and clever (and brave), you can operate both yourself. It is also possible to add a third cab to control some essentially discrete area such as a freight yard or a group of long, interwoven industrial sidings. More cabs actually can be added through various switching schemes, but manual operation quickly becomes a practical nightmare.

Walkaround control consists of a power supply in a fixed location and a hand-held control unit to govern the speed and direction of one locomotive. The control unit is connected to the power supply by a long, flexible cord, allowing the operator to follow the train wherever it goes, setting the turnouts and flipping the block switches as necessary. You can install a fixed cab to begin with, then add walkaround units later if you wish, and use both as you desire. This system is more expensive than ordinary fixed cabs, and doesn't prove much on a small layout.

Command control is a complex and fairly expensive system that controls the locomotives with high frequency signals superimposed upon the track and picked up by receivers in the trains. It too uses hand-held controllers that plug into jacks located at various points around the layout. It is not made for Z scale and is problematical for N scale, because the receivers are too large to fit into most locomotives or rolling stock. The system may become more affordable and practical in time.

There are published plans available for making your own power supplies of various sorts, if you wish. Otherwise, consult the manufacturers' literature for units that will fill your needs and are designed for your scale, and purchase a versatile, top-quality unit. This is not a place to scrimp on price.

THE TRACK WIRING PLAN

No real plan is needed to wire the layout accessories like lamps, switch machines, and assorted gadgets as you just run the wires to them as necessary. Unless your trackage is only a simple loop or two you'll need a well thought out track wiring plan, or you'll get lost in a thicket of connections.

First, there are two model railroad conventions (FIG. 6-6) that are confusing at first but have their purposes that will eventually come clear. One is that one rail of the track is called South and designated "S," the other is North and designated "N." South is considered plus electrically, and North is minus, they are connected to the power supply in that fashion, and never the twain should meet. Usually the rail closest to the front edge at the lengthwise midpoint of the layout is the S rail, the back one the N rail. Then, no matter what direction the rails take, they *always* keep their relative positions, even though in many instances the N rail will physically be the forward one.

The other convention is that trains travel in East and West directions. From a selected point on the layout, trains going forward to the right are considered Eastbound, to the left, Westbound. An Eastbound train backing up is not going Westbound, it is an Eastbound train in reverse, and vice-versa. An Eastbound train is always that, no matter where it is on the tracks. On an oval track plan the East direction is counterclockwise in general. The selected starting point is usually a terminal. Then all trains pulling out of the Wagonwheel Falls station headed right are Eastbound, headed left are Westbound.

If you have a single or double simple oval and only one train to run, all this is immaterial. Hook two wires to the rails and you're off and running.

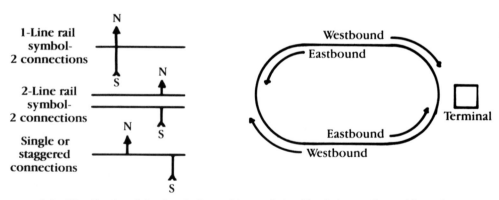

6-6   The South rail is electrically positive and the North is negative, while trains headed to the right and traveling counterclockwise are Eastbound and those headed left and going clockwise are Westbound.

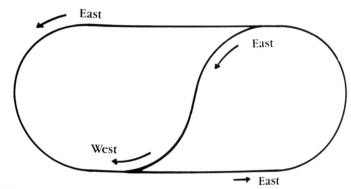

6-7 This track plan contains a turning track; if an Eastbound train swings onto the loop, it "swaps ends" and becomes Westbound when it exits.

But most layouts are more complex than that, even small ones. If there are any loops or turning tracks, or if you want to run more than one train at a time (and also for some other reasons to be covered later) you will have to divide your trackage up into a number of electrically isolated sections called *blocks*. This is done by leaving or cutting gaps in the rails at certain locations. In some circumstances both rails must be gapped, in others only one. You can cut gaps with a razor saw and caution, but the best method is to use a very thin, large-diameter abrasive cut-off wheel in a motor tool. Or, if you know where the gaps must be before you lay the track, you can easily cut them then with nippers, and insert insulating rail joiners.

The first step is to find the parts of the trackage that are called turning or reversing tracks. Sometimes they are obvious. The track in FIG. 6-7 includes a turning loop. The Eastbound locomotive can run around the outer oval forever and it will always be Eastbound—counterclockwise rotation. But if it swings onto the loop, as soon as it comes out the other end it is suddenly a Westbound locomotive, clockwise rotation. This is a turning loop. An oval with a figure-eight in the center is another, loop-to-loop dogbones containing two reversing loops, and return crossovers are reversing tracks also. A wye section is always a turning track. If you can spot these sections (FIG. 6-8) on your track plan, fine. But if the plan is complex some of them may be disguised, especially big loops and widely separated crossovers.

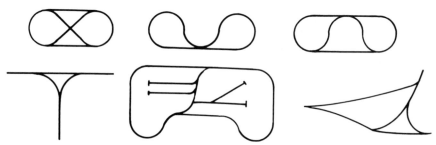

6-8 These are all common turning track configurations; they often become hidden in a complex trackage maze.

There are several ways to sort this all out, including trial and error, but the system devised by master model railroader Linn Westcott years ago is probably the best, although is a bit simplified here. Get out your layout plan. If it is detailed and finished you might want to make a new tracks-only tracing that you can mark up and use as a wiring diagram. Pick a starting point and find all the pairs of turnouts whose tails point toward each other, and wrap a circle around the line about midway between them. Then find all the pairs of turnouts whose branches face one another, and make a thick slash across the line about midway between them. Disregard the turnouts facing the same way. Figure 6-9 shows a sample result of this exercise.

You have just divided your trackage into a series of blocks, with their boundaries marked by the slashes. You could in theory attach feed wires at the circles and cut gaps at the slashes and operate the railroad, but it probably wouldn't work too well and so far you haven't uncovered the turning tracks either. So, wherever there is a circle, pencil in an "E" for Eastbound, along with an arrow pointing counter clockwise. From each circle, follow along the track in a counter clockwise direction until you come to a slash, or gap. Pencil in an E to the near side of each one. With all those done, start at each circle and follow the track along and mark a "W" just shy of each slash. Take care here, as the lines may cross each other or you might miss a slash. At most slashes there will be an E on one side, a W on the other. But wherever there

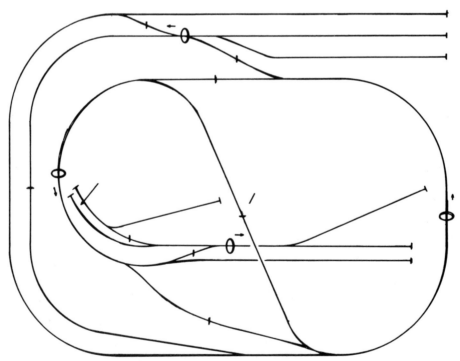

6-9   Here the basic blocks have been identified and their initial boundaries located on the track plan.

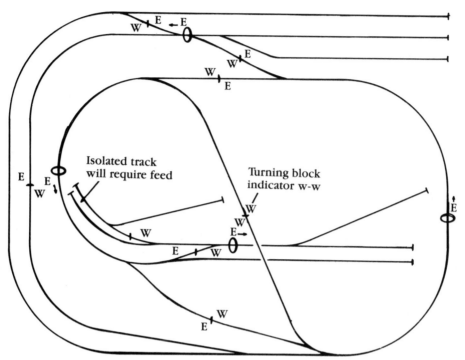

6-10 Here the East and West sides of the block boundaries have been identified, pointing up the turning-track blocks.

are two Ws or two Es, you have a turning track that requires special wiring. Figure 6–10 shows a completed block diagram.

There's another way to do this, which some prefer, but it's trickier and more work. Figure 6-11 shows why turning tracks must be electrically isolated—they will short-circuit! Make a sketch copy of your track plan, but instead of single lines indicating the centerline of each track, draw in each rail, including turnouts. Draw the North rail (minus) in black, the South rail (plus) in red. All black/black and red/red rail junctions are okay. All black/red junctions are short circuits and that track section must be gapped and isolated.

The next step is to determine the most advantageous block boundaries and gap locations. To begin with, all the turning tracks must have a block called a turning section or a return block (FIG. 6-12). This block should be longer than the longest train you expect to run through the turning track, but should not be much longer, perhaps two or three carlengths, at most. Both rails must be gapped. If there is a long enough stretch of track between the reversing turnouts, that makes a good block. If not, include one of the turnouts and some of the track beyond in the block. If a wye has a long leg off the main line, that's a good block. Usually wyes are short-legged, so one leg, the turnout, and the tail track become a block. A turntable must be isolated for control purposes.

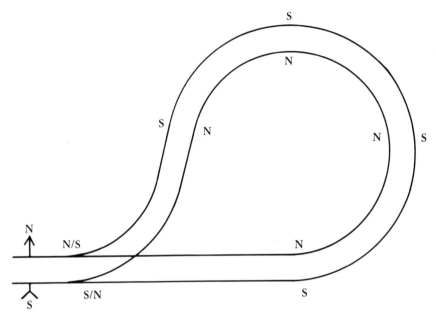

6-11 If a turning track is not gapped and electrically isolated and separately controlled, a short circuit will occur when the line is energized.

The other blocks in the trackage are set as a matter of convenience and operating interest, not electrical necessity. On any plan you must have at least three blocks for two trains, so there is always a free one for the trains to move into, and five should really be considered the practical minimum (FIG. 6-13). Most layouts will have more than this, even small ones.

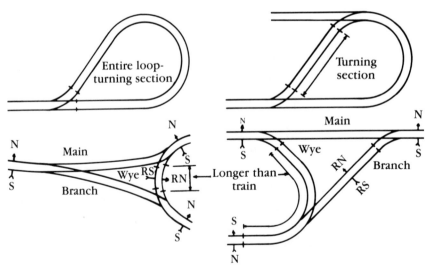

6-12 Make your turning sections a bit longer than the longest train you expect to run through them.

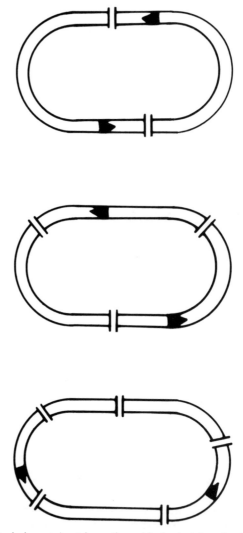

6-13 Any two-train layout must have three blocks, but five should be considered a practical minimum for adequate control.

Consider also the blocks shown in FIG. 6-14. Every passing track or passing siding should be a separate block, with a comparable block in the main line. One train can wait on the siding as another passes, then move out and continue while the other is still running along. An entire single-ended yard is usually considered a single block, so switching and main-line running can go on at the same time. A large yard might be broken into two blocks, as might a set of locomotive service tracks with enginehouse and a yard. In a double-ended yard the through tracks are cut into blocks. Long parallel runs of track are often blocked separately for two-train operations in the same area. You might want to consider a stopping block, too. This is a control block, usually located near a station. A gap in one rail is all that's needed.

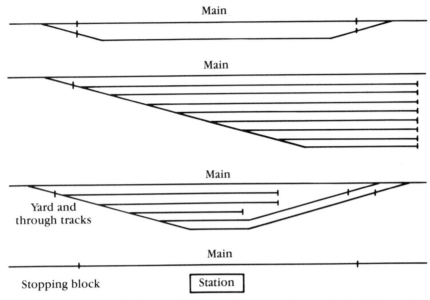

6-14   Added blocks of this sort will increase interest and operating flexibility on the layout.

Flipping a switch cuts the power to that block and the train coasts to a stop. Note that nonadjacent and noncontinuous sections of track, such as two or more separated spur tracks, can be combined in a block if there is no chance of simultaneous use of the sections by two locomotives. If you want to run or dead-park a second locomotive on any of the tracks, the arrangement won't work.

Once you have added these desirable or more-or-less necessary blocks, consider all the trackage again, including the sections already blocked. The rule of thumb is that each should be longer than the longest train that you will run on that part of the line. There are four possible exceptions. On long, high-speed stretches the blocks should be perhaps two train lengths long because they are cleared rapidly. In places where trains will pass the same point in rapid succession but on different routes, like a crossing, the blocks can be short so the trains can move along quickly. At the tops and bottoms of helper grades, the blocks can be short so that the road engine and the helper engine can be independently controlled. If a yard or a siding is next to a main line where a switcher might have to come out onto it, a short block on the main line will allow the switcher to complete its maneuver and move off while a main-line train is approaching close. Any long stretches of track can be cut into train-and-a-half-long blocks for convenient control. Mark in any additional blocks that seem worthwhile.

By now you should have a variety of hash marks peppered all over your track plan. The block boundaries, and the rail gaps, should be located at logical points. Sometimes you can saw through existing metal rail joiners. Often the best spots are close to the turnouts. Here they should be placed between the fouling point and the frog of the turnout. This is the area in which a car or engine cannot be left standing without being hit by another passing along the other track (FIG. 6-15). Do not cut gaps in places where trains are likely to be standing frequently. Both of these practices reduce the possibility of short circuits caused by standing metal-wheeled cars or engines. On long, open tangents, place gaps so that you can remember where they are, such as at a road crossing or opposite a particular sign or building.

Don't be concerned about having too many blocks. The only consequence of that is extra switches. You can leave any one block switched to join either adjacent block indefinitely. You can always eliminate a block simply by jumper-wiring it back to an adjacent block. You don't have to put in all the blocks on your plan right away. Start with just the major ones if you wish, leaving expansion room in the wiring and control panels for more later.

With the block boundaries all marked on your electrical plan, you now can locate the feeders. The designation is an arrowhead pointing away from the North rail and an arrow tail pointing into the South rail. These symbols represent the pair of power feed-wires and connection points that each block must have in this kind of wiring system. Usually each arrowhead has the letter "N" beside it, and the tail the letter "S." If the block is a return section, use "RN" and "RS." This is a good time, too, to number all the blocks. You can code them however you want, in some sort of logical progression. On a small layout, just B-1, B-2, etc., will do the job. Then you can tag the wires and terminals, which makes keeping track of them a lot easier.

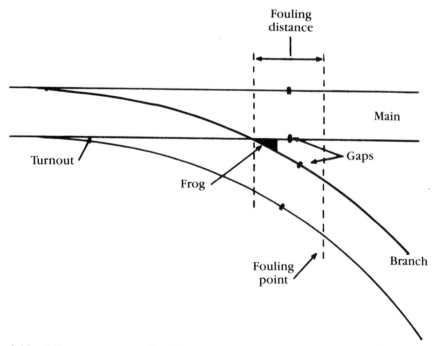

6-15 Rail gaps at turnouts should be placed within the fouling area to avoid possible short circuits; it's also easy to do here.

Once you've sorted out and noted all of these details, the track wiring diagram is complete. Depending upon its complexity, you might find it helpful to draw up a clean and perhaps larger copy to serve as a working wiring plan. (A typical diagram is shown in FIG. 6-16). The next step is to proceed with the wiring itself.

SAFETY

Wiring up a model railroad doesn't sound like it should be a hazardous occupation, but in fact it can be. And potentially lethal. The load side of a power pack has assorted low voltage output terminals, always DC and maybe AC as well, that can range anywhere from 6 to 24 volts and sometimes up to 50 volts. The amperage is usually limited to 3 or less. This combination is only enough to give you a bite, albeit sometimes a hefty one, if you get your fingers across it. A little bite if your skin is dry or calloused, a bigger one if thin or moist. The line side, however, is 115 volt AC, as are the outlets in your house. This voltage can kill easily. A short circuit flash can burn you, start a fire, put out an eye. Take care when you mess around with the innards of any power pack or power supply. A capacitor-type switch machine power supply, incidentally, can rattle the fillings right out of your teeth if you get hold of it the wrong way.

Another danger point lies in the inclination to just do a little wiring in the layout room to add a light or two or some extra receptacles. If you are

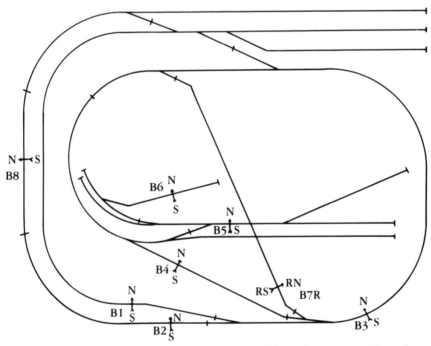

6-16   A typical track wiring diagram includes all the information you need to make the connections easily.

comfortable with this sort of work and have some pertinent knowledge and experience, fine. If not, don't try to save a buck and instead start a fire or blow yourself away. Hire an electrician.

There are two other hazards. One is in using cut-off blades in motor tools to cut rail gaps. Apart from the fact that you can lose a fingertip by handling the tool carelessly, when in use these blades can not only send up a shower of hot grit and metal filings, they can explode into shrapnel. These tools are almost always used in close quarters with your nose right down on the work, so eye protection is essential. Safety glasses, please.

The other hazard is the soldering iron, from two standpoints. One is burns—they can be severe if the iron slips through your fingers or you drop it and automatically make a grab for it. Sometimes little globules of molten solder can drop or fly off and hit you. Another way to lose an eye. The other danger is inhaling fumes from hot flux, simmering oil or grease, melting plastic or paint, or whatever. Be cautious.

WIRING THE TRACK

There are several kinds of wire you can use for wiring your layout. Solid conductors are best for most purposes, stranded when there is a reason to have limp, flexible conductors, such as in a walkaround throttle cable, and both must have an insulating jacket. The wire sizes used mostly are #18, #20, #22, and #24. The higher the number the thinner the wire and the smaller its current carrying capacity. There are some occasions when single conductor wire is best, but two conductor wire is most suitable for the two-wire system and for general purposes. When a single conductor is needed, it can be split out of the two conductor cable.

As a rule of thumb, keep total conductor lengths and currents, from power source to load, to the maximums shown in FIG. 6-17. If you must run farther with, say, your #22 line than the listed maximum, upsize to #20. Or instead of a single #22 wire, run two in parallel. This will give you twice the current capacity for the same length, or half the resistive length (practically

Size—AWG (Copper)	OHS/100 FT. (68F)	Feet/OHM	Sug. Max. Current (A.)	Dist. From Panel (FT)
14	0.25	400	18	50
16	0.40	250	13	30
18	0.64	156	10	20
20	1.02	98	7	12
22	1.61	62	5	8
24	2.57	40	4	4
26	4.08	25	3	3
28	6.49	15.5	2.5	2

Assumes 1 ampere of current at 12 volts in a 2-conductor cable.

6-17 Use these conductor size/length figures as a rule of thumb in wiring your layout, whether on the layout proper or in the control panel.

speaking) for the same current. Two conductor wire is readily available in electrical supply and many hardware stores in #18 and #20 as thermostat or bell wire, in 250 or 500-foot rolls or in shorter cut lengths. Single conductor wire in sizes #18 and up you can get at hobby shops, by mail order, or at Radio Shack or other electronics stores in small rolls, typically 25 feet.

Figure 6–18 shows the most common track wiring arrangement for small layouts, a two-wire system for wiring the track, using two power packs for two-train operation. (The physical arrangement of the components will be covered in the upcoming section on control panels.) All of the mainline or normal blocks are wired just the same, and all of the blocks with return tracks, including a roundtable block, are also wired alike. This is essentially a repetitive exercise that (despite an outrageous number of conductors snaking hither and thither) is really a simple task.

Mount a terminal strip first, containing a pair of terminals numbered or coded for each block, then run a pair of feeder wires from the strip to each block connection point (FIG. 6-19). Attach them to the proper rails, North and South. Of the several ways to do this, the pigtail method is perhaps the best. Cut a short length of solid #24 or #26 wire, strip about ½ inch of insulation off each end, and crimp an ell in one end with needlenose pliers. Drill a tiny hole down through the roadbed, between ties and right next to the rail, on the *outside*. Push the straight end of the wire down through the hole and cock the elled end in so it lies flat against the rail base. Solder the wire to the rail with rosin-core solder, using just enough heat to get the job done without melting anything (FIG. 6-20).

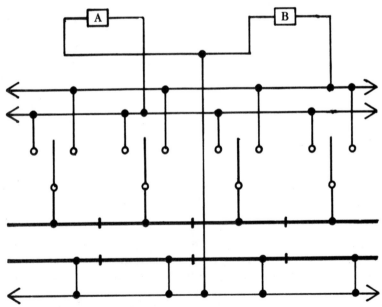

6-18   In block form, this is probably the most common track wiring setup for small layouts.

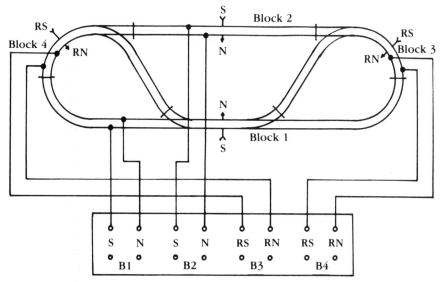

6-19   The terminal strip to track blocks wiring.

Then, underneath the layout, attach the feeder wire to the pigtail. You can support the wire here with a small hook screwed into the benchwork. You can make the connection by soldering, but I prefer to use a tiny wirenut. This simplifies wiring changes later if necessary, it's easier, and troubleshooting goes faster. Keep the feeders properly polarized by wire color. For example, always red to South and white to North. The total length of rail supplied by one such pigtail should be no more than about 5 feet. If the block is longer than that, attach more pigtails as needed and connect them to the

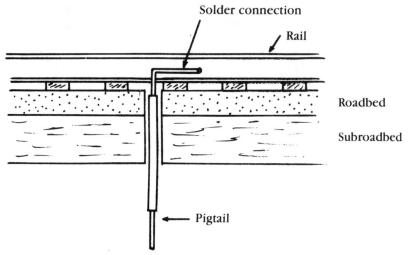

6-20   This pigtail method is one of the best for making track connections.

block feeder. The reason is that rail resistance is so high you have to compensate for the consequent voltage drop in order to get effective operation. For this reason, some modelers run feeder jumpers to each 3-foot rail section and don't bother with metal rail joiners, or leave them unsoldered.

Next, from each pair of mainline or ordinary block terminals at the strip, run a pair of conductors back to the center terminals of a double-pole, double-throw (dpdt), center-off toggle switch. These are the block selector toggles (FIG. 6-21). Then, for each turning section you have, cross wire a dpdt center-off switch in an X on the outside terminals. Then run a pair of conductors from the terminal strip to the center terminals of those switches. They are combination block selector and direction controller switches for the reversing blocks (FIG. 6-22).

Now, on the block selector switches, run jumpers across like outside terminals from switch to switch. From the first switch in line, run a pair of wires to the center terminals of a dpdt switch on the A cab side. From the last switch in line run another pair of wires to the center terminals of a similar switch at the B cab side. These are duplicate main direction controllers. Cross wire the outside terminals of these switches just as you did the block direction controller switches. From one pair of corner terminals on each, run a pair of wires to their respective cab throttle output terminals

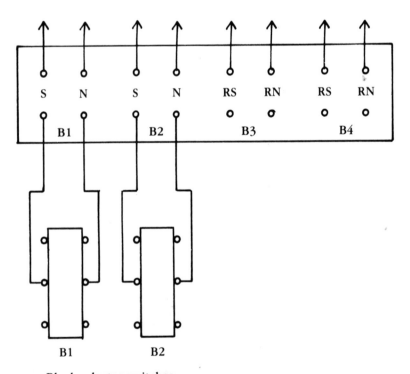

Block selector switches

6-21   Wiring between the block terminals and the block selector switches.

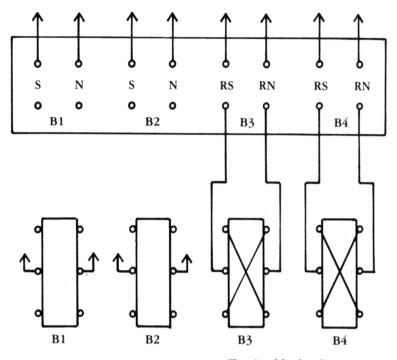

**Turning block selector
and direction controller
switches**

6-22 Wiring between the turning block terminals and the combination turning block selector and direction controller switches.

(these terminals each will have two conductors attached to them, as in FIG. 6-23).

Wire the reversing block selector toggles similarly. If there is more than one, parallel them with jumpers from outside corners to matching outside corners. From one corner pair of terminals, run wires to another pair of dpdt switches, one at each cab side, to their center terminals. Parallel wire jumpers from the main feed side of the main direction controllers at each cab to comparable terminals on the new switches. These switches are the auxiliary direction controllers (FIG. 6-24).

That completes the basic track wiring. Be aware that there is another wiring system called *common return* or *common rail* wiring, wherein many of the North rail jumpers are connected together on a common bus beneath the layout while the South rails are individually fed. Though fairly popular, the system is more complex for beginners even though there can be somewhat less wiring. There are some drawbacks too, so that system will not be covered here. Another item to be recognized is that much fancy electrical work can be done with relays, lamps, and switches in the way of warning signals, indicators, semiautomatic train operation, and functioning accessories.

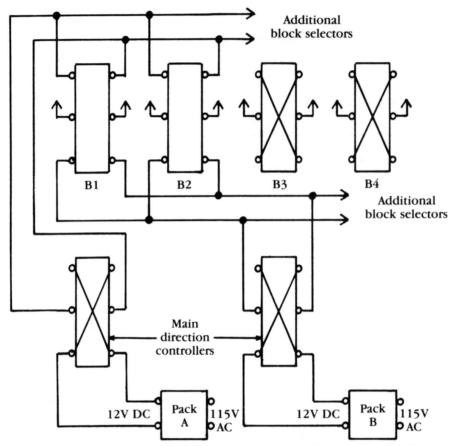

6-23 Wiring for the block selector switches to the main direction controller switches and the power pack outputs.

Another area not considered here that you might like to investigate has to do with *selective control* turnouts, where the points can be fitted with auxiliary wiring to energize one or the other branch with the points and/or appropriate auxiliary contacts. This means a lot of games can be played, such as "floating" reversing sections. It also means special rules for gapping rails and some interesting jumper-wiring. Note too that if you use crossings with insulated frogs, you can ignore them electrically. If they have solid frogs, special gapping and wiring procedures are needed. By contrast, the wiring discussed here presupposes installation of the more common *fixed control* turnouts, where each branch of the turnout is electrically connected to the rails ahead of the turnout points.

SWITCH MACHINES

You can operate the turnouts on your layout by pushing the points closed with your finger, or by operating a tiny mechanical lever, called a *ground throw,* attached to the turnout throw rod. You could also use the old tried-

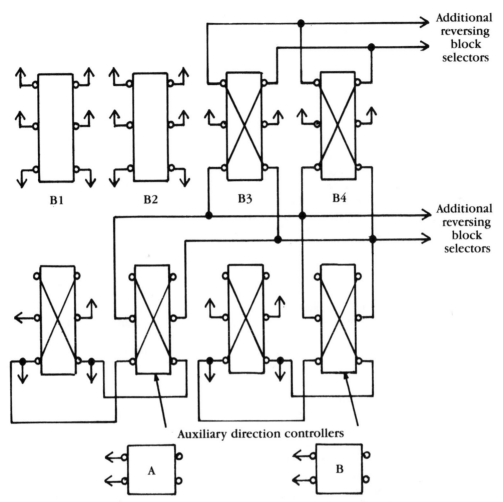

6-24 Wiring for the reversing block selector switches to the auxiliary direction controller switches.

and-true mechanical method of connecting automotive choke cables or strings run through screweyes for remote control. Or a commercial system like the one made by Locomotive Works. Or, you can operate the turnouts electrically from the control panel with toggles or pushbuttons actuating switch machines. Though more expensive, this method affords excellent mechanical and electrical reliability as well as remote operation from a central or several locations.

There are two types of switch machines in common use today. One is the twin coil type, and is activated with a momentary contact pushbutton. This type is positive acting, but acts unprototypically fast, requires a great deal of current and accordingly can burn out quickly if the juice gets left on a bit too long. It is rather noisy, and requires indicator lights installed somewhere to show which way the turnout points are set. Nonetheless, twin coils are popular. The other, newer type is the motor driven switch machine. This type operates the turnout slowly, is positive acting and relatively quiet, takes less current, and requires a toggle or similar switch to operate it. The direction of the toggle lever shows you which way the points are set, or you can install indicator lamps.

Either type can by mounted atop the layout beside the turnout and hidden by a chunk of scenery or a building, or beneath the layout on a mounting frame. In some cases it is easier to mount the machine, the linkage brackets, and some of the wiring on a small baseplate and then attach that to the benchwork. It is always easiest to do as much of the setup work as possible on the workbench before installing the machine, rather than afterward under the layout. The machine is connected to the turnout by a mechanical linkage that is adjustable to fine-tune the point closure. When you position each machine, set it to the center of its travel and the turnout points to the midway position, so you have about the same amount of travel and degree of spring tension in each direction. These machines also have auxiliary electrical contacts for powering indicator lamps, or turnout points for the selective control mentioned earlier. There are numerous differing installation details for different brands of machines, so follow the manufacturer's instructions.

Twin coil switch machines operate on 12 to 20 volts AC or DC and take so much power—as much as 4 or 5 to 9 or 10 amps—that they are best operated from a separate power supply. This can be the auxiliary terminals of a regular power pack, but a better arrangement is a capacitor discharge power supply made for the purpose. You can buy them, and there are published plans for building your own.

The usual arrangement for wiring a twin coil switch machine is to connect a pair of normally open (n.o.) pushbuttons in the circuit, one for each coil. A quick push on a button sets the turnout to one direction or the other. Use #20 wire out to about 15 feet or so, and #18 beyond that. The problem with pushbuttons is that they don't indicate which way the turnout is set. There are a couple of ways around this. One is to wire indicator lamps into the circuit, using the auxiliary switch machine terminals. The other is to use two pushbuttons and one single-pole double throw (spdt) toggle switch. The switch handle shows the direction the points are thrown to. Flip the switch to select the appropriate coil of the switch machine, then push the button to activate it. Figure 6-25 shows these wiring arrangements.

Mechanically, motor driven switch machines are installed in the same general fashion as twin coil units. Details vary with brands, of course. You can take the power from the accessory terminals of a power pack, or provide a separate supply. Generally the latter is better, and some machines require only a transformer with a suitable output voltage, perhaps with some voltage-dropping diodes in the circuit. The voltage might be anywhere from 1½ to 32 volts, AC or DC. Current needs are low, so you can use #24 wire out to about 20 feet, #22 beyond that. The usual wiring arrangement is to take a pair of conductors from the power supply to a dpdt toggle switch, the handle of which indicates the direction of turnout throw. The switch should be cross wired at the outside terminals, because it acts as a reversing switch for the motor in the switch machine. Another pair of conductors runs from a pair of

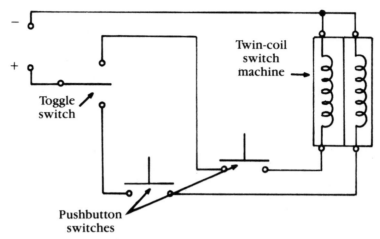

6-25 A typical wiring arrangement for twin-coil switch machines.

switch corner terminals to one side of the motor and one side of the machine limit switches (FIG. 6-26). Three wire switch machines are treated a bit differently, so follow the wiring instructions provided.

WIRING LAMPS AND ACCESSORIES

There is a grand array of electrically operated accessories available for model railroads of all scales. For the most part, though, not much need be said about them here. The requirements almost always are low voltage and low current from the accessory terminals of a power pack or an independent accessory power supply (always a good idea if you have more than just a handful of accessories). Power is supplied by a pair of conductors that pass through an actuating switch of some sort. Even if the internal circuitry of the device is complex and sophisticated electronic wizardry, not many wires are needed for operation. So there are generally only a few simple connections to be made, and those are spelled out in the instructions that accompany the accessory.

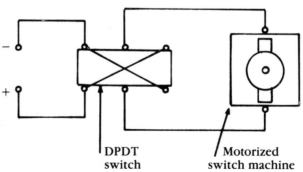

6-26 A typical wiring arrangement for a two-lead motor-drive switch machine.

There is one area, though, where you will probably want to do a lot of wiring, and that is lighting. Lights on your layout—crossing lights, stop lights, street lights, lights in and on buildings, radio towers, and fuel tanks, lights anywhere there is a logical place for them—can really bring a layout to life. Certainly there is an excellent selection of tiny light bulbs (properly called lamps), resistors, light-emitting diodes (LEDs), and associated components. These are available for the purpose, from hobby supply houses, by mail order, and at electronics supply outlets like Radio Shack.

The basic hookup for a lamp is simple enough: two conductors, running from each side of the power supply to each side of the lamp. To turn it on or off, introduce a switch connected in series with the plus (hot) leg, as in FIG. 6-27. The switch can be a toggle, slide, electronic strobing circuit, photocell, whatever. Your power supply can be AC or DC and the conductors are usually small, such as #24 or #26 (there is no harm at all in using larger).

A key to layout lighting is bulb longevity. Lamps are fairly expensive and installed in places where replacement is difficult if they go out. Miniature lamps are particularly susceptible. Each lamp has a rated voltage; 1.5, 6, and 12 are common numbers. If you feed much less that the rated voltage to the bulb, it will glow reddish-orange and last a very long time, but won't produce much light. Jack up the voltage a bit and the color will turn yellowish. As you get to the rated voltage, the light color will turn progressively whiter and the lamp life will be progressively shorter. When you get above the voltage rating the color will be brilliant white and burnout can occur within minutes or even seconds. One trick is to run all bulbs at less than rated voltage, about where they produce a yellowish, reasonably bright glow that looks suitably prototypical.

This sometimes takes some experimenting, and you will end up using various kinds and sizes of lamps to accomplish your purpose. Running a 16-volt bulb at 12 volts might do the trick. You can attach three 6-volt bulbs in series to a 12-volt supply (FIG. 6-28) and each bulb will get 4 volts (one-third of 12), but remember that if one burns out, they all go out. To operate a lamp at less than rated voltage or on a voltage of higher rating than the lamp, you can series a dropping resistor with the lamp. First estimate how much voltage from the supply you want to "waste" as heat dissipated from the resistor. Then, using Ohm's Law, figure the number of ohms of resistance that you'll need to achieve that voltage drop. You can use this system to adjust the bright-

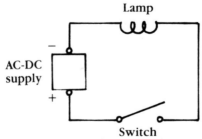

6-27 The basic lamp and operating switch circuit.

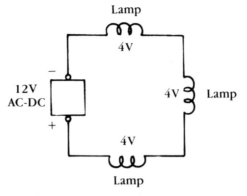

6-28 Lamps connected in series will each operate at a voltage equal to the supply voltage divided by the number of lamps.

ness of one or a whole string of lamps, or tune the voltage to any other accessory. Don't exceed the current output capacity of your power supply, and a fuse in the output line is a good idea. Yet another possibility is to run a lamp at its rated voltage on AC and connect a 1-ampere, 50-volt diode such as a 1N4001 in series with it. Light output will be reduced by nearly a third.

BUILDING A CONTROL PANEL

There are numerous ways to build a control panel and hundreds of variations. However, one of the most popular and also most satisfactory for a small home layout is a single, centrally located, all-inclusive, slant-front unit (FIG. 6-29). The central portion of the panel features a graphic diagram of the track plan. At each side is a set of reversing switches, and sometimes a voltmeter

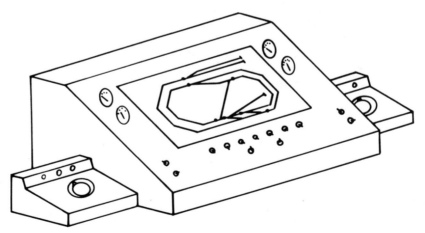

6-29 A conventional control panel like this, whether with the front slanted or not, is probably the most popular arrangement for a small home layout and is very workable.

and an ammeter. In small layouts a commercial power pack/throttle is set on a ledge on each side of the panel for dual cab control. Inserted in the track diagram at their appropriate locations are the block selector toggles and the turnout switches. Indicator lamps may or may not be included at various points for various purposes. An alternative to placing the turnout and block switches in the track diagram is to arrange either or both in rows or banks, all numbered or coded as to purpose. In this case, corresponding indicator lamps are sometimes installed right in the track diagram.

The first step in building a control panel is to make a panel-sized drawing of the track plan. Use diagonals instead of curves, and locate all the switches and lamps (FIG. 6-30). Adjust the overall size of the face panel so that there will be plenty of room beneath for all the switch bodies and ample "drape space" inside for the conductors. Then build a suitable cabinet onto which you can mount the face panel. I suggest an attaché case shape perhaps 6 or 8 inches deep, made of plywood or pine, braced at the bottom corners with gussets and open backed. You can then mount the panel vertically, flat, or at whatever angle you wish by attaching it to brackets. You can easily move the entire panel to another location and/or set it a different position at any time later without any problem, such as when you move or enlarge your layout.

The face panel should be less than ⅜-inch thick in order to accomodate switches and lamps. Tempered Masonite ¼-inch thick works well; the ⅛-inch thickness is okay for smaller panels but lacks rigidity in larger expanses. Plywood is usable but not overly satisfactory, and plastic works well but scratches readily and looks shabby after a time. Standard practice is to spray paint the panel to a glossy, neutral finish (white, yellow, most any very pale tint), then do the layout and install the components. However, I suggest the reverse, to lay out and drill the required holes first, then paint. But for a top-notch job, don't paint at all. With nonflammable contact cement, bond a piece of smooth surfaced, matte or semigloss finish, plastic laminate like Formica to a piece of ¼-inch-thick tempered hardboard. Then do the layout and hole drilling. Or, because this requires carbide cutters for trimming and carbide tipped drill bits for the holes, you might want to have the panel made up at a cabinet shop. Alternative: Buy the laminate already cut to exact size, trim the hardboard to suit, and figure on wearing out, or at least dulling, several ordinary steel drill bits while boring the holes.

Lay out the track diagram and locate all the hole positions on the face panel, then drill the holes. For a hardboard or plywood panel, apply the finish next—several coats of a good spray enamel or lacquer. On the finished surface, lay out the track diagram again, this time with colored tape. Narrow tape seems most effective and mainlines can be wider than branches or spurs if you wish. A combination of ¼-inch and ⅛-inch tape is a good one, but the difference should be emphatic. Some modelers like to color code the blocks, too. You can use chart or graphics tape from art or graphics supply outlets, or pinstriping tape from automotive accessory stores. Lay the tape on straight and smooth, leaving narrow gaps to indicate at the block boundaries. Use a dashed tape line to indicate hidden trackage. It's easiest to tape right over the holes, then cut the tape out later with an X-Acto knife.

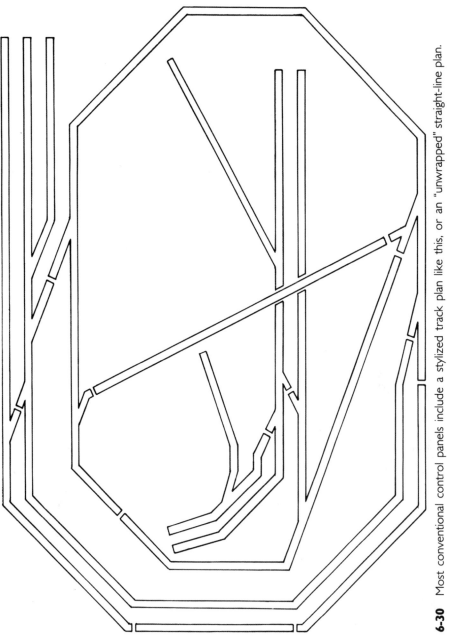

6-30 Most conventional control panels include a stylized track plan like this, or an "unwrapped" straight-line plan.

For a finished effect, you can add lettered designations to the diagram, such as station names, block codes, or track designations. One effective method is to use dry transfer letters for this, set directly on the panel surface. Another is to stick on Dymo labels, apply decals, or type or print adhesive labels with self-stick stock and stick them on. In any case, the completed panel should be covered with two coats of a clear finish such as urethane. Make sure it is compatible with the paint finish and lettering.

The next step is to install all of the switches, and meters and lamps if those are used. Then attach the panel to the cabinet with a pair of butt hinges, or better, a strip of piano hinge. You can arrange the panel to open up and back like a school desk, or open forward and flop down. The latter allows easier access to the innards. Either way, you can also install a standard drop leaf or drop front hinged support at each side to hold the open panel in place. The cabinet can be finished any way you wish, but paint is a prevalent option, and no finish at all is also common.

Depending upon the complexity of the control panel, you may want to start wiring the components as you install them in the face panel, rather than installing everything and then wiring. There's no reason not to. Leave some slack in the wires, route them cleanly, and bundle them with plastic wire ties or flex jacketing (available at Radio Shack) in a neat fashion, or slip them into cable clamps. You can use crimp-on terminals or not, as you wish, but they do make a neater job and better connections as well. It's a good idea to label all the leads at the terminal strip ends, too. That can save a lot of time later on when trouble shooting becomes necessary, or if you want to move the control panel. Leads can be run into the control panel from the power packs as necessary, or to the terminal strips mounted on the benchwork and then back into the control panel.

SWITCH OPERATION

Operating the railroad requires flipping a lot of switches, and doing it at the right times. While this may seem confusing at first, it's really simple and you'll get the hang of it quickly enough. Here's how to work them; assume you're alone and at the Cab A (left hand) throttle.

As a train rolls along through a block, check the block selector switch for the upcoming block. If the handle points toward you, the block is powered under your control. Straight up, it's dead, the train will stop. Headed away from you, the block is under Cab B power and control but that cab is turned off so you must flip the switch toward you to put the block in Cab A control. And so on. If you are operating alone with one train running, you can set all the block switches where you'll be running to Cab A. If you are running two trains, you'll have to operate Cab B as well, flip the switches, and keep the trains apart.

As the train rolls along, plot its movements ahead of time. Check the next turnout coming up. Is it set right? It may indicate main or branch by point direction, toggle direction or indicator light, either at the turnout itself or on the control panel. For a twin coil machine you will have to push a button to shift the points, or throw a toggle and then push a button. For a motorized switch machine, you'll flip a toggle.

Your main direction switches control the direction of travel over the entire trackage except any turning sections. With the switch one way the locomotives will go Eastbound, the other, Westbound. Test this out for direction when you install and energize the switches, and orient them in the panel so that when the toggle handles point to the right, the trains go Eastbound. Label the switches to suit. In normal running, all cab main direction switches are set to the same direction.

There is another direction control switch on each power pack. Once connected through a main direction switch, this becomes a forward/reverse control for the locomotives. It does not change the direction of travel around the layout, only the direction of motion of the locomotive, and that is its purpose. As was stated earlier, an Eastbound locomotive backing up is not a Westbound locomotive.

The auxiliary direction switches come into play on turning sections only. As the train approaches the turning block, check the block selector to make sure the block is energized to the proper cab. Then check the auxiliary direction controller. The toggle lever should normally be left set to indicate the usual direction of travel into the turning section. Set it the opposite way if the train is entering the section by the other, less used direction. These directions are established during initial testing and operation of the circuits and the switch handles physically aligned accordingly, so you can tell which direction is which. The actual positions are up to you. Labeling is a good idea, so you'll know at a glance which is the commonly used position, such as "front" and "back" perhaps, as in doors. Now the polarity in the turning section is the same as in the approach block where the train is. When the train is completely within the turning section, you quickly flip the main direction switch to change the polarity on the main line. The train will continue on without a hitch, now Westbound. If you run the train through another reversing section and go through the same control sequence, it will become Eastbound again. Otherwise, you will have to bring the train back to the first turning section and run it in through the back door in a reverse procedure to turn it around again.

While you are attending to all these details, of course, you are also manipulating at least one throttle, perhaps two, and possibly three. But you can always park a train or two if you get tired, and leave a block selector switch straight up. This is a good way to protect trains, too—leave a moving dead block somewhere between them. There are a lot of other things you can do by switching switches, too, as you'll discover in due course. It's a little like playing the piano. Practice helps.

Chapter 7

Structures

A substantial part of a model railroad layout is made up of the structures of various sorts that add emphasis and realism to the scene. But not all of them are there just for effect or decoration. Some play a part in the operation of the trains and the functional effectiveness of the layout.

TOOLS AND SUPPLIES

There are some structures available that are factory made and all ready to plunk down on your layout, especially the side of the track type, but this varies depending upon the scale. But most, especially buildings of all sorts, come as kits that you have to put together and/or finish yourself. You can get by in modelmaking of this sort with surprisingly few tools, but those few are basic and essential. Certain supplies are also required.

At least one hobby knife is a must. The pencil-sized type is the best general purpose type. X-Acto is perhaps the most popular because they have a sizable hobby-tool system, but there are other brands as well. If you have two of the same size you can keep a different shape of blade in each and won't have to stop to change them every few minutes. I find the most useful blade to be the No. 16, with No. 11 second best. Some modelers prefer the No. 10. Having a package of each on hand is a good idea (you'll use up a lot of them), and you might like to add a No. 17. Also keep a box of single edged industrial-type razor blades handy.

Measuring tools are also a must. You will need a good steel (preferably stainless) rule graduated in inches, for both measuring and to use as a straightedge. You should also have a steel scale rule. The Model Railroad Reference Rule made by General is probably your best bet and you can get one through your hobby shop. You'll also find a clear, flexible plastic 1-foot ruler handy at times, but not essential.

Needle files, also called Swiss or jeweler's files, see a lot of use. You can buy a full set, but a round, triangular, and flat in medium or fine cut will see you through. You will want at least one pair of tweezers, and probably a pair of miniature needlenosed pliers. You'll need a small screwdriver with a slot-type blade about 1/8 inch wide, too. And, a No. 0 or 1 artist's brush, inexpensive type, for applying liquid cement. For clamps, you can use the spring-type clothespins, and it's hard to beat an assortment of rubber bands, paper clips and paper clamps. You can also purchase various kinds of special modeler's clamps.

For a work surface, you can cut out a piece of ⅛-inch or ¼-inch tempered hardboard, 1-by-2-feet minimum. When it becomes too scarred up, pitch it out and cut another. I prefer a sizable pane of ¼-inch plate glass, as it remains perfectly flat and ideal for squaring up, leveling, and similar tasks.

Beyond this, there is a world of tools that are great to have, like a set of jeweler's screwdrivers, an airbrush and compressor, more knives and pliers, a hobby motor tool and assorted accessories, razor saws and a miter box, a clamping system, more tweezers, hemostats, miniature diagonal cutters, picks, rifflers, taps and dies, drill bits, miniature wrenches, and on and on. Nice, but get them only as you need them.

You'll need supplies, too, that vary with the kind of models you are making. The basics are masking tape, Scotch Magic Tape, a plastic cement like Testor's Liquid Plastic Cement, and miscellaneous other adhesives for gluing other substances, such as Duco Cement, Hobsco's GOO, Goodyear Pliobond, a cyanoacrylate ("crazy glue" or ACC), or a 5-minute epoxy. Some of these have a limited shelf life, so buy as needed. You will also need hobby paints of appropriate colors, such as Pactra, Floquil, or Polly-S, perhaps some stains, and weathering supplies. There are various other items that you will need from time to time, but there's no point in trying to stockpile them.

STRUCTURE TYPES

Model railroad structures can be broken down into three groups. The first and often the largest on a layout is composed of *nonrailroad* structures. This includes all the miscellaneous buildings that don't pertain to the operation or function of the railroad but are part of the overall picture. They might be factories or coalyards or stores or churches, barns and farmhouses, bungalows or ranch houses, garages or service stations, warehouses, lumberyards, feed mills, rowhouses, hotels or motels, prisons or restaurants—you name it.

These structures are included in greater or lesser numbers on every layout to add interest and realism to the overall scene. Because of space restrictions this can seldom be done in prototypical fashion. For example, modeling a complete town, even a small one, would be difficult at best and maybe pretty boring too, both to do and to observe. So the usual practice is to model a judicious selection of buildings and place them at strategic locations on the layout to provide the sense of scene and flavor typical of the locale or area. An exception might be an arrangement like an industrial layout, for example, where the structures are actually most of the scenery.

The second group is made up of *trackside* structures (FIG. 7-1). These are buildings and associated structures that are located beside the tracks. They may be owned by the railroad or by others, but their collective purpose is in serving the railroad's function of moving passengers and goods. The railroad structures include stations, freight docks, ramps and platforms, freight warehouses, roundhouses and locomotive sheds, car shops, associated boiler plants, water tanks, sand towers and similar servicing facilities, yard master's

7-1 Trackside structures are located close to the tracks and serve the direct needs of the railroad, like this one-stall engine house and the water tank.

office, trackside shanties and storage buildings, and section houses. The customer-owned structures might be anything. A coal or metals mine, logging camp, or gravel works are all typical. Others might be a packing plant, sawmill, oil tank farm, warehouse, any kind of factory, grain elevator, brewery, or any other kind of business that requires railroad service. These are the structures that denote and fulfill the purpose of the railroad, to which its rails travel and from which its revenues flow.

The third group is made up of *right-of-way* structures (FIG. 7-2). These belong entirely to the railroad and are essential to its daily operation. They are not buildings, but structural assemblies of various sorts that are located

7-2 Right-of-way structures include such items as bridges, signals, and tunnel portals and their retaining wings.

directly on the railroad right-of-way. They include signs, signals and associated relay boxes, turntables or transfer tables, bridges, viaducts, trestles, tunnel portals, snowsheds, culverts, and anything else that can be considered a part of the right-of-way. Some of these structures placed along your right-of-way will add interest and realism to the layout, especially if you get to the point of installing operating signals or an automatic turntable.

WHAT TO USE AND WHERE

The decisions about what structures to use and where to put them must be governed largely by the concept of your railroad. There's a tremendous range from which to select, but the key is to choose the structures that appeal most to you while at the same time do the most for your layout. They should not just fit into the general scheme, they should enhance it.

Right-of-way structures like viaducts, bridges, and trestles must be made part of the plan early on, because they have to fit into the trackwork. Kit-built trestles can be trimmed to fit a roadbed in many cases, but most of these structures must be dimensionally planned for so the roadbed can be made to order. It's best to actually have these items on hand when you build the roadbed. Turntables and tunnel portals need to be located in the planning stage, but can be installed later without much trouble. On the other hand, snowsheds, telephone poles, and signals can be added any time, and signs are part of the detailing process that usually comes last.

Usually it's necessary to preplan for the trackside structures. For some, you need the specifics ahead of time, and often having the structures on hand is a good idea. This is true of engine houses, roundhouses, and industrial buildings that have tracks going inside them. In other cases, you can get along with dimensions for width, length, and sometimes clearances. Oftentimes just approximations are sufficient, so you can make a space allowance. This is true of most stations, platforms, and freight docks, for example. For many of the customer-owned structures, just a general idea —such as a medium sized sawmill here, a small warehouse there, so you can leave room for them—might be all you'll need.

Usually the nonrailroad structures that are included to flavor the layout are not preplanned in detail. You may have a good idea of what you want, or you can leave that somewhat to chance. These structures can be located after the layout is partly built, and often even after the scenicking is under way.

All of the structures should fit the time period that you're modeling. You can use any kind of structure or construction that would plausibly have still been in existence at the time setting of your layout. None, though, that surely would have disappeared by then (unless you can come up with a convincing reason), and nothing from a later date. An old barn, a Pizza Hut, an Exxon station, a truss bridge, and a Toyota billboard would all fit nicely on a 1980s layout. Only the barn and the bridge would fit a 1940s layout, and you'd have to change to Dixie's Diner, Esso, and Hudson for the rest. Wagons and buggies scattered about, wood sidewalks, a livery stable, and gas lamps wouldn't fit either one. Nor would radio transmission towers, poured concrete grain silos, fuel tanks, and a movie theater work too well on a layout set in the

1890's. These examples are obvious, but there are many that are not and it's easy to get tripped up. When did plate glass storefront windows first appear? When did poured concrete railroad overpasses come into common use? Was chain link fence around in 1937? Have you got something that doesn't fit? Finding accurate answers can be a challenge sometimes.

The structures have to fit the setting, too. Obviously there are few modern ranch houses in an industrial environment, and a tank farm seldom occupies the center of a town. But there are subtleties involved here, too. For example, derelict log cabins are common even today in the high Rockies, but you're not likely to see one in New England. Certain products, such as gas stations, stores, restaurants, etc., are common to certain parts of the country. Conoco gasoline in Colorado, Gulf in Vermont. Certain architecture is typical of certain parts of the country. Cape Cod houses in New England, Spanish Mission in the Southwest. You won't see a Swiss chalet-style Kansas farmhouse, or a four-square Colonial perched on a ledge in the Tetons. Fortunately many structures are almost universal. A brick factory is a brick factory anywhere, and regional differences are few. Still, you have to be wary of mismatches.

The structures also have to match up with the theme of your railroad. If the main revenue producers are coal and lumber, it stands to reason there should be a coal mining operation and a logging outfit or sawmill on the layout. An industrial theme requires some industries. A steam-era pike might have steam locomotive servicing facilities, but not diesel, and vice versa. But you could have both, during the transition period. The structures should be typical of the region as well as the theme. Grain elevators are typical of midwest towns, sugar beet processing is done on the Colorado plains, lumbering takes place in forested areas, gravel can come from almost anywhere.

If you are modeling a prototype, then you must be extra careful. The right-of-way structures must be of the kind actually in use at that time, and on that branch of the railroad. So must the rolling stock and the locomotives, and their paint schemes, lettering, heralds, and like details. The trackside structures that you use should be as prototypical as possible, which can be difficult. The flavor is sometimes the best that can be done, from a practical standpoint. The nonrailroad structures should also be closely matched so that they typify, or at least are in keeping with, those that actually existed at the time. All of this usually takes some study to get an authentic effect, but the result is worth the effort.

REDOING READY-MADES

There are ready-made structures of numerous kinds available, and just about none of them look real. There are some that suffer from being poorly made, grossly out of scale, misproportioned, or bearing no recognizable resemblance to any prototype. Those aren't worth bothering with. A lot of the very good ones, and there are many, don't look right either. The reason is surprisingly simple, and easy to correct. The colors are wrong, the coloration is boringly uniform, often the combinations are awful, and everything is slick and shiny. Structures are not shiny.

If the color scheme is okay, perhaps just killing the shininess is all you'll have to do. First, wash the structure in warm water and dishwashing detergent, using a small brush (an old toothbrush works well). Rinse it thoroughly under running water and allow it to dry completely—keep your fingers off it meanwhile. Then spray the structure with a very light, mist coat of Testors Dull Cote. Do this outdoors in bright shade, temperature 70 degrees or over. Outdoors because of the vapors, and so you can see well. This lacquer is not compatible with most plastics, so mist very lightly from 18 inches or so away, so the finish is almost dry by the time it hits the plastic surface. You might want to try it on the inside, bottom, or back of the structure first, to see how it will work. Another possibility is to brush on Poly S Flat Finish, which is compatible with plastic and is water based—not flammable, no fumes. Or, if you have an airbrush, you can spray it on.

Another way to modify ready-mades is to repaint, partly or wholly. This can make a surprising difference in the appearance of a structure. I recommend doing this with Polly S paint or Pactra Acrylic Enamel (or equivalent), both of which have no fumes and are nontoxic. You can brush or airbrush, with a huge variety of colors available. Always use flat or matte paints. Wash and dry the structure before application.

Another way to change ready-mades is to make simple alterations to the structure itself. This works especially well if you want to adapt one of the many European-type structures to an American flavor. Lopping off gingerbread and trim protrusions usually is easy. You can trim off a porch or entryway, reduce the size of a cornice, lop off a balcony. You can change window and door openings, or block them off. You can cover a tile roof with strips of sandpaper to simulate roll roofing. You can add or subtract chimneys or stovepipes. You can cover window openings on the inside with clear plastic, or clear cellophane from a candy bag, to simulate glass. Ingenuity is perhaps the main ingredient here

MAKING STRUCTURES FROM KITS

There is a huge variety of structures available in kit form. A few are shoddy, off-scale, and cheap, so be sure of the quality level before you buy. Some are simple, snap-together models, and while not of the best quality most are passable, and can be made better with some adjustment, refitting of parts, repainting, and weathering. Most of the kits are made of molded plastic parts, typically styrene but others are used as well. Usually the plastic is precolored in a more or less prototypical fashion. Most plastic models require only a modest amount of skill and patience to assemble, and the result is good to very good, occasionally excellent if realistically weathered (FIG. 7-3). The overall quality level and realism is generally good and the instructions are complete and understandable. That, however, can vary.

Some kits are composed mostly or entirely of wood parts, such as the Campbell trestles. Some of these kits are no more difficult to assemble than plastic structures, though the techniques are different. Others, like the John Rendall models, are called "craft" or "craftsman" kits (FIG. 7-4), and they are aimed at the experienced modeler. Instructions may be minimal and terse

7-3 This railroad hotel is typical of the many plastic structure kits available; finished results can be very good.

and there are few precut or manufactured parts, but mostly stock materials from which the parts must be fashioned and then assembled. They can be difficult.

Making plastic models is fun, and easy. If you take your time, include a few steps beyond just those in the instructions, and work carefully, you can turn out some mighty fine models. Start by laying out all the parts and check-

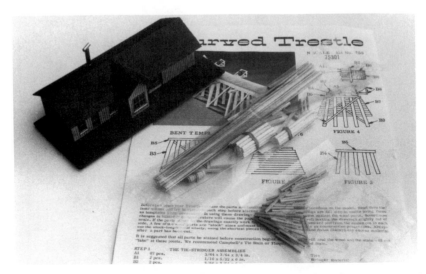

7-4 Craft-type kits, like this completed station and the curved trestle not yet started, feature raw materials, brief instructions, and few ready-made parts.

ing them against the parts list or exploded diagram, and familiarize yourself with all the bits and pieces for a few moments (FIG. 7-5). Read all of the instructions before doing anything, and get a sense of how the structure is supposed to go together and what it looks like when finished. Lay all the parts out in your work area, out of harm's way, but where you can check them over as you proceed.

Many of the parts, especially small ones, will be attached to a rod-like framework, the *runners,* by tabs or cylinders, and these are called the *sprues.* Leave all the pieces attached until it's time to work on them. As the time for each part comes along, cut it off the sprue with a razor sharp blade; *never* twist the part away. Then trim the sprue remnants off and smooth the surface. Check each part, whether from a sprue or an individual molding, for *parting lines* and *flashing.* The former mark where the mold parts came together, the latter is excess plastic that squeezed out when the mold was filled. Trim the flashing away, and gently scrape away the parting lines until the surface is uniform and smooth. You may also want to remove some of the small casting alignment pins and smooth out mold marks.

Note: depending upon the part, often you can remove flashing and smooth parting lines more easily with the part still attached to the runner, or at least to a sprue, that can serve as a handle. Some parts can also be almost completely painted this way, too, and the sprue attachment points touched up after installation.

Many parts need to be test fitted to make sure they align or slot in properly. Often a bit of scraping or other adjustment is needed. No kit fits together perfectly all the way through, no matter how good its quality otherwise. The

7-5 Most plastic kits feature a wealth of detailed parts and good assembly drawings and instructions.

parts must fit accurately, because glues won't make up the difference satisfactorily. Align individual mating parts and check them. Where there are several to be fitted together, like the walls of a building, set them up and bind them together with masking tape on the outside (low tack type if the parts are painted) or any tape on the inside, hidden surfaces. Scrape, file, and trim until everything is flush and snug—this is where the patience comes in, because sometimes the process seems endless.

The next step might be painting, or might be assembly, or perhaps some of each. Any time you can prepaint some or even all of the parts of a structure, that's a plus because it makes the job easier. Then whatever touchup is needed can be done after assembly, and it will blend right in, completely unnoticeable to anyone except perhaps yourself. An exception to this is when an assembly consists of several parts all to be painted the same color. They can be put together and then sprayed all at once. When you prepaint, try not to paint over places where glue will join parts, because you'll have to scrape the joints clean later. Allow painted parts to dry and cure for at least a day before applying a second coat, and preferably three or more before handling them to any great extent.

To assemble parts, fit them together and clamp them gently in place—rubber bands work well, but don't get them too tight—and apply the plastic cement. Apply cement from the inside of the joint, or the back, or any hidden location, with the tip of an art brush or the needle of a microapplicator made for the purpose. The watery substance will shoot along the joint lines and be sucked into the joints by capillary action. Use as little cement as you can, as it "melts" the plastic and joins the pieces as a weld does, by fusing them. You don't want the stuff leaking out of the seams. If you have a loose, gappy joint or two with no hope of close mating, use a thick glue like Duco Cement or Ambroid, but sparingly, and beware the droozles and strings. After it cures you can brush on a little liquid cement to smooth and rebond the joint.

Liquid cement does not work on some plastics, and that fact is usually noted in instruction sheets included in kits containing such materials. Other materials must be cemented with different adhesives. Five minute epoxy is a common choice for these purposes. This is a two part glue, very strong and bondable to nearly anything, with good gap-filling properties. It usually has to be mixed and used within 3 or 4 minutes. Duco Cement can be used too, and ACC is popular for bonding any smooth, nonporous surfaces. All of these must be applied sparingly and carefully, but boo-boos can usually be scraped or pared or otherwise smoothed over. Cementing clear plastic can be ticklish because so many glues turn it opaque, especially liquid plastic cement. I recommend tiny dots of Hobsco GOO or Duco Cement placed with a toothpick and spread just a tad. Some modelers use Elmer's Glue-All; it dries clear, but the bond is weak.

Once the assembly is complete, you can do the painting, or final painting, or touchup, as required. Sometimes a little backpedaling is needed, to readjust something that was put together earlier. If you have some parts left over (this is frequently the case), save them, along with some of the runner and sprue material. Toss all spares in a junk box for later reference, as you'll use a lot of them eventually.

When you make buildings, it's a good idea to leave the bottom at least partly open. Then you can set the structure down over a switch machine, or install lights inside it later. An alternative preferred by some modelers is to make the roof removable. If you plan on lights, the lamp(s) are best installed in the roof peak so that only the light can be seen and not the lamp(s). Also, you might want to install heavy paper baffles inside, so that you can't see entirely through a structure, or to direct light to certain windows, or to close off certain "rooms."

KIT-BASHING

This is the model railroading term for the creative (rather than destructive as the name implies) process of combining two or more kits, like or unlike. Combined with or without added odds and ends of other parts and/or stock materials from the junk box or hobby shop shelves, you can make a kit-based structure that is entirely new and unique. Such projects range anywhere from simple to complex, including entire industrial blocks, refineries, and such. Simple bashes require only minimal modeling skills and a little imagination. They usually have no reference to anything prototypical in particular at all, and are fun to do. They will also give you structures like no one else has, along with a certain self satisfaction.

Structure kit-bashing is most often done with buildings of all sorts. There are a few things you should not change, such as the separation between floors, the height (except perhaps upward slightly) of doorways that loco-motives or cars will run through, the height of ordinary passage doorways, and window sills or top edges if that runs them close to or into floors and ceilings. Beyond that, you can do practically anything you want to. Adding wall moldings together end to end make a longer building, or stacking them for a two-story (or more) effect, are common practices. Changing roof lines, peaked to flat, flat to gambrel, or whatever, will change the entire appearance of a building. You can add or subtract skylights, doors, windows, porches, loading docks covered or uncovered, retaining walls, half-basements under-neath, platforms, chimneys, smokestacks, roof water tanks, signboards. You can change window styles, door styles, add railings, take off steps, shingle the roof, tar paper a wall, and on and on.

To give you an example of a simple kit-bash, consider Heljan kit number 702 in N scale, which contains a pair of identical small cottages or bungalows. Perfect for a small, old, company owned mining or railroad town, which always had rows of little 4-room bungalows for the workers, sometimes alike and sometimes in three or four slightly different styles, and often painted different colors. As you can see in FIG 7-6, these kit houses are supposed to look typically European. Scandinavian, really.

So. Put a couple of them together about as the directions show, but forget the roofs. Cover the insides of the windows with cellophane. Cut pieces of thin cardboard—a manila file folder or oaktag will work well—for the main and porch roofs, with some overhang. Eliminate the white trim pieces at the roof edges. Glue 400-grit 3M Wetordry Tri-M-Ite waterproof silicon carbide sandpaper (which is already a grimy black color) to the pieces

7-6   These houses, a popular kit, have a typically continental appearance.

and attach them as roofs. Put one chimney in a different spot than shown in the directions, with a smoke pipe on top. On the other house, install a stovepipe and no chimney. Paint in aluminum flashing at the chimney and stack. Use a fine-point black marker pen to draw tar seams for roll roofing, one horizontal, one vertical. Paint the two houses different colors, with contrasting trim. Then weather them both. Figure 7-7 shows the results. Compare this with FIG. 7-6.

7-7   These houses were made from the kit shown in FIG. 7-6, using most of the kit parts but with a few changes.

From another kit, build a third house. This time, leave the front porch off, but retain the stoop. Put the chimney in a different spot. Cut the roof pieces from a stock sheet of styrene "metal roofing" from your hobby shop, and paint them aluminum, and weather the roof with Grimy Black and Rust. On the fourth house, cut the front stoop away. Add the porch to the side door, making it the front. Put an outside stovepipe up the back wall and have no chimney. Simulate a shingled roof. Paint these two houses differently from the first two, and weather them. You could go on to a third pair by using like pairs of end and side walls, fitting both porches together on one house as a veranda, and adding a lean-to ell on one, or make whatever other changes your imagination suggests. The result will be a half dozen somewhat alike but individualistic houses, without much extra work.

SCRATCH-BUILDING STRUCTURES

To scratch-build means to start from ground zero and build up a structure (or anything else) from stock materials. It could be a freelance design, or follow a set of plans, or be entirely prototypical from detailed drawings. Whatever the case, such models are built to scale, and often as not are more detailed than kit-built structures (although kit-builts can easily be modified by detailing).

There is a tremendous array of stock materials available in all scales that you can use for scratch-building. Some of the supplies are bulk, and you buy them by the standard sized sheet or bundle or length. They include materials like wood or plastic sheets simulating novelty, V-groove, and board-and-batten wood siding, brick or stone walls, and corrugated steel roofing. Scale lumber is available in many prototypically standard sizes, cut and packaged. Stock lengths of stripwood in many sizes, plastic structural shapes like I-beams, columns, and channels, and similar materials abound. You can buy stock ladder lengths, skylights, window and door frames, stair rails, steps, screening, chimneys, and a host of specific detailing parts.

Scratch-building a model steel mill, a locomotive roundhouse, or some such thing is a long, complex, and difficult job. A lot of modelers look at photos of marvelous prize-winning scratch-built models and think, "There's no way I can do that." Maybe not. Especially if you don't try. Those prize-winning modelers do have a lot of time, experience, and expertise behind them. But even a raw beginner can scratch-build. The key is to start small and simple.

How about a trackside tool storage shed? You don't even need plans for this, and any layout can use at least one. Pick a stock siding material, say, board-and-batten. Cut a back wall 8 scale feet high and 16 long. Cut another for the front. Cut two end walls 8 feet wide, 8 feet high at the rear, 10 at the front, for a shed roof effect. From a sheet of roofing, perhaps corrugated metal or ribbed seam, cut a piece to fit atop the walls with about a 6-inch overhang all around. Cut an opening in the front wall to fit a freight door, and perhaps one window as well. (Figure 7-8 shows the parts outline.) Glue stripwood corner blocks to the end walls, then glue the front and back walls to the blocks (FIG. 7-9). Fit the roof in place. Paint or stain the walls, but paint

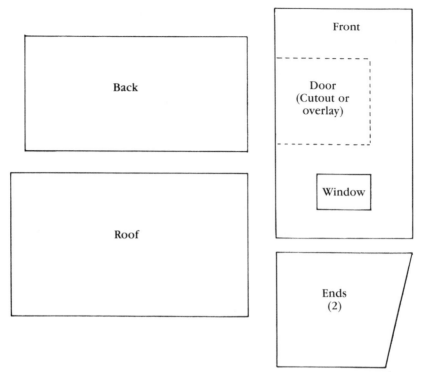

7-8   A small storage shed consists of only a few simple parts.

the door and window separately. Install the door and window, then weather the whole outfit. Make a stovepipe from a piece of plastic runner or a length of soda straw if you wish, and glue it to the roof. Bingo! You have a storage shed (FIG. 7-10).

Once you get the hang of scratch-building, and if you enjoy making models, you'll find yourself doing more and more of it. It's a great way to dress up your layout with structures that just aren't available any other way.

WEATHERING

Probably the most important thing you can do to any structure, though, is weather it. If you look closely at the various structures in your neighborhood and town, you'll see that all of them bear various effects of the weather and the immediate environment. You'll see dirt, rust, peeling paint, scars and scratches, faded and chalky colors, grease, grime, soil of all colors and particularly those of the immediate surroundings, graffiti, stains and splotches, soot streaks, and a hundred other manifestations of age, use, and abuse. The trick is to replicate this in reasonably realistic fashion on your structures, which probably will involve you in some first hand observations of the real thing.

The classic case of pursuit of such realism is the modeler who scratch-built a complex building, then set it afire. He carefully monitored the progress of destruction, put out flames here and there, and finally extinguished

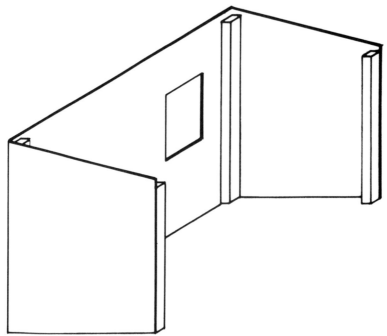

7-9 Glue stripwood corner blocks to the end walls to provide gluing surfaces for the sidewalls. Stripwood stiffeners can be glued in lengthwise for greater rigidity, too.

7-10 A few pieces of cardstock and/or styrene and some bits of stripwood plus some finishing touches results in a scratch built shed-type building of universal design that is suitable for any layout.

them to leave a realistically burned out hulk, complete with genuine char and soot. A couple of such buildings are now available as model kits (but they don't have to be torched).

Weathering takes an eye for detail and color, some patience, and some time. Some practice is needed to acquire all this, too. But it's also fun, and not difficult, and you can't really wreck anything. There are lots of ways to go about it. I prefer to use repetitive washes of acrylic paint for the overall, cover-everything weathering. I use mostly light and dark earth, grimy black, light and dark gray, dust, and rust. I sometimes mix two shades for something different, or wash on one color and immediately work in a second in splotchy fashion. I make a wash by putting about 8 or 10 drops of water into a soft drink screw-top cap and adding an unmeasured blob of paint off the tip of a No. 0 art brush. The water usually is from a container that starts with about 4 to 5 ounces of water and 4 or 5 drops of dishwashing detergent to make the water wetter.

The process involves washing the color onto the surface, usually streak-ily or splotchily, blending it along as realistically as possible. Too much color, wash on some water to cut and spread it. Not enough, wash it again, maybe after drying, maybe not. To dirty the mortar joints in a brick wall and tone down the brick color and mottle it a bit, try a grimy black or a medium gray wash. It will zip right along the mortar joints of its own accord and you can splotch-wash the brick faces. Soot streaks from a chimney can be made with black or grimy black that fades and spreads as it crawls down the stack, or down the chimney onto the roof or wall. Apply this as paint thinned with about 4 parts of water, using a fairly dry brush. Earth splashing up onto build-ing walls from dripping eaves takes washes of suitable earth tones flowed on the bottoms of the walls and diminishing upward.

Once the major weathering is complete, you can add the little touches like a graffito, a splotch of grease, a paint spill, rust streaks, mud splatters, bird droppings, whatever. When all is complete, you can leave the structure "as is" if it will not be handled much, or coat it with Testor's Dull Cote or artist's fixative to preserve it.

There are many other approaches to weathering. Commercial prepara-tions like Blacken-It and Weather-It are useful for various purposes. Many modelers like to use earth tone artist's chalks. There are commercially avail-able sets of just earth tones, and also assortments specifically for model weathering. Scrape a little chalk dust off a stick, load it onto a dry brush and work it around. It's infinitely changeable, and what you don't like you wipe off. Fix the final result with a sprayed flat finish. Another alternative is to work from a multi-hued set of women's blush or eye shadow makeup cakes, apply-ing the material with a brush much like the chalk dust. Sounds strange, but it's a very effective and easy method.

Yet another method is to use mixes of artist's basic colors in acrylics, available by the tube from art supply outlets. Cake-type watercolors have also been used to good effect. Another art item, artist's felt tip pens are especially useful for doing finish, detail weathering after the basic work has been done. The ones to use are the Eberhard Faber Design Art Markers, and the key to a pleasing result is to use blends of various colors and shades, as well as light washing plain with mineral spirits or Floquil Dio-sol thinner. Use earth tones, especially for weathering wood, and variations of the basic colors for weathering painted surfaces.

Don't hesitate to experiment with any of these techniques and materials, alone or in combination. There are other methods as well. With practice and experience, as well as real life observation, you'll soon be able to add a great deal of authenticity to your layout structures.

SCALE AND SIZE

When you build a layout, no matter its overall size, certain questions crop up with regard to the structures installed on the layout. The concern is not with the right-of-way structures, but rather with the trackside ones to some degree and with the nonrailroad structures in particular. What is involved is scale, dimensions, proportions, and placement, all of which interact. The larger the layout, the more important these factors become, but they are important on small layouts as well. This subject can get a little deep, but the purpose here is to give you the short form, so you can be aware of it and investigate further if you wish.

You might reasonably think that when you build a model layout, you should make everything to the same scale. Not necessarily. For instance, there are ways to use Z scale track to simulate narrow gauge N scale. You can also use structures of a different scale to create an impression of distance. A farmhouse in a back corner of an HO layout might be N scale, giving the impression that it is far away on the horizon.

Scale also implies proportion. If something is out of proportion to its surroundings, like a four story apartment building on a street of bungalows, it looks out of place and we say it is out of scale. Keeping everything in proportion on a layout is not always easy. It might be fun to build a big-city station, but it would be out of place at a branchline stop. It's also easy to make warehouses or factories too big for the overall size of the layout. Unless a structure is actually the focal point of a layout, the sizes should be compatible. Small layout, small structures, and not too many of them.

This goes back to dimensions, the measurements of the structures. They can't be overly tall, overly wide, overly long, for the size of the layout. Just as importantly, they can't appear to be too bulky, to take up more room than the apparent or implied size of the area covered by the layout would warrant. Remember that on a layout you're working in part with the old smoke and mirrors, so appearances and illusions count heavily.

This leads to structure placement. Where and how you position the structures will make a big difference in the illusion of reality. An industrial scene is crowded, busy, hardly an open spot left for a bush to grow. A country branch line scene is small town, or pastoral and peacefully spread out. A mountain mining scene is rough, craggy, rugged, structures precariously positioned, perhaps crowded in a cluster on a cliffside, otherwise sparse. Put the wrong kinds or sizes of proportions of structures in the wrong places, and you throw the scene out of whack. Give placement some careful thought, and don't just slap your structures down any-old-where.

Chapter **8**

Making the Scenery

A model railroad without scenery is like a hot dog without relish—a lot of the flavor is missing. It's the Dullsville & Drab City R.R. When there's not much to look at but a cat's cradle of trackage, a bunch of bare wood strips, and a spaghetti patch of drooping wires, you can lose interest in the whole works pretty easily. A lot of modelers wander off in pursuit of some other activity at this crucial turning point. They are loath to become involved in the mysterious business of scenicking that so obviously requires the talents of an artist. The pike gathers dust and becomes the Goodstart & Coodabin Primo.

Making scenery doesn't require a ton of artistic talent. There's a whole new world opening up here for you to exercise your creative abilities and imagination. There are several general methods for building scenery and a tremendous number of variations on each theme. Far too many to cover in this book. Some of the most commonly employed techniques will be explained here, with emphasis on those that produce the greatest amount of believable scenery for the least amount of cash, time, and mess. The tools, equipment, and supplies required are widely varied and often a bit out of the ordinary, and are not your usual workshop items, so they will be covered as the need arises.

PRELIMINARY DESIGN AND PLACEMENT

As was explained in Chapter 3, the basic scenery concepts are best developed early on and evolved along with the plans, because scenery that is just cobbled up and stuck in place as an afterthought invariably looks like just that— an afterthought. Nothing blends in properly, and there may also be operational problems, insufficient clearances, not enough working room, or other difficulties as a result.

Most people have trouble visualizing exactly how the scenery will go together, even if they have a fairly clear mental picture of how it should eventually look, and it's almost impossible to draw up scenery plans on paper. Plans are one dimensional, the actuality is three dimensional. Some modelers resort to making a scale mockup of the layout, but making a model of a model still doesn't convey well the finished layout and seems a waste of time.

But with the completed benchwork and trackage, you have a full sized base on which you can begin to convert your ideas into reality.

There aren't any rules in scenery building, but there are some usual practices that have come about to skirt some potential problems. First, assess your overall plan to see that it is workable. List all the major scenic elements of the layout, such as a cliff, mountain, trestle, pond, swamp, river, or gorge. Include anything that requires specific, detailed construction, as opposed to just general landscape that merely fills in the blank places. All of these major elements are focal points with a scenic purpose. Will they fit in naturally, without being forced or looking peculiar? Is there room enough at their appointed locations to build them, and will you have room enough to work? Should any be shifted, or eliminated? Have you tried to jam too much in? Now is the time to make any needed changes.

Next, double check to make sure you have avoided some common pitfalls. Where two tracks that are not a double-track main line run parallel on the same level, they should be separated by two or three track-widths so you can place believable scenery between them. If two tracks are on different levels, separate them horizontally by at least 1.5 times the difference in elevation (FIG 8-1). This allows for a reasonable slope between the two lines that approximates the natural angle of repose (roughly 36 degrees) of loose materials. Check all portal, bridge, and structure placement clearances to make sure your long overhang locos or rolling stock won't clip some edges or sides. Test run all trackage for proper operation.

Solder jumpers across metal rail joiners at all locations where the track will be hidden. Turnouts or crossovers and such in hidden and inaccessible locations mean trouble for sure. Ascertain that a proposed piece of removable scenery, access hatch or other similar device will actually work for you when installed. If questionable, make a change. Check that the proposed scenery does not interfere with any trackage and does not visually obscure tracks, structures, or other scenic details, or does so effectively if that is its purpose. Successively higher tracks are usually placed successively farther back on the layout with the scenery downsloping toward the front (except for layover or storage tracks deliberately hidden behind scenery).

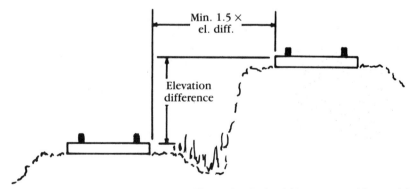

8-1   Parallel non main-line tracks on different levels should be separated by a minimum of 1.5 times the elevation difference.

After this checkout, consider the compatibility of the proposed scenery with the overall concept of the railroad, and the compatibility of the various scenic elements with one another. Everything should fit together, but a common problem is that they do not. Make sure your geology, topography, and flora all are complementary and suited to the assumed layout location.

PROPORTIONS AND COMPRESSION

As you plan the scenery, and as you construct it, keep in mind the business of correct proportions, selective compression, and selective omission, all of which work hand in hand. There is no possible way to build everything to scale, and you don't want to try. The trick is to create the illusion that everything is real, convey the perception of truth, even though close examination will turn up many a falsity. You can do this in a variety of ways.

For example, it might seem logical to "plant" tall trees toward the back of the layout and gradually reduce their height as they near the front. Actually, if you position tall trees toward the front and make them gradually smaller toward the rear, perhaps also increasing the overall density of the foliage at the same time, you will create the impression of distance by manipulating linear perspective. A smaller-than-scale structure placed toward the back will help in creating a similar effect, and a properly painted backdrop can add to it.

Compression has to be widely used in scenery building. If your prototypical mountain has a vertical rise in elevation above your freightyard of 2000 feet and you model it faithfully, it would soar through the roof of your house—23 feet high in HO scale. Prototypically, a mile of track hardly gets you beyond the city limits, but in the N scale that's clear out of the basement and into the backyard, over 33 feet. If you place your telephone poles every 150 scale feet or so along tracks and roads, they'll look mighty lonely. That's every 21 inches in HO scale.

Obviously a lot of the scenic elements must be built or arranged in a different way and to a different scale than would be prototypically correct. The mountain must be just a shoulder of a mountain, sloping up and back, perhaps to blend with a painted backdrop, or a series of cliffs and ledges that can be carried up and back to the backdrop top. The trackage leaving the city must in a short distance pass through a compressed scene that makes a quick but unobtrusive transition from city to country. The telephone poles must be set closer together, at some distance that appears to the eye to be believable. Everything has to be selectively shrunk, but not entirely and not in complete proportion. Selective addition may play a part. More telephone poles than there really should be, for instance, and selective omission may also be needed, as you can't possibly set up all the structures that would really be present in the city-to-country transition.

There are many tricks and techniques that can be used, many of which you can learn by further reading. For example, rolling hills take up a lot of space on a layout, and if they are to look real, they have to sprawl. Mountains don't, and you can get a lot more variability and more scenery that's more impressive by building vertically. Much of learning about scenicking, depends upon actually doing, often by trial and error, and by experimenting with different techniques and materials. Learn to trust your eye. It will tell you more often than not when something is either just right or not quite.

THE MOCKUP

Because finished scenery is so difficult to visualize, especially if lots of focal points like rivers, gulches, and ledges are involved, making a preliminary mockup is a good idea. All you need for this is wadded up newspapers, cardboard cartons or sheets, scraps of wood, wrapping paper, a towel or two or some rags, or whatever else is handy. Tack or staple the materials to the benchwork and roadbed, pile up paper wads, drape fabric, stack boxes, and do whatever it takes to set up a rough, tentative representation of your scenery. Lay in substitute trestles and bridges with wood scraps, form a mock creek or river with ribbons of twisted plastic bread wrappers, spot your tunnel openings, set cardboard boxes for the principal structures. Model all the lesser elements like between tracks, drainage ditches, shallow cuts and fills, flat spots, and bankings with sheets of paper cut, shaped, and stapled to suit.

Let the whole affair stand for a while so you can ponder. Make some changes, poke it apart here and pinch it together there, and whatever you do, don't rush the job. Be picky, be choosy about what you leave in place. There should be a reason for every ledge, valley, flat, and gulley, and especially for every cut and fill along the rail grade. Justify everything. Keep in mind that while you are building the scenery to the tracks, in real life the scenery was there first and the tracks were built through it, and that's what your model should look like. When you're finally happy with your mockup, quit.

Now you can start in earnest, which means tearing out the mockup. When it goes, so does your representation of what the scenery should ultimately look like. There are two ways to get around this problem, and the best arrangement is to use them both. One is to take a few close-up photos of the mockup. Black and white is fine and Polaroid is okay, but regular negative film is better so you can have enlargements made. With a few overlapping 8- × -10-inch glossy prints you can follow your mockup quite well. The second method is to mount some contour templates as you remove the mockup materials. You can use pieces of corrugated cardboard from old cartons if you don't mind some rugged scissoring. Otherwise, buy some sheets of fairly rigid posterboard, that cut a lot easier. Section by section, draw rough outlines of the mockup contours on pieces of cardboard and staple or tack them to the benchwork and roadbed (FIG. 8-2). As each template goes up, the adjacent mockup materials come down. You can also number each space between templates and make notes on exactly what you have in mind to go there. When this is done, you can start building the foundation.

THE HARDSHELL FOUNDATION

This technique was developed many years ago and remains a widely used and effective one. It is based upon a U. S. Gypsum plaster product called Hydrocal. This is very dense and strong and can be applied in thin layers, and it does not shrink or crack. When cured it actually becomes alabaster rock.

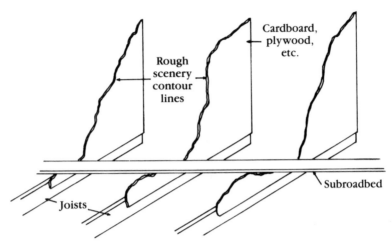

8-2 Cardboard templates attached to the benchwork will give you a visual reference for the finished scenery contours, and are easy to revise if you don't like what you see.

The resulting scenery is tough and lightweight. It is not expensive, not available everywhere, and it is messy (but simple and fast) to use. Local hobby shops often carry small packages, and bulk materials can be obtained through U. S. Gypsum suppliers.

First, cover every bit of the trackage with wide masking tape to protect it from the plaster that certainly can get around. Stick it lightly to the rail tops and it probably will pick up little if any ballast. Then mount a few 1-×-1-inch posts to the benchwork, spaced about 18 to 20 inches apart in any direction and set to the heights indicated at those points by your contour templates (FIG. 8-3), or just by eye if you can visualize the contours you're after. Now if you wish, you can fill in the spaces with crumpled paper to indicate the approximate contour lines, but it's not an essential step.

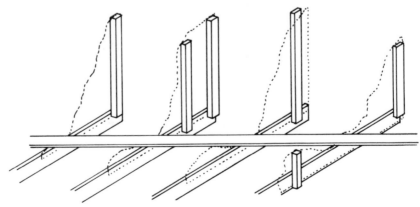

8-3 A few support posts, alone or along with cardboard or plywood contour templates, are the starting point for hardshell scenery construction.

Next you need a cat's cradle, which you can make out of strips of post-erboard or a similar cardboard about 1 inch wide, or from 1-inch masking tape. Many modelers use both, and that's an effective method. String the tape around and about in criss crosses, sticking the lengths to the posts, to one another, and to roadbed edges (FIG. 8-4). Or do the same with the cardboard, stapling and bending it into place. Or, do both. You can leave the cardboard contour templates in place and use them for props, and you can also attach sturdier plywood formers at strategic locations on the benchwork if you wish. The object is to keep fiddling around until you get a conformation that you like, and that fits well. Most of this web will be self-supporting. Nonetheless, prop it wherever there's a need with crumpled paper, or suspend it from a guy tape. Supports can be pulled away later.

Arm yourself with a spritzer bottle full of water and a roll of top quality, soft, absorbent kitchen towels. Drape towels, whole or in torn strips, over the cat's cradle and spray them until they go limp and you can work them into the approximate shapes you like, refining the broad scenery contours. Again, keep working them until you are satisfied with the basic realism (the lines will still be soft). If there's something you don't like, pop a strip or a tape off and reposition it, or slice out a section and redo it. Let it all stand for a day or two or more while you study it.

When you're done with this phase, start with the Hydrocal. Mix small batches, according to the directions. You won't have much working time before setup starts, probably about 15 minutes. Have a stack of paper towels ready to go. Use the tough, folded, brown commercial type you find in public dispensers, or cheap, rough, single ply kitchen towels. The recycled-paper type works well. Whichever, tear them into strips about 4-×-6-inches for convenient working, or whatever other size best suits you. Make sure every place the plaster can drip, which it will do in plenty, is protectively covered.

Dump the Hydrocal into a pan of cool, clean water and let it soak through, then stir it smooth. A rectangular pan like a Pyrex baking dish works

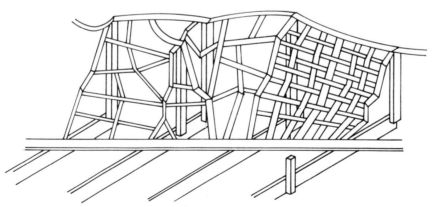

8-4 A cat's cradle of tape, cardboard strips, or both forms the underlayment for the scenery shell. The crazy quilt pattern (left) works well for rocky, craggy mountains, the woven pattern (right) for smoother, rolling countryside.

well (and cleans easily). The plaster mix should be the consistency of thick cream or a heavy texture paint. Take a piece of toweling and slip it through the mix with a sawing motion so that both sides get evenly coated. You must do this slowly enough that the towel becomes saturated. If the plaster runs off when you hold the piece up edgewise, it is too thin, and you should add just a bit of plaster. If it clumps and does not cover the surfaces well, it is too thick. Add just a tad of water.

Plop the coated towel onto the cat's cradle at one of the high points. Poke it into place with a finger as necessary but don't fuss with it much— there's a lot to do yet. Keep laying on the pieces, working downhill and over-lapping them just a little (FIG. 8-5). Wherever you cover a support post, make sure the top is completely covered and add a second small piece on top of that right away. As soon as the mix starts to set up (it won't work properly or "feel" right), scoop the remainder onto a scrap of cardboard and try forming it into a rock outcrop, a boulder, a little ledge, or whatever appeals. Or you might want to cast something in a mold, like a bridge abutment. This will give you some practice working with the material without affecting the layout. Save the cured pieces for experimenting and practicing with later with paints and dyes. You might well end up with some usable chunks that you can later graft right onto your layout scenery.

As you lay the plastered pieces of toweling onto the cat's cradle, you can manipulate them to some extent by poking them into general shapes like gullies, cuts in a rock wall, ledge protrusions, and the like. As soon as the plaster starts to stiffen, leave it alone. It should cure quite hard in about an hour, and then you can add other layers along the edges if you're careful. Full

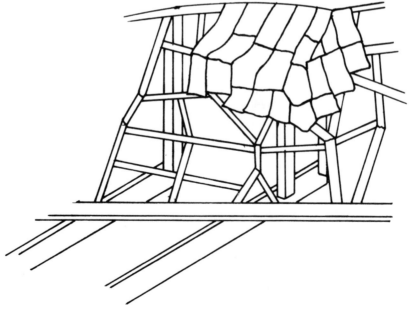

8-5 Lay the plaster-coated towel strips in overlapping layers, starting at the high points and working downward.

strength does not occur for some while. Give it a day or two, then inspect your work. The shell will be very thin, which is normal, and it's also very strong. Pull out any loose newspaper, strips, or other supports from beneath the shell. Put a light inside, then look over the outside surface. You'll quickly spot any missed areas, gaps, or obviously weak points. Circle them lightly with a pencil.

Now look over the shapes you have engineered and see if you want to make any changes or additions. You can break out small pieces with a scratch awl or a screwdriver, saw out larger ones with a saber saw and a fine toothed metal-cutting blade. Take care, but don't worry about a crack or three. If you want to add something, just wad up paper in the approximate shape and tape it to the shell. Then mix up some more Hydrocal. Spritz the shell surface in the fix-up areas with clean water until it is well soaked, then lay on some more plastered towel pieces, covering your holes and cracks and building up over the new shapes. Put a second layer over all the particularly thin spots. It's a good idea to add a second layer all the way along any roadbed/scenery joints, and any places where you think there might be unusual weight or pressure placed on the scenery. Plaster ridges, where new covers old, can be smoothed in by lightly swiping your finger or a small brush over them. Keep an eye on the patches, especially at the edges. If the fresh plaster starts to turn powdery and dry out, it's not curing. It has to stay damp for a full hour, usually, so mist it gently as often as necessary.

One of the advantages of the hardshell method is that you can chop out or add pieces to your scenery any time, now or later. You can rework it any way you want to, just by adding more Hydrocal in a thick paste for small changes or as coated towel pieces for more major ones. If you need substantial strength at some point, embed a piece of metal window screening. This is also an ideal material for building removable scenery sections or hatch coverings, and for take-down layouts.

SUPPORTED SHELL FOUNDATION

There are several variations in the way a supported shell foundation is made. In all cases the skin is weaker and less self-supporting than a Hydrocal shell, therefore it must be reinforced with an internal support skeleton and a skin underlayment. This type of scenery is also heavier than hardshell, because of the added weight of the skeleton and also the additional plaster thickness needed to create a suitably strong skin.

The support skeleton is easy to make, and usually consists of a combination of several materials, chiefly scrap. The starting point is a series of contour boards screwed to the benchwork at strategic points. You can cut these out of ½-inch plywood or any similar material, using your cardboard mockup contour templates as patterns. Or you can leave the cardboard templates in place and add wood risers right next to them, with appropriately angled cross pieces attached. An alternative is to install risers and cross pieces alone, with no profile boards or templates. You can also run narrow strips of wood, either straight edged or profiled, at right angles to the risers or templates. All of these wood pieces will serve as attachment points for the skin underlayment, so fasten them securely to the benchwork, roadbed, and each other (FIG. 8-6). Remember that all will be hidden beneath the finished skin, so every part of each piece must lie lower than your desired final effect.

There are several materials that you can use for the skin underlayment, and again, combinations are often used. They may depend upon the material selected for the skin. Some modelers use cardboard strips bent to rough shape and stapled in place, the same as for the hardshell cat's cradle. Burlap or jute or a similar heavy fabric can also be used, but is expensive and not easy to work with. Starching the material greatly helps, but it works best where it can be draped into rolling, gentle topography rather than rocky crags.

One of the most popular and effective materials is metal window screening. You could use plastic but it is limp and won't form well. Metal screen you can shape even to sharp contours by crumpling, bending, and pinching it as much as you wish, or to gentle, undulating shapes equally well. Hardware cloth with a mesh of ½-inch squares makes a good underlayment but is difficult to work with. It must be cut with wire cutters or tin snips, and it doesn't shape well because of its stiffness. Chicken wire works better, in a small mesh and smaller gauge wire. Whatever material you select, shape it to suit your desired contours as much as you can, and staple it to the support skeleton (FIG. 8-7).

Probably the most commonly used skin material is a plaster other than Hydrocal. There are several kinds, and not all of them work satisfactorily. Gypsum molding plaster, which you can buy in bulk, is a good bet. So are gypsum wall plaster and gypsum patching plaster, also inexpensive and readily available, but both are a coarser grade than molding plaster and do not

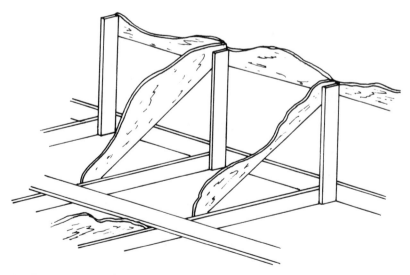

8-6 The underlying framework for the supported-shell scenery skin is ruggeder, stiffer, and more complex than for a hardshell construction because added strength is needed.

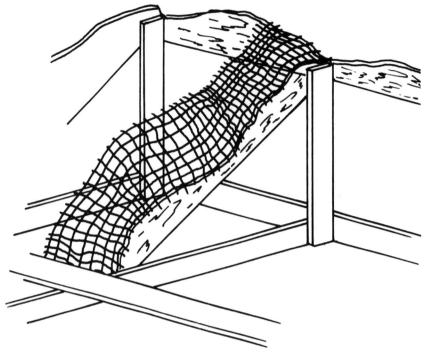

8-7 Small mesh chicken wire or metal window screen works well as underlayment for the supported-shell scenery skin.

sculpt fine detail as well. Wallboard joint compound, available ready mixed in 1- and 5-gallon pails, works and sculpts beautifully but must be applied in several thin layers because it shrinks and cracks open. For an outdoor layout you can build with portland cement plaster, but it is seldom used on an indoor layout. Furnace cement has been used with reasonable success, and so has lime plaster (which can be tough on your skin). Neither will detail well. Ordinary wood-fiber plaster, Keene's cement, and plaster of paris are generally unsatisfactory. Before applying any of these materials, be sure to cover all the trackage with wide masking tape.

One method of applying the gypsum plasters is to begin by making up a soup and coating pieces of paper towel. Lay the towels over the underlayment, just as in the hardshell method. In this case the underlayment can be any of the open mesh or cat's cradle types. Then, after allowing 48 hours or so for the plaster to cure, mix a paste of plaster and spread it over the skin about ¼-inch thick. Dampen the surface first with water.

Another method, which must be used over a fine mesh underlayment, is to start with a fairly thin but not runny plaster paste. Spread or brush it onto the underlayment and let it cure for a day. Mist this coating with water, then spread on a second layer about ¼-inch thick of plaster mixed fairly thick.

If you want to avoid the splattery mess of plaster, you can substitute the sticky mess of glue. Glued paper laminate is a good scenicking method, easy and cheap and relatively fast. The resulting shell is lightweight and suffi-ciently strong provided it is not heavily stressed, and is not susceptible to cracking. Don't use newspaper, as in papier-mache. Strong paper towels will serve, but heavy brown wrapping paper or shopping bags are best. Soak strips in wheat wallpaper paste mixed a bit more watery than usual, and lay them up in the same fashion as for hardshell. In this case, though, you will need four to six layers everywhere, depending upon the weight of the paper used, and six to eight wherever there might be any stress or weight. The first layer can be set on any kind of skeleton, and subsequent layers built up immediately or piecemeal, whichever works best for you. Usual practice is to apply a final coating of plaster about ⅛ to ¼-inch thick.

To avoid the messes of both glue and plaster, consider working with plaster impregnated gauze. This is a medical supply item, available from those sources, used for making certain kinds of plaster casts. It comes in rolls 2, 3, and 4 inches wide, packed in standard cartons of 12 rolls. It is expensive, but works very well, creates no mess, and is fairly fast, resulting in a reason-ably strong shell. You don't even have to mask the track. To apply, just cut off strips of gauze, dip them in water briefly to activate the plaster, and drape the pieces, slightly overlapped, over strips, screen, or crumpled newspaper. Run your finger lightly over the lapped edges to set them tightly. Let the plaster cure for several hours, and apply a second layer if you wish, damp-ening the shell surface first. Here too it is common to apply a final coat of plaster. Mask the track if you do.

Yet another option, also mess-free and also relatively expensive if you need a large quantity, is to use one of the proprietary products especially formulated for making model railroad or diorama scenery. Perhaps the best-known is Sculptamold, an American Art Clay product, which is compounded of plaster and wood fiber. There are similar products for the same purpose, like Form-A-Mountain or Perma-Scene. These materials are applied as a paste over a screen underlayment, so follow the manufacturer's directions. They are very workable materials and allow more open time before setup than most others.

COMPLETING THE CONTOURS

There isn't much likelihood that your completed scenery shell will much resemble any landscape now known to man. There's work yet to be done. Any of several general techniques can be employed to finish the surface in whatever combinations seem most appropriate for the kind of landscape de-sired. As you might expect, there are dozens of little tricks and hints and kinks in making a better landscape.

In most cases at least part of the final layer of plaster, which could also be the first, must be sculpted. Or, a commonly favored alternative is to apply more plaster as needed after the basic skin (or sections thereof), whatever its construction, has been completed, for the specific purpose of sculpting. On a laminated paper skin this might mean coating the entire surface, on a plaster shell it would only have to be applied in the areas to be worked. In fact, this is usually done piecemeal and plaster buildups here and there on the skin may take numerous coatings before you are finally satisfied.

You can use Hydrocal for this, but it sets fast so there isn't much time to work when it is soft, and when cured it is too hard to carve easily. It's fine for preliminary buildups, though. Molding plaster is a good bet, because it can be applied in any reasonable thickness, cures fairly rapidly, can be shaped and formed while soft, and carves nicely and smoothly when cured. Joint compound is excellent as long as you can keep the layers fairly thin, as it shrinks and cracks if too thick. But such damage is no problem to fix, either. It carves very nicely and holds a good contour, and can be smoothed and also reshaped with a wet sponge even after curing. Sculptamold and equivalent products are also excellent for final contouring. Such materials work and carve well, are not awfully expensive for this purpose, and are available through hobby and craft shops.

In spots where the scenery skin will be completely obscured by a roadway, heavy shrubbery or trees, or a structure, the surface can be left to cure or dry smooth. Elsewhere, the surface must be worked in some fashion. There are few completely smooth surfaces in nature, no straight lines, and certainly no putty knife or spatula swirls and ridges. In all areas that will be essentially bare, rough, and/or rocky ground with little or no vegetation, when the plaster is still wet or damp stipple the surface. Roughen it up by jabbing the tip of a stiff bristled paint brush into it with sharp, short motions, and not too deep. Where there will be grass and shrubbery, partly vegetated open ground, pat the damp surface with a fine-pored sponge or a piece of foam rubber, just enough to break the smoothness. Where there will be simulated rock, whether outcrops, ledges, cliffs, or cuts, swipe the wet plaster with the tip of a brush, or several brushes of different bristle consistencies and sizes. The motion should be mostly sideways, but include some angular and vertical swipes as well. Light stippling is also in order in many instances.

Most of the sculpting is needed on the rock formations, all types of which exhibit a myriad of cracks, crevices, little shelves and ledges, and striations of all sorts. As much as anything else, a web of tiny hairline cracks and fissures will lend realism to rockwork. Study the real thing, or good photos, to see what sort of character your particular kind of rockwork should have, and try to model it. Good tools for this are your old, dulled hobby knife blades (always save them for such purposes), both Swiss and riffler files, dental picks, a penknife, a pointed-tip table knife, and of course professional sculpting tools.

Another technique, generally used in combination with others, is to add materials to the skin by gluing them on or sticking them in fresh plaster as it is being worked or sculpted. All such add-ons must be blended in thoroughly so they don't look stuck-on. One good example is precast rockwork. There are many commercially available molds for different kinds of rock facings and you can also make your own molds from likely prototype specimens you yourself locate. Casting the rock sections with plaster is a simple procedure, much faster than sculpting, and gives realistic results.

There are two casting methods. To wet cast, you fill the mold, allow curing to begin, then while the plaster is still damp press it gently onto the scenery skin at the desired location. Use just enough pressure to make it merge with the skin surface, which should be rough enough to provide "tooth," and either hold or secure it in place until curing is well along, then peel the mold away. Dry casting is easier for beginners, works better for hard to reach spots, and affords a bit more control. Just fill the mold (or several at a time) with plaster and scrape the surface off fairly smooth (but not slick). After allowing plenty of curing time, peel off the molds. Arrange the pieces on the skin for the best fit—you can trim them however you like—and glue them on. You can use a thin plaster bed for this, and acrylic latex caulk or a silicone adhesive or caulk also works well. In either case, meld the separate castings together as necessary with a bit of plaster so the joints and seams don't show.

Another possibility is to preform chunks of plaster and stick them on the skin while it's wet and while you're working fresh plaster, then fashion them into ledges, boulders, or outcrops by stippling and carving (FIG. 8-8). This works particularly well where there are isolated features that stand up in a relatively empty area. Precast items like tunnel portals, bridge abutments, wings, and retaining walls are glued onto their supports or backings and faired in with plaster in much the same way. Some modelers like to embed pieces of actual rock, too, and if done carefully and sparingly this can be effective and realistic. But it's tricky (and heavy).

While all this is going on, you should be shaping in whatever fashion is necessary the streambeds and any pond or swamp or marsh areas—wherever there will be water. Line out your roadways, trails and paths, and structure pads.

8-8   Isolated features like a rock outcrop or a boulder can be preformed, stuck onto the still-wet plaster scenery surface, and faired in with a bit of fresh plaster.

GROUND COLOR AND COVER

That expanse of white plaster has to be colored to resemble earth and rock, then textured with various materials to simulate bare earth, loose dirt and rubble rock, native grasses, or other cover. This is perhaps the most difficult part of building scenery, and unfortunately the simpler the process, the less realistic the results. Getting good results does take some time, some practice, and some experimenting and experience. There are several approaches and dozens of variations, and lots of different materials that can be used. Two commonly used and effective methods will be covered here, with a few variations.

As you go through this process, keep three points firmly fixed in your mind. First, there's no way you can make a mistake. You can only create some effects that you're not happy with, and in that case you can cover them over with little effort and do something else. Second, the most common error is making the colors too intense, bright, heavy, and also too uniform. The colors you use for the most part should be thin, subdued, pale, subtle, and variable in tones, and only strengthened as needed by means of repeated applications (a couple of exceptions will be noted later). And third, probably the next most common error is to make the ground cover materials too coarse or bulky and out of scale, or otherwise unrealistic in overall appearance.

Latex texturing

The first method of adding color and cover, often called *latex texturing*, is relatively quick and simple. It is most effective (and easiest to do) where nearly all the scenery will be covered with vegetation and there is a minimum of exposed rockwork. I recommend it for modelers of non-rocky scenery who want the best appearance for the least amount of work and fuss.

First, determine the most prevalent soil color of the area or kind of terrain you are modeling, and select a paint color to match it. The best way to do this to actually collect a sample of the soil, get some strips of color chips that approximate those colors from your local paint store, and lay them all out right on your layout. Make a match or two under the lighting conditions that will most often prevail there. Failing that, you'll have to work from color photos (which are often off-tone), or just make an educated guess. The more accurate you can be, the more realistic the result. If you are doing a western scene, there may be a couple of predominant earth colors, such as deep, rich red and buckskin tan. Eastern scenes are more apt to be a neutral brownish-gray. If you're not sure, select a medium tan-beige. Have the paint mixed in your chosen color in an interior latex flat enamel. Depending upon the porosity of your scenery skin, you'll get from 100 to 200 square feet of undiluted first coat coverage per quart of paint.

If the ground color in your modeled locale is mostly uniform, that's all you'll need for paint. If there are striations of different colors, as is common to western buttes, for example, you will need more for a creditable job. Select some appropriate earth tone acrylic colors. You can use basic acrylic artist's colors, available in tubes from any art supply outlets. Yellow ochre, burnt and raw sienna, burnt and raw umber, black, ultramarine blue, and white are the common choices. You'll have to experiment some to get used to the way these colors work, unless you're an artist. An easier course is to choose some appropriate acrylic modeling paints at the hobby shop, such as Pactra or Polly S . Another good source is the Ben Franklin stores, which carry a wide range of earth tone and pastel acrylic craft paints.

Next, assemble your loose ground cover materials (also called scatter material). There is a wide range available from hobby shops, and select those appropriate for your purposes. Lawn grass and field grass comes in various shades and combinations, such as fall or spring. Plain ground foam (ground up and dyed foam rubber) comes in a variety of colors for various purposes, even to stimulate dust or raw topsoil. You can use the different colors and grades of scale track ballast material spread, scattered, or piled for gravel, sand, or rock. Many modelers prefer to use sorted and sifted grades of real soil and pebbles they collect themselves. This works well and adds to the realism, and it's cheap. Whatever the material, select several colors and grades that can be randomly scatter-mixed. There's no uniformity in nature.

You'll also need a pump spritzer bottle, preferably one that will mist well. Fill it with a mix of 1 part acrylic matte medium (available at art supply stores) and 3 parts water, plus liquid dishwashing detergent at a rate of about 10 drops per pint. Set out a few paper cups and a small kitchen strainer, and you're ready to go to work.

Mix some of your base paint 50/50 with water in a second, closable container. Work in areas of about 1 square foot, 2 at most. Brush the paint on, covering the plaster completely. If the paint soaks in quickly, go right back over it with another coat. Have any other needed colors opened and ready, and immediately work them into the wet base paint with an artists brush—a wide flat works well. Have a container of plain water handy, so you can wet your brush when necessary to merge and wash the colors together. Blend and streak and wash the colors into a natural looking pastiche. Then add the ground cover. Sift the principal fine material, representing grass, straight down from above with the kitchen strainer, so it lands fairly even onto the flats and slopes without drifting, but misses sharply angled and vertical surfaces. You may want the cover sparse in places with earth showing through and thicker in others, such as alongside a watercourse. Mix the colors so there is no uniformity. A light sprinkling of yellow foam will give you a field of dandelions, white for daisies, blue/purple for alfalfa or lupine. Use some different sizes.

Trickle or tap ballast, fine dirt, or tiny pebbles from a paper cup to make a rocky field, a rock pile, a gravel bank, a pathway, a spill of soil or gravel at the base of a cutbank. Spread a layer of dirt on a banking and trickle diluted color down through it to simulate erosion effects. Arrange gradations of ballast or pebbles to form a scree slope. Here and there you might want to brush on some added color, either your base or some washed-in acrylics. This might mean sprinkling on a little more ground cover. Where the surface is supposed to be bare earth, sift on a thin dusting of fine soil, almost floury. Experiment with as many different but prototypically appropriate effects as you can think of.

Now mist everything you've done with the matte medium solution.

Spray above and across, not downward, so the moisture will settle onto the landscape without disturbing it. This will impregnate the ground cover and bond it in place, along with the wet paint beneath it. Finally, place some bits of coarse ground foam or lichen here and there as appropriate, to simulate vegetation that is larger/taller/bulkier than grass but not yet large shrub size. This might be weed patches, rushes, small shrubs or low hummocks of grasses. Again, vary the size and color. Then spray the binder on once more to lock in this material. Several light mist applications might be needed to tie everything down well.

Dye texturing

The second method of applying color and cover is sometimes called *dye texturing*. This is a more difficult and time-consuming procedure that often requires some experimenting to find the right color combinations, but the results can be very impressive. It is also a recommended method for making rockwork and mountain country look real, and for those with an artistic bent and/or who enjoy the fiddling around and don't mind spending the time to achieve better than average results.

You'll need some packages of household dye like Tintex or Rit, available at supermarkets and houseware outlets. Cocoa brown, yellow, green, and black serve for most purposes, along with brick red and buff for some western scenes, and perhaps some orange for irony, rusty soils and rock. You'll also need some screw-top storage jars, a few mixing sticks, and some smaller jars or old margarine tubs or something similar to work from. Load a spritzer bottle with water and 10 drops of liquid dishwashing detergent per pint.

You will be coloring three different types of terrain in whatever patchworks are necessary on your layout, and blending them together: bare rock, bare earth, and grass (which includes any kind of similar low growing vegetation). Each of these will probably be composed of two or three or more colors, washed and blended in a mottled, streaked, striated, or sometimes stratified fashion. Eventually all the plaster surface will be dyed. Your first chore is to mix all of the dyes in the large stock jars. Ignore the undissolved, settled-out material at the bottoms of the jars; the liquid will be a saturated solution at constant strength. Each time you use some, add more water and stir again. When all the dye powder has dissolved, throw the solution away and start over.

Next, start experimenting to find the dye tones you will need. Pour a measured amount of water in each working container and add a certain, counted number of drops of the stock dye solution. Each solution should be very dilute, especially black and dark colors. Some dyes you might want to use alone, others you might need to mix to produce the right color. For example, a diluted black will be a neutral gray, which can be warmed with brown or reddish brown, cooled with blue, dirtied and toned off with yellow. Also, the straight colors can be applied over and washed into one another on the plaster to create different effects. Another trick—try diluted coffee (the blend doesn't matter!) to color bare rock; add some dye to change its tones. When you arrive at some tones you like, make a note of the formulation so you can repeat it. Jot it on the plastic tub with a Sanford Sharpie permanent marker as it won't wash off.

You can color as much surface at a time as you wish, moving from spot to spot as you wish. Thoroughly spray each area with the wetted water, until the plaster can hold no more. Then apply the dye. You can spray it, daub it on with a small piece of sponge, or use fine bristled ½-inch or 1-inch paint brushes. Keep a jar of clean water handy for further diluting and washing already-applied dye. You can dribble it from a drinking straw used as a pipette, or drizzle it down a draw or gully from a spoon. However applied, it will flow out, follow cracks and crevices, and entirely change the appearance of the plaster. Each application should be thin; build color density and tone with repeated applications, and make sure all the strokes are in random directions with no hint of uniformity.

If you need a speckled effect, like granite or certain other rocks exhibit, splatter the color on a dry surface by zipping your thumbnail back along the bristles of a dye-loaded toothbrush. If you need small concentrations of color, use a small diameter pipette and drip onto a damp surface. If you need to lighten an area, mix water and household bleach at a rate of 1 drop to 1 ounce of water and wipe it onto the surface; the effect is controllable by washing with plain water just before you think you've lightened enough.

Once this process is finished to your satisfaction, you can go ahead with the texturing, applying the ground cover in the same way as was outlined for latex texturing. The only difference is that you will not be scattering the materials on wet paint, but rather you'll start with a dry or damp dyed surface. As you arrange the materials, dose the heavier ones like ballast and pebbles with dribbled-on matte medium solution, and soaking it well. Here you might prefer a 50/50 mix, rather than 3 to 1, and add a few drops of detergent to wet the water. Anchor the lighter materials, like flock or ground foam, with a mist of the solution.

WATER

Modeling water can be a tricky business, but there are a number of techniques that will give you creditable results without much difficulty. The approaches vary, depending upon the kind of water you want to model.

To model a river, fairly wide and deep and running fast and relatively smooth without much vertical drop, try this. The "water" will be a very thin layer, so first build up your river bed to the desired final level. Fashion the bankings, and also put in any items that need to be bedded in the plaster, such as rocks that will protrude, stumps, logs, or pieces of junk. When the plaster has cured, spread a layer about ⅛ inch thick of joint compound over the riverbed, where the water will be. Let the compound begin to set up. Then work it with a synthetic kitchen sponge, the kind that has small but random-sized holes in it. Keep the sponge damp. By patting, jabbing with an edge or corner, and swirling or sweeping in various ways, you can make different kinds of ripples, eddies, and waves. You can keep this up quite a while without bothering the compound. Take care, though, that the waves stay in scale and realistic. When you have a satisfactory pattern, let the compound cure. If some shrinkage and cracks appear, gently brush them full of fresh compound on an art brush.

Next, paint the banking and the extreme outer edges of the riverbed with a suitable earth tone acrylic that matches in with the rest of your earth colors. Then paint the riverbed with acrylic black (flat or gloss). Leave the center black and fair in a dark blue along the edges. For the best effect, work outward with a lighter blue, perhaps to a bluish green, and gradually fade into the earth colors slightly before you get to the edge of the water. You might want to add some yellow-green or blue-green streaks to represent moss or algae. The result should imitate the gradually changing colors from shallow to deep water. This is most easily done by spraying the paint on, but brush washing will work, too.

After the paint has dried, add river rocks, sand, gravel, bankside vegetation, or whatever else you want. Sand and small pebbles, or perhaps mud, might extend outward into shallow water. Some of these could also be placed before you paint, so they become partly obscured by color. When you finish arranging, lock everything into place with an acrylic matte medium solution, just as you did with other ground cover. Now paint on a coat of undiluted acrylic gloss medium. When that has dried, add a second coat. That usually is sufficient, but if you want the feeling of more depth, add as many coats of the medium as you wish. If some gloss creeps in where it is unwanted, kill it with matte medium or any clear flat acrylic.

You can use the same method to make a fast running river or stream where the water is deep or murky enough that the bottom can't be seen. This requires substantial shaping of the plaster streambed, then more shaping with a joint compound overlay to form the waves and roils and foamed-up patches of "water." Then, after painting and applying the gloss medium, you will have to create the effect of white water (or greenish-white, or some other tone depending upon the nature of your stream) and foam by dry brush painting those areas.

To create a shallow, clear mountain creek with either slow or fast water, some changes are needed. Here, most of the creekbed is visible, along with underwater sand, pebbles, rocks, and if you're lucky, rainbow trout. Fashion the bankings as usual, and mold the creekbed with plaster and/or joint compound. No need here for sponge work, just mold the general contours. As you do, mold and bed in rocks, boulders, pebbles, perhaps a downed tree trunk or part of a beaver dam. Paint the surface with appropriate shades of acrylics, washed together and mottled in realistic fashion. These colors may range from yellowy-gold to reddish and rusty browns; often they consist mostly of a range of gray tones. When finished, you should have a representative creekbed with no water.

One way to simulate the water is to brush on a couple of coats of acrylic gloss medium, undiluted, with curing time in between. Then partially mix a very small amount of acrylic white paint with about 1 teaspoon of gloss medium. As the second coating begins to set up, tease this fresh mix into the places meant to be white water and foam. Let it cure, coat again with medium, and tease in more white as needed. Repeat this until you're satisfied.

The problem with this method is that there is little illusion of depth. You can correct that by using a pouring plastic instead of gloss medium. A two part epoxy such as is used for decoupage, available at most craft and many hobby stores, works very well. You could also use a polyester resin mix, intended for making clear castings and embedding items, but be warned. The odor is horrendous, and lasts quite a while. Mix according to directions; both materials are applied in much the same way as gloss medium, using cheap, throwaway applicators.

The "water" will be at least ¼-inch thick, so prepare the creekbed with that in mind. Add any materials that you want to embed, like logs or boulders or weeds, and anchor them. Allow at least a couple of days for everything to dry out completely. Then apply the plastic by brushing, ladling, dribbling, pouring—whatever is most appropriate. Smooth it into place and work it into crevices, about ⅛-inch or so thick. Allow this coat time to cure, keeping it dust-free meanwhile, and apply a second coat about as thick as the first. The material sets up slowly, and as it does you will have a chance to sculpt in ripples or waves or eddies, and to tease parts of the surface into rough roils with a small stiff brush. In a third (or fourth, etc.) go-round you can add plastic in selected spots, building up surges and eddies, or adding small patches of plastic tinted with dyes to yellowish or brownish or whatever, or tipping spots with whitish plastic for foam and white water.

You can model still water using these same methods. Nearly all ponds and lakes are opaque except for right along the shores. Shape the area to be covered with "water," then paint it black in the center, feathering out through dark to lighter blue and into greenish to mud or sand shores. Or, go quite abruptly from black to charcoal gray to rocky banks, as mountain lakes usually do. Gloss medium works well for most flat water scenes, especially when the underlying plaster or joint compound surface has been worked with a sponge to make ripples and wavelets. Pouring plastic works better if you want to model a marshy edge, have some rocks rising above waterline, or want to plant tree stubs and stumps out in the water. The "underwater" parts of those features will remain visible and a good illusion of depth is created because of the greater thickness of the plastic.

TREES AND SHRUBBERY

Outfitting a layout with trees and shrubbery has always been a problem. For a sparsely vegetated layout, only a little problem. For a heavily forested one, a big problem. There are lots of trees in many simulated species, flowering and plain, spring, summer, and fall foliage, even leafless or dead, available through hobby suppliers. But they seldom cost less than a dollar each, and can run as much as ten. If you only need a few, fine, but if you need several hundred . . . There are a few tree kits on the market, but they are also expensive. There are lots of ways to make your own, too. Bulk materials are cheap, and some techniques use materials you can gather or scrounge at no cost. Many of the methods are time consuming and tedious for more than a few trees, and some are difficult as well. Even so, if you need lots of vegetation, this is the way to go. Here are some relatively quick and simple forestation methods.

For shrubs, try this. Pick up some rubberized fiber scouring pads at the supermarket, like Scotch-Brite. Cut or tear them into chunks and tease them into shape with tweezers or a hobby knife (FIG. 8-9). Paint them with acrylics in believable shrubbery tones, by brush or spray or dipping. Add flowers to some with tiny dots of bright color, or fall foliage with more color. Glue them onto toothpicks or other "stems" painted a gray-brown or other bark color for individual, larger, open-branched shrubs. For smaller ones or a dense thicket, just leave the material in clumps. Alternative: use precolored foliage lichens, available in bulk from hobby shops, instead of the scouring pad material.

One of the most effective and easiest ways to build a flock of individual deciduous trees—the ones that lose their leaves in the fall—is to start with copper electrical wire. Depending upon your scale and the size of trees you want, the most useful wire sizes and types are #10, #12, and #14 single-conductor stranded Type TW or similar, and #14, #16, and #18 flexible cord like Types SJ, SJT, SPT, SO, or similar. The larger sizes are best for bigger trees with heavy limbs, the smaller (that have more, finer strands) are good for any size tree that has many small limbs. If you don't know typical tree species, sizes and shapes for your prototypical area, get a copy of *The Audubon Society Field Guide to North American Trees,* which tells all.

Start by cutting a length of wire about 2 inches longer than the total height of the tree. Allow about ¼-inch at the bottom for "planting" and determine the length of the trunk, which will remain largely exposed. Strip the insulation from this portion, and make sure the strands are twisted snugly

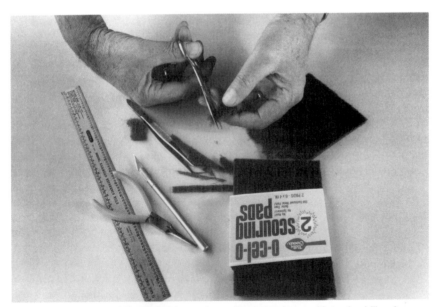

8-9 Certain kinds of fiber scrubbing pads can be cut and teased into shrublike shapes, and strips make great hedges.

together. Solder the strands together here. Hold a sizable, hot iron beneath the wire, just touching, and flow the solder onto the topside. It will quickly chase into the strands, and you're done. Or, coat the wire with a slather of Duco Cement or dip it in varnish.

Then, pull off the remaining insulation. Unravel the wires loosely, and recombine them in two and threes and fours, twisting and trimming and bending until you arrive at a satisfactory bare-limbed tree shape (FIG. 8-10). At this point some modelers prefer to coat the trunk and perhaps parts of the lower branches with joint compound or plaster, that sometimes is dyed gray- ish brown, to represent a rough bark. Alternative: wrap a piece of masking tape around the trunk, positioned vertically and trimmed to just overlap at the rear. Paint the whole affair with flat grays and blacks in a mottled effect.

Allow plenty of drying time, then apply ground foam or fine lichen to the branches. You can use either white or yellow glue to attach the material, but Duco Cement will do it faster. Use mottled greens for colors, with per- haps some specks of brown or yellow here and there, or reds, rusts, browns and yellows for fall foliage. If you stand a batch of trees in holes drilled in an old board, you can spray mist-droplets of assorted colors onto them from 2 or so feet away with a selection of spray enamels like Rust-Oleum. To plant, bore shallow holes in the scenery skin and set the trees in. If you don't glue them, you can remove them for maintenance, repairs, changes, or reuse else- where.

8-10 Unraveled copper stranded wire, with a "trunk" length soldered together at one end, can be easily worked into bare limbed tree shapes ready for covering with foliage.

To make a deciduous forest, plant all the trees in the foreground as individuals, unless the forest is to be dense. In that case, set only the first couple of rows so the trunks show. Behind them, or behind some other sort of hiding foreground if the forest is toward the back of the layout, attach a span of metal window screen to the scenery skin, blocked up to a suitable height. Cover the screen with lots of variegated clumps of lichen and/or ground foam, forming a solid canopy. Lock the clumps in place with GOO, Duco Cement, or a silicone adhesive.

There are lots of ways to make conifers, most of them difficult and tedious. Here's a fairly easy way, especially if you need bunches of firs and spruces. Go to a crafts supply shop and buy a length (or a whole roll) of a material called "bump chenille." There are several sizes, but buy the biggest (in green color), which you can trim to any size you want. If you want all small trees, buy the closest size, for the most bumps for the buck. Clip the bumps apart somewhere near the middle but in varying lengths, and trim off the tails. Then trim the fuzz as necessary while shaping it to suit the desired tree form (FIG. 8-11). Remember that all trees of the same species are far from identical or symmetrical—some raggedy and misshapen spots add realism, and this material you can also bend to simulate a windswept stand or individual trees that had growth problems.

Now there are several possible procedures, and you might want to experiment. One is to stick their bases into a block of Styrofoam as a rack, and mist-spray them with various colors of flat spray enamel. At the same time you can dust them lightly with finely ground foam, grass flock, or fine lichen bits (all of which should be slightly varicolored) for "needles." Another method is to spray them with the cheapest hair spray you can find, or a matte

8-11 Bump chenille is an ideal material for cutting, bending, and trimming to evergreen tree shapes, and you can make a whole forest for pennies.

medium solution, then dust them. Or, you can dip them in full strength matte medium, cut shellac, or even satin varnish. As the coating starts to set up, tease the fibers around into whatever shape you like until they stay put. Then dust, or spray paint.

Considering the small expense of cash and time, this is also about the best way to create a conifer forest. In this case, though, it may be more practical to "plant" a whole section of unfinished trees and then spritz and dust them in place. Then you'll catch the visible top portions of the trees and blend them together, without wasting time on the hidden lower parts.

Bare but living deciduous trees and any kind of recently-dead trees are difficult to model accurately. Unraveling multistranded fine wire is about the best bet, then fashioning a suitable bark coating. Such models usually look most realistic when partly shrouded by conifers if they are bare winter trees, or any kind of greenery if the trees are meant to appear dead. Old dead trees are easier to do because they have lost most of their small branches, leaving only a few large limbs. Again, wire will do the trick. A better possibility, though, is to search around your neighborhood for weeds or shrub branches that look a lot like miniature trees. There are many kinds that do, such as some kinds of sagebrush, privet, and spirea. They are delicate; clean and trim with extreme care. Then dip them in matte medium, varnish, or shellac. If necessary, spray them later with Testor's Dull Cote or equivalent.

SNOW

Modeling snow scenes poses a couple of problems. First, simulating a white, dead of winter landscape is easy enough, but making it look truly realistic is difficult. Second, once you've embarked on this course, there's no turning back. Scenes that are modeled for spring, summer, and fall can be shifted about and changes made easily, but snow is a more permanent covering, especially when bonded to the roofs of your buildings. There's a third problem that can occur. The fine materials used for snow cover can get into the working parts of equipment and raise hob, and/or cause corrosion of metal parts. There are a couple of alternatives to covering the entire layout with snow that are less problematical. One is to use mountain scenery and confine the snowy areas to the peaks while the valleys are still spring-green or fall colored. The other is to model patches of snow and slush from a recent late spring or late fall snowstorm, with appropriate foliage covering most of the landscape.

A wide variety of materials has been tried to simulate snow, including baking flour, baking powder, flour and salt paste, sugar and flour, and ordinary gypsum plaster. Though a lot of modelers persist in trying them, none really work well. Nor does a plaster scenery shell with other materials sprinkled on, even though the effect is white. But there are three materials that do work: Hydrocal plaster, by U. S. Gypsum; white marble dust, by Builders In Scale; and Snow by Vintage Reproductions in "Fluffy, Wet" or "Cold, Dry" or "Slushy." Get the first from a building supplies outlet, the other two from a hobby shop.

There are three different approaches. For a winter snow cover ranging from a dusting up to perhaps a scale 6 to 12-inches of depth, build up the scenery skin in the usual fashion, add trees and vegetation in the winter colors, and position the structures. For a mid fall or mid spring snow that has already partly or mostly melted and is patchy and slushy, make the scenery in the usual way, add trees and other vegetation in spring or fall colors, and position the structures as usual. For a midwinter heavy snow cover of a scale foot or more, and especially a 5-foot or more depth in a mountainous location, form and sculpt the scenery framework and skin the represent snowdrifts; cornices, snowbanks and cuts along shoveled pathways and plowed roads, and the smooth but undulating surface typical of a deep and perhaps windswept snow cover. Add only the tops of vegetation that would logically protrude through the snow, shorten trees accordingly, and arrange for structures to base at an appropriately lower point than the snow cover.

In all cases, all of the surface areas that will not be covered with snow, such as rock faces, should be painted or dyed as usual. All uncolored surface areas, if plaster, should be given a very thin wash of light gray dye or acrylic. If the shell surface is some other nonwhite material, coat it with a barely off-white paint. Then when you apply the snow cover you'll be able to tell where you have covered and where you haven't. Before applying any snow cover, mask off and cover up the trackage and anything else that should not get treated.

To apply a Hydrocal snow cover, first prewet the surface with a thorough misting of wetted water. Load a fine-mesh kitchen or tea strainer with plaster, hold it several inches above the surface, and tap it gently. Sift the plaster out and let it drift down in natural fashion over trees, shrubs, and structures if you want the appearance of a dusting. For a heavier snowfall, you can dust a bare landscape first. Then plant trees and other vegetation, rewet with a very light mist, and sift on another layer of Hydrocal. Another trick is to sift with one hand, not far above the surface, and poof air out of a syringe with the other, blowing the snow into ridges or against walls. Hydrocal has no sparkle. To introduce this feature, before the plaster sets up sprinkle on sparingly and evenly a very fine silver glitter powder, which you can get at most crafts stores. Be sure to completely vacuum up all excess materials.

The Snow by Vintage Reproductions is best applied in conjunction with Hydrocal, or at least on a pure white surface. You can eliminate the glitter dust, though, because this material already has a good sparkle. Proceed as above, applying the plaster first. Then immediately dust the snow on with the puff applicator provided; the "Cold, Dry" is probably the best bet here. To apply alone on the scenery skin, spray first with dilute matte medium, then puff the snow on. For patchy, melting snow, model the patches first with Hydrocal or acrylic white bathtub caulk, then puff on the Snow—"Fluffy, Wet" or maybe "Slushy" around the edges—and shape it to suit with a brush or your finger. A little experimenting will turn up some positive results.

Marble snow is best applied in two separate operations. Wherever there are relatively flat, open surfaces that are to be covered with an unbroken layer of snow, including building roofs, the easiest approach is to paint the snow on. Mix acrylic matte medium at 1 part to 3 parts water. Blend the powdered marble into the solution until you have a workable paste about like pancake batter. Adjust this consistency to suit the thickness of the coating you want and the slope of the surfaces you're applying it to, such as more watery for a thin coating, gooey for a thick or slanted one. Dampen the surface with a mist of wetted water. Apply the paste with a brush, spatula, or palette knife. Go right back over it to smooth out brush, tool, or lap marks. You can do this by sticking your hand in a plastic sandwich bag and smoothing with the backs of your slightly curled fingers. This will leave a surface that is too smooth, and there are two ways to correct the situation. As the paste sets up, but well before it hardens, rub your fingertips around on the surface to raise a slightly rough, fluffy dust. If your finger raises a water glaze, wait a bit longer. Or, sift a very light coating of fresh marble dust from a tea strainer down onto the still-wet paste surface to create almost the same effect. Either way, vacuum up any loose residue after a couple day's drying time.

The second application method can be used over the entire layout to simulate a light dusting of snow, or along with the paste method in those places that couldn't be painted. It might also be used, with patience, to create a snow cover of considerable depth and realism. The basic procedure is to spray the surface with matte medium, mixed about 1 part medium to 4 parts water, until it is saturated. Sift marble powder down onto it from a strainer held several inches high, until the surface moisture is absorbed. You can resoak with medium and resift marble onto it in successive applications wherever it's needed, and push the mush around with your finger or a small, stiff brush to make whatever shapes you like. Build the depth as necessary, and keep the surface nonuniform. After everything is dry, vacuum up the excess dust.

With all of these methods, it's a good idea to experiment with the materials and practice your techniques a bit before you go to work on the layout. A little of that will teach you much more than a lot of words will. As you complete parts of your snow scenes, don't neglect to include details. You might need footprints, a shoveled path, wheel tracks, or a plowed road. Old snow might need to be soot covered or dirty, or perhaps you need some slush. Visualize a typical snow environment, and use your imagination.

DETAILING

Another aspect of scenery building where you can let your imagination run is in the detailing process. Some of this occurs during the building stages, but much can be done afterward by adding bits and pieces. The process covers a whole lot of ground, and it means different things to different modelers and takes various forms on different kinds of layouts. The basic purpose is to add to the layout as much as is reasonable of the minutiae you ordinarily find in the real world. This might range from such obvious elements as telephone poles to lesser ones like adding glass insulators and wires to them, or from big items like a billboard to a hornets' nest under a station eave. Just think of all the little detail items that might be, or could have been, present in the real world that you're modeling, and let your layout reflect that scene. Here are a few detailing suggestions.

Install some fencing. This could be board, chain link, wire, or post and rail, around a yard or business or field, or it could be snowfence.

Plant weeds everywhere they might normally occur in real life, including between the rails of little-used track and along roadsides, maybe in sidewalk cracks.

Find spots for old junk—tires, wheels, abandoned car bodies, barrels and drums, an engine block, refrigerator, any likely detritus that might be thrown into a pond, dumped over a banking, left in a field, pitched out in an alley.

Add railroad junk and used parts and equipment to trackside, at section sheds, in yards or near engine houses. This could be car wheelsets, locomotive drivers, gears, short lengths of rail, a stack of new tires, a scattering of old broken ties, a grease drum near a turnout, lengths of pipe and culvert.

Make some baggage wagons for your stations, add a Coke machine, place a stack of wood pallets or a group of welding tanks or an air compressor or fuel tanks.

Model a cellar hole or two, a burned out house or shack, a tumble down log cabin, a derelict barn.

Scatter plenty of litter around—papers, cardboard boxes, broken boards, bits and pieces of trash windswept against a fence.

Make up instrument cases, relay boxes, battery cases, and cable sets to go along with the trackside signals.

Add switch stands to your turnouts.

Put "window glass" in all your buildings, along with curtains, shades, and drapes, and in your rolling stock as well.

Add appropriate signs and billboards of all kinds and sizes.

Try some unusual details like a farm windmill and stock watering tank, cattle guards, rocker oil pump, high tension or radio towers, stock pens, a campfire, a log or ore loading platform.

Liven up the layout with lots of figures, both human and animal. Repainting stock figures often helps realism.

Chapter **9**

Motive Power and Rolling Stock

*T*he animate heart of a model railroad layout, the element that provides the action and the major focal point, is comprised of the motive power, the engines or locomotives, and the rolling stock, the freight, passenger, and specialty cars. For most model railroaders, this is the starting point. The acquisition of a locomotive, or a car or two, or a "train set," by purchase or as a gift, perhaps as a model kit to be built or a factory-finished piece ready to run, is the spark that lights off the desire for a full fledged model railroad layout. Many would-be pike operators accumulate a good many pieces of such equipment before even planning a layout. You can lay those plans to incorporate whatever equipment you already have. Even better, you can plan for a layout early on, then acquire motive power and rolling stock that will fit that scheme. Either way, the equipment and the layout should complement one another, and that means making choices that are sometimes difficult.

SELECTING MOTIVE POWER

For many, the locomotives are the most fascinating pieces of the model railroad equipment roster. This is where the action is, this is what the tracklaying and the electrical wiring was all about—to allow these tiny reproductions of huge machines to rumble along the rails. There is an endless attraction, not to mention a special mystique, in these scale behemoths, and there is also a wide variety. The earliest steam locomotive bears no more resemblance to one made 50 years later than a stage coach does to a Dodge Caravan, and the diesel locomotives are entirely different again. How do you select appropriate models?

There are several points to consider. First, the age, or era. The period setting of the layout and the age of the motive power should be compatible (FIG. 9-1). Steam locomotives were used from the inception of railroads until shortly after World War II; by 1950 there were very few steamers left. The exception is tourist or excursion steamers, a handful of which still operate today on a regular basis. Depending upon your plans, you may have to differentiate between locomotives that burned wood and those that burned coal. Both fuels were in concurrent use, even by the same road (though not in the same locomotives) for many years. The earliest engines burned coal or coke, and wood came into use because it was cheaper and more readily available in many areas, and also because it was much cleaner for passenger service. The details of locomotive tenders were different for the two fuels. Diesels first appeared in 1924. They were tiny, and only used for light switching duty. By about 1940 some bigger units were being used for light freight and even some light passenger service. By about 1950 almost all trains were headed by diesels.

The locomotive type is also important. Steam locomotives are designated by the Whyte system of wheel notation, which is the primary factor in the differing appearances of locomotive types. For example, a 2–8–4 has a two-wheeled leading truck, eight much larger driving wheels that power the machine, and a four-wheeled trailing truck. In symbol, each small "o" represents a small leading or trailing truck, and each large "O" stands for a driver. The symbol for a 2–8–4 is "oOOOOoo." Most types also have special names. Thus, the 2–8–4 is always a Berkshire locomotive, a 4–8–4 is a Northern, and so on. These steamers were first manufactured at various times. The Berkshires appeared in 1925, so should not be used on a 1910 pike. A 4–6–2 Pacific, though, could be, as it was introduced in 1902. Figure 9-2 lists some of this information.

9-1 There's no mistaking that these locomotives are from different railroading eras that would require appropriate layout settings.

Wheel Format	Symbol	Name	Date
0-4-0	○○	Four-wheel switcher	Pre-1840
0-6-0	○○○	Six-wheel switcher	1840
0-8-0	○○○○	Eight-wheel switcher	1840
0-10-0	○○○○○	Ten-wheel switcher	1905
0-10-2	○○○○○ ○	Union switcher	na
2-4-2	○ ○○ ○	Columbia	1892
4-4-0	○○ ○○	American	1837
4-4-2	○○ ○○ ○	Atlantic	1895
2-6-0	○ ○○○	Mogul	1863
2-6-2	○ ○○○ ○	Prairie	1901
4-6-0	○○ ○○○	Ten Wheeler	1847
4-6-2	○○ ○○○ ○	Pacific	1893
4-6-4	○○ ○○○ ○○	Hudson	1927
2-8-0	○ ○○○○	Consolidation	1866
2-8-2	○ ○○○○ ○	Mikado	1903
2-8-4	○ ○○○○ ○○	Berkshire	1925
4-8-0	○○ ○○○○	Twelve Wheeler	1882
4-8-2	○○ ○○○○ ○	Mountain	1911
4-8-4	○○ ○○○○ ○○	Northern	1927
2-10-0	○ ○○○○○	Decapod	1867
2-10-2	○ ○○○○○ ○	Santa Fe	1902
2-10-4	○ ○○○○○ ○○	Texas	1925
4-10-0	○○ ○○○○○	Mastodon	na
4-10-2	○○ ○○○○○ ○	Southern Pacific	1925
4-12-2	○○ ○○○○○○ ○	Union Pacific	1926
2-6-6-0	○ ○○○ ○○○	Articulated	1906
2-6-6-2	○ ○○○ ○○○ ○	Articulated	1906
2-6-6-4	○ ○○○ ○○○ ○○	Articulated	1935
2-6-6-6	○ ○○○ ○○○ ○○○	Allegheny	1941
4-6-6-4	○○ ○○○ ○○○ ○○	Challenger	1936
2-8-8-0	○ ○○○○ ○○○○	Articulated	1916
2-8-8-2	○ ○○○○ ○○○○ ○	Y6b Mallet	1906
2-8-8-4	○ ○○○○ ○○○○ ○○	Yellowstone	1929
4-8-8-4	○○ ○○○○ ○○○○ ○○	Big Boy	1941

9-2   Steam locomotive types, names, and dates of introduction.

Not all Berkshires, or Pacifics or any other type, were created equal. There were numerous intra-type classes depending upon available tractive effort, the types evolved over the years with many detail changes occurring along the way, and different railroads ordered locomotives with various features. Many modelers ignore these details, but purists and bugs on prototypical realism research and model them as faithfully as possible. True enough, if you are modeling a prototype railroad, you should in the interest of veracity model your locomotives as closely as is practical to the real thing, in the proper time setting.

The designation system for diesel locomotives is different. First, a unit with an engineer's cab is designated as an "A" unit, while a cabless booster unit is a "B." Unlike steamers (for the most part), road diesels are routinely run in combinations of two to several units, as well as singly. So, a locomotive complement might be an "A," an "AA," an "ABA," and so on. A wheel arrangement designation is also used. "A" means a 2-wheeled, single powered axle, "B" means a 4-wheeled truck with all axles powered, "C" means a 6-wheeled truck, all axles powered, "D" means an 8-wheeled truck, all axles powered, and a numeral means an unpowered axle. Thus, a B-B diesel has two 4-wheeled powered trucks, a C-C has two 6-wheeled powered trucks, and an A1A-A1A has two sets of 2 powered axles with an idler axle between.

Because of the widely different appearances and characteristics of the diesels that have been manufactured over the years, these designations are not definitive. Instead, the actual model numbers of the units are principally employed as designations, along with the manufacturer's name. The Alco RS-1 or PA-3 or S-2, the EMD SD-7, the Fairbanks-Morse H-10-44, and the GE U-28C are all familiar to railfans and modelers alike. As with the steamers, it is important to select those that are compatible with the modeled time period. The EMD SD-45, for example, didn't appear until about 1965, so shouldn't be run on a 1940's pike. The EMD SW-1, introduced in 1939, could be. Some of the better known locomotives are listed in FIG. 9-3.

Another point to consider is the kind of service that your locomotives, either steam or diesel, will be used for. Though there was, and is, a lot of overlap, many locomotives were designed for certain kinds of service. A little 0-4-0, for example, is a light duty yard switcher, period. The first 4-4-2 Atlantics (1896) were stubby workhorses, but the final models (ca. 1936) were beautiful streamliners, one of which pulled the famous Milwaukee Road crack passenger train *Hiawatha*. The Alco S-1 diesel was intended for general switching service, while the EMD FP7 was designed for heavy duty passenger service.

As with the steamers, if you are modeling prototypically you should endeavor to use the same models of locomotives and for the same purposes as the prototype road did, or does. You can, however, introduce certain different locomotives with different road names if those lines might have occasionally used your prototype road's trackage, or if you include a common interchange point where several roads can pass through. If you are modeling a road you dreamed up, you can run just about any kind of locomotive for which you can also dream up a plausible justification, or even an excuse.

SELECTING ROLLING STOCK

Any modeler intrigued by railroad rolling stock, such as the passenger, freight, and special purpose cars, has to feel like a kid in a candy shop. There is an enormous array, constantly (though slowly) changing, from which to choose. If you were able to start at age 4, you could build a car every day for the rest of your life and not have all of them. Therefore selectivity is a key. For most of the rolling stock an essential criterion is compatibility with the layout time period.

The rolling stock of the very early days was crude and highly variable, and best left to the historians. Little if anything from this period is modeled today, though it certainly is fertile ground for a railroad-historian/model-scratchbuilder.

Year	Maker	Models
1931	Alco	HH600
1939	EMD	SW1, NW2, FT, E6
1940	Alco	S1, S2, RS1, DL109
1940	GE	44 Ton
1944	F-M	H-10-44
1945	EMD	E-7
1945	Alco	FA1
1946	Alco	RSC2, PA1, PB1, RS2
1946	EMD	F3
1948	EMD	BL2
1949	EMD	SW7, F7, GP7, E8, FP7
1950	Alco	S3, S4, RSD5, PA2
1950	Baldwin	S12
1950	EMD	SW8
1950	F-M	H-12-44
1954	EMD	SW1200, GP9, SD9, E9, FP9, F9
1954	Alco	S6, RSD12, RSD15, RS11, RSD7
1959	EMD	GP18, GP20
1959	GE	U25B
1963	Alco	C420, C628
1963	EMD	GP28, SD28, GP35
1963	GE	U25C
1965	EMD	SD45
1966	EMD	SW1500, GP38, SD38
1966	Alco	C430
1966	GE	U28B, U28C, U30B, U30C
1967	Alco	C636
1969	GE	U50
1971	GE	U36C
1972	EMD	GP38-2, SD40-2
1974	EMD	MP15, SD40T-2
1976	EMD	GP15-1
1977	GE	B30-7, C30-7
1980	EMD	GP50, SD50
1984	GE	C39-8, B39-8
1984	EMD	SD60

9-3 Some of the better known brands and models of diesel locomotives and their dates of introduction.

Passenger-type rolling stock is only moderately popular with modelers, and not a whole lot of variety is available in either kit or rtr form. An enthusiast in this area will have to do some research to see just what was used where and when that will fit his or her scheme, then do some kit bashing and modifying to come up with the requisite model rolling stock.

There are five distinctly different general forms of model passenger train rolling stock available (FIG. 9-4). Typically, for modeling from the 1860s into the early 1900s, more or less depending upon location and particular railroad, one could use the "oldtimer" coaches and combines. These stubby, high riding affairs were about 45 feet long, built of wood and with characteristic vertical wood sheathing. The next group would be suitable, again de-

9-4 These passenger cars were used at different times and for different kinds of service, though there was considerable overlap.

pending upon road and location, for a period from the late 1800s into the 1920s and 1930s on mainlines and 1940s in short line service. These are the so-called "standard" 65-foot coaches and combines. From the early 1900s on, and especially through the 1920s into the 1940s, the larger railroads used the standard all-steel heavyweights, ranging from 70 to 85 feet long, in mainline passenger service. These are available in coach, combine, observation, dining, and sleeping cars. The fourth group saw mainline service from the mid 1940s through the 1970s. This includes various kinds of streamliners in the 85-foot range, smooth sided and corrugated sided, in coach, bi-level commuter coach, Pullman, baggage-mail, full baggage, railway post office, observation, dome, dome-observation, and dining car forms. The last group consists of the various types of modern Amtrak cars, including the Superliners, ViewLiners, and mail and express cars.

These cars will serve realistically on some layouts, but for many others they will merely give the flavor of passenger service. Numerous other forms and sizes of prototype passenger cars with a wide range of color and lettering schemes actually saw service. The hotel cars, parlor cars, and private cars of the late 1800s are examples, and there were cars in the 70- to 80-foot range on the mainlines well before the turn of the century. The modeler intent upon authenticity and prototypical realism will have to research first, then modify or kit-bash existing models, or scratch build.

The situation is different with freight cars. They are the most popular rolling stock by far, and there is a tremendous range of model kit and rtr cars available. Box cars in various forms certainly head the list, followed by hoppers, covered hoppers, gondolas, flats, tanks, stocks, and cabooses. Many different road names and paint schemes are offered. In addition, any kit model or rtr "undecorated" (no paint or lettering) can be finished to represent any of hundreds of other road names, numbers, and paint schemes, all of which varied from time to time, even on the same railroad. Any decorated car can be refinished as well. Only a part of the freight cars that were actually built and operated somewhere in this country are represented. Model kits or rtr cars can be kit-bashed or modified to model some of the more unusual, custom built, or limited production prototypes, or to upgrade or update by adding or subtracting various features that appeared or disappeared during various time periods. All of this can be confusing and sometimes frustrating, so the selection of freight cars for a given layout should be made with care and foreknowledge of what units would be appropriate for the modeled time period and kind of service.

There are lots of points to consider. You can reasonably expect to see any or all of the general types of cars on any railroad—box, flat, tank, etc. You would only see specialty cars on a given layout if there was a local or other logical reason for them to be there, such as sugar beet, stock, chemical, log buggy, hot metal, milk, 70-ton ore, etc. The time periods during which different kinds of freight cars were run should coincide with your modeled time period. Truss-rod gondolas were very early, ice refrigerators didn't roll in the 1960s, piggyback flats are relatively recent and so are auto transporters. You have to look at the design of the car too, especially box cars, because they evolved over the years (FIG. 9-5). The 40-foot double-sheathed single-door box is typical of the 1920s through the 1940s, while the 50-foot peak-

9-5 The evolution of boxcars, as well as other kinds of freight cars, from the small, crude early models like the 34-footer at the to through the many variations of the "standard" 40-footers (center) top the big modern ones like the 50-foot peaked-end at the bottom is a study in itself.

ended box didn't show up until the mid 1960s. The many distinctly different forms of general purpose cars appeared at different times and remained in service for variable time periods on different roads, so to be authentic you have to be careful not to run a car that is too early or too late for your layout.

This is also true of road names. Freight cars get shuffled all over the country, so any road is likely to appear anywhere. Except. If your layout is 1960, no way will you see a Fort Worth & Denver City box car. If it's 1920, there won't be any Burlington Northern rolling stock around (that's later) or a Colorado Midland reefer (that's earlier). Paint schemes can cause problems, because roads changed them from time to time. Same thing with lettering schemes and heralds (logos). All of this can mean some research, if you want to be prototypically correct. Sometimes there's an easy out. Some rtr models and decal sets that come with kits include, as part of the car data lettering, the prototypical date the car was built ("Blt 4–27," for example), and you can use that as a guide.

Apart from all this, as freight cars evolved there were many detail changes made, and the dates when they occurred are important for prototypical modeling. For example, early trucks (wheel sets) were wooden beamed supplanted by archbar trucks (the use of which was outlawed after 1938), which gave way to Andrews trucks, which were followed by Bettendorf friction-bearing trucks, which are now mostly roller-bearing and all of them have a different appearance. Brake systems and components show a series of obvious changes down through the years, and so do the styles of car ends, car sides, door sizes and arrangements, and roof walks. All such details have to be sorted out and included or not, as the time frame dictates.

There is generally more flexibility involved with the specialty cars (FIG. 9-6), especially if you are not faithfully modeling a prototype railroad. You

9-6 Every model railroad can find a need for certain specialty cars. They add a lot of flavor and interest.

might have need for a string of modern 70-ton ore cars or a series of hot metal or slag cars. You might scratch build a few early-type wooden ore cars. Log, piggyback, coil, depressed center flat, milk, and early wood-sheathed reefers are other possibilities. You might want to work up some of the more unusual cars that appeared on some roads, especially short lines, like ventilated box cars for carrying produce, freelance logging cabooses, transfer cabooses, mine concentrate, liquid sulfur, pulpwood, four-truck flat, two-dome tank, or pickle cars.

You can probably have the most fun with non-revenue cars, most of which were, and are, part of the "work-train" complement (FIG. 9-7). They are collectively known as *maintenance of way* cars, or *MOW*, or *MofW* units. Some large and affluent lines use cars especially made for various MOW purposes. Many lines, and especially small, poor shortlines, made do with whatever they could build, rebuild, scrounge, or cobble up. Along with some decent (and not so decent) specialty equipment, this is where a lot of rolling stock too old and tired to make regular runs finally wound up, still good enough (sometimes barely so) to make occasional track maintenance and repair trips.

This group includes crew, kitchen, repair, machine shop, relief, dormitory, supply, and tool cars, often made from old box or passenger cars, as well as rotary snowplows with tenders and perhaps extra water tenders, wedge snowplows, flat cars for rails and ties, a big Brownhoist crane or other wrecker and accompanying boom car, ballast gondolas, small Burro crane, an even smaller hoist or crane car, water tank car, ditcher, pile driver, flanger,

9-7 Work train cars afford a lot of opportunity for some unusual treatments and different looking rolling stock.

and for modern railroads, numerous kinds of specialized track repair and test units. With all of this rolling stock, you can follow prototype patterns, and you can also improvise and freelance to your heart's content.

KIT VS. RTR EQUIPMENT

All of the so-called "toy" or "tinplate" equipment is rtr, ready-to-run. These items are not part of the scale model railroad picture. In Z scale, all locomotives and rolling stock is factory finished and rtr, and the variety of that is small. In N scale, all the locomotives and nearly all the rolling stock is also rtr. There is a small selection of good quality car kits. In addition, many locomotives and cars are available as "blanks" that must be painted and lettered, so they are kits of a sort. In HO scale and up, kits are available in tremendous variety. There are many rtr units as well, and you can also have kits assembled and finished by a professional model maker if you wish to.

Which is better? Neither one. Rtr units you can put into service immediately, while kits obviously take time to assemble and finish. For this you will need model makers' tools and equipment and some supplies, and you will have to develop some experience and expertise. But after all, that's what model railroading is all about, at least in part—making models. The time and effort is offset by the satisfaction and the ultimate finished product. Factory finished units usually need some tuning up to look good and run well, but they also form handy bases for customizing or remaking into a slightly different model that fits your scheme better. Kits, on the other hand, offer great flexibility because you can make modifications as you proceed and end up with a different model than the one pictured on the box lid.

There are some instances were rtr units are of better quality, appearance, or operating characteristics than can possibly be managed by a kit builder, but that's rare except in Z scale. In other scales the finished kit can be at least as good as, and often better than, a factory finished unit, especially if done with care. As to cost, that's not usually a factor. You won't save by buying kits, and you won't go broke by buying rtr units. Some kits are more expensive than similar rtr units, and vice versa. If you count your time as money, only then is there much difference, and the rtr units come out ahead.

COUPLING

Effectively coupling cars together, and to locomotives, keeping them coupled during operation, and uncoupling them on command, has been a perennial problem since the hobby began. Though still far from perfect, many advances have been made over the years and the current arrangements are at least reasonably workable and reliable. They are also confusing to beginners.

There are three coupling systems (FIG. 9-8). One consists of *dummy* coupler heads, which are cast or molded models of the prototype and have no working parts. To couple or uncouple you have to lift one car end up and engage or disengage the fist-like coupler heads manually. These couplers are suitable for static displays and dioramas, and could in theory be used on a layout to connect a series of cars that normally would not be separated, like a string of coal hoppers or ore cars.

9-8   These are the three common types of couplers; nonscale automatic (left), semi-scale automatic (center), and dummy.

The second arrangement is the most common, and uses *nonscale automatic* couplers. They are bulky and oversize and allow too much space between cars, and bear only a vague, passing resemblance to prototype couplers. But they do operate. Designs vary in the larger scales; in HO scale the *horn-hook* type is common, and the *Rapido* style is used in N scale. Most cars and locomotives, both rtr and kit, are furnished with this kind of coupler.

The horn-hook style operates with a sideways motion, which sometimes causes derailment when reversing. A push will couple two cars, and they can be uncoupled manually, or by means of a manually remotely operated mechanical ramp positioned between the rails. Rapido couplers operate with a vertical motion, one sliding up over the other and dropping into place. They slip together fairly readily, even on curves, with a solid push to the car. Automatic uncoupling is accomplished with mechanical or electrically operated ramps, that can be positioned on either tangents or curves. The lifted ramps do sometimes cause derailments. To uncouple where there is no ramp, you can manually disengage the coupler heads without disturbing the car by inserting a hook-ended length of wire, positioned from directly above, beneath one coupler and gently lifting it free of the other.

Nonscale automatic couplers do get the job done. They are simple, adequate, and workable, and are often recommended for beginning model railroaders. However, the *semiscale automatic* type of coupler makes a better installation from several standpoints. These couplers look much like prototype couplers, and have spring loaded operating knuckles. By far the most common brand is Magne-Matic by Kadee, which are furnished on all Kadee model freight cars and are available in several forms for installation on other brands of rolling stock, and in conversion kits for popular locomotive models. Some skill is required to make the conversions and there is expense involved, but the result is worthwhile.

Coupling on tangents requires only a slight nudge of one car; on curves coupling is seldom possible because the knuckles do not align. Automatic uncoupling is done with special electromagnetic ramps and delayed uncoupling is an added feature, so that cars can be separated after actuation and away from a ramp. Cars can be manually uncoupled by lifting the cars and slipping the couplers apart, or with a special tool that opens the knuckles when it is inserted between two cars. The key to good operation is precise installation and adjustment, after which the couplers will perform smoothly and reliably. They also afford the most realistic appearance of all small scale coupling systems, particularly in the much shortened space between cars.

Though conversion of all (or most, anyway) your rolling stock and motive power to semiscale couplers takes time and money, I recommend this course unless you plan on little or no switching operation and are not concerned with the unrealistic appearance of the nonscale couplers. Accordingly, you will want to figure on installing an uncoupling ramp and operating switch, or perhaps several of them, so make allowances in your layout plans. During the conversion process, keep two or three cars on the layout that have a new type coupler on one end and an old one on the other. That way you will always be able to interface and couple up any combination of cars and engines.

The best way to ensure reliable coupler operation and a minimum of derailments, random uncoupling, and associated problems is to "tune" each piece of equipment before putting it into service. Make sure the trucks, and their wheels, are correctly aligned. Check all moving parts of the couplers for bits of flash or other foreign matter caught up in them, make sure springs are centered and operational, and check screws or retainers to see that they are tight and aligned. Coupler and/or trip pin height must be set exactly to specifications, so make whatever bending or shimming adjustments are necessary. All coupler pockets and mating parts should be smooth and bare of paint; polish as necessary. All pivoting parts must swing freely and easily. Lightly lubricate the mating surfaces with a dry lubricant made for the purpose like Labelle's Teflon or graphite; never use an oil or grease.

MODELING THE EQUIPMENT

When it comes to modeling the equipment, you have several choices, and most modelers eventually use all of them. The first is to buy rtr models off the shelf. You can set them right on the rails, and that often happens. Usually there is work to be done on any model, if not now, then later. Converting the couplers and/or trucks is a common occurance. Replacing grab irons, roof walks, ladder rungs, and similar items for a more realistic appearance are all common alternatives. There might be reason to modify the car, slightly or radically, to convert it to another time period, another road style, or even another car type. Repainting and relettering to a different time period or a different road, often called redecorating, is also popular. Often inexpensive units of only modest quality can be substantially upgraded into very nice models by rebuilding them, so don't overlook this opportunity.

A large percentage of rolling stock, along with many locomotives, is built from kits, the "shake the box" models. The locomotives are made up of both metal and plastic parts, and the kits are moderately complex but for the most part are not really difficult. Most car kits are made up of preformed plastic parts (FIG. 9-9), and assembly ranges from easy to somewhat difficult. Instructions range from sketchy to very well done. There is also a group of kits generally classed as the "craftsman" type. They consist mainly of appropriate kinds and quantities of raw materials which have to be cut, shaped, fitted, and assembled as per instructions, which are often vague and imprecise but sometimes detailed and excellent.

Building models from kits is not only fun and satisfying, it affords you the ready opportunity to diverge from the instructions and modify or improve upon the intended finished result if you wish to. This ensures that your model won't be just like everybody else's, and also lets you tailor it to your own layout requirements. Much of the modifying takes place in using paint and lettering schemes other than those provided, and this will be covered a bit later.

The best way to learn how to build rolling stock models from kits is to go ahead and do it. The general process for working with the plastic models is much the same as for building structure kits, and so are the tools, equipment, and supplies. Practically everything you'll need for structures you'll eventually use in car kit building, and vice versa. Purchase a quality kit with top notch instructions to begin with, for a good initial familiarization with the procedures. After doing one or two of these, you'll be able to tackle any plastic kit. As for the craftsman type, you'll probably need to puzzle your way through a couple of them as an initiation, using as much care and patience

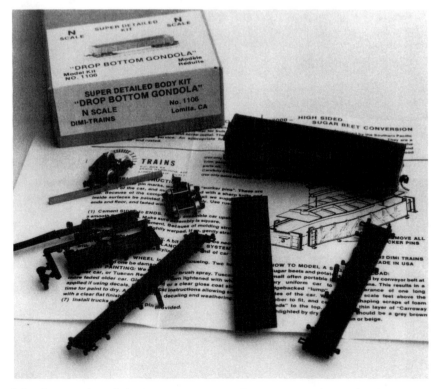

9-9 Construction of plastic kit cars like these Dimi drop-bottom gondolas is not difficult, the quality is good, and the finished result is fine.

as you can muster. Be aware that they never do go together easily—they aren't meant to.

Another possibility is that fun exercise in miniature creative engineering known as kit-bashing. This is the same process as discussed in Chapter 7, but involving cars instead of structures. Whenever you build from kits, save any leftover parts or bits and pieces, including some of the plastic sprue material, and toss them in a "junk box." All of this stuff comes in handy during kit-bashing projects. The object is to use the materials and parts from two or more kits, perhaps along with junk box items, to make up something that is not commercially available (FIG. 9-10). For example, a flat car kit plus parts of a box car or caboose might result in a crane boom car, or a logging caboose. You could make a 60-foot chip gondola from a pair of 40-foot standard gondolas. Two flat cars might end up as a longer, heavy duty, four-truck flat.

The final possibility is the ultimate in model making, scratch building. You start from scratch with the raw materials and build the model, usually to reasonably accurate scale from scaled plans of a prototype, but sometimes as a freelance project (which also must be kept within realistic scale proportions). Supplies for scratch building, such as scale stripwood, plastic structural shapes (channels, column, beams) brass and aluminum shaped stock (rod, tube, angle), sheet building materials (sidings, roofings, glazings, masonry), and detail parts (windows, doors, ladders, grab irons, wire and pipe, etc.), are readily available from hobby supply outlets. All this material is also helpful in modifying rtr equipment, or kits, or in kit-bashing.

9-10 A flatcar body, some new trucks, a stack of stakes, and recombined pieces of a wrecked caboose come together here to make a kit-bashed logging work caboose for Lufkin Logging & Lumber.

DECORATING, WEATHERING, AND DETAILING

Decorating a model is the process of painting and lettering it. You can buy certain rolling stock rtr models as "undecorated," meaning they are not painted and have no road name lettering at all. You must take care of that. Kit models of rolling stock may or may not include lettering decals, or may or may not be partly painted or lettered, and this varies. Usually, though, you can do whatever you wish in that line. Some locomotives are sold undecorated, but they may be painted flat black and perhaps include a trim stripe or two. Most brass locomotive and rolling stock models are unpainted. You can always repaint and reletter any decorated piece of equipment; in fact this is a standard procedure.

Schemes

If you are modeling a particular prototype road, most (if not all) of your motive power and passenger cars, as well as a large proportion of your freight cars, will be painted and lettered according to that particular scheme. The more popular roads, like "Pennsy" or Sante Fe or New York Central, are often available right off the shelf. Decal or dry lettering sets are available for those and many, many more lines. Model paints, especially those in the Floquil line, are available in specific shades that match the colors used on rolling stock by various railroads. By researching the requirements and matching them with available supplies, then applying the correct paint and lettering to appropriate pieces of rolling stock, you can come up with authentic representations of all but the more obscure road names. Of course, there are a lot of those, and they can be difficult.

If you are modeling an imaginary short line, then you need to name it, perhaps devise a herald (not all lines used them), and pick the color(s) you want to use on your equipment. Here you can have some fun. Steam locomotives need not be black, even though you usually see them that way. You can use a silver smokebox and black boiler, or vice versa, red or blue cab, and green, blue, maroon, red, and other colors have been used on boilers or entire engines. Whitewalls on the drivers, and sometimes the trucks as well, have long been popular, too. Diesel engines have had all kinds of bright and wild color schemes — the Santa Fe "Warbonnet" is a classic example.

Passenger cars have also been colorful at times, though deep green is the traditional color. Red, maroon, yellow, light green, and other colors and combinations have been used. The traditional colors for box cars are Tuscan red and box car red, but you can pick anything. The New York Central has used jade, the Boston & Maine bright blue, Burlington Northern bright green, and others are possible. They can also be two-toned, or even three-toned like some Bangor & Aroostook cars, in various ways. Many lines use different roof and side colors. Yellow, orange, and white are traditional for reefers. Coal hoppers are usually black for obvious reasons, but could well be other colors in other service. Black is typical for tanks, but white, silver, and others have been used. Flats might be anything.

Lettering

The lettering for your own road poses no problems except perhaps a little added expense. For simple lettering schemes you can use stock decal or dry lettering, numbering, and striping, as well as car data sets (of limited selection). These are available in hobby shops as stock sheets of different kinds and styles. You have to apply each piece individually, which is a chore. The work is tedious and positioning and alignment can be tricky. But, the cost is low. You can also mix up prototype railroad lettering decals to create your own custom set if you plan ahead, and this makes application much easier. The key is to find decal sets with matching lettering styles.

For example, you might reverse Illinois Central, add a lower case "of", and make it Central of Illinois. You could change Pacific Fruit Express to Pacific Express Ry., or the Denver & Rio Grande Western to the Denver & Western or the Rio Grande R.R. With matching type styles, you could make up the Great Southern from the Great Northern and the Southern Pacific, or the Sante Fe & Texas Central, the Chicago & Lake Erie, the Spokane & Pacific, or dozens of others from various road names. Then you can use various combinations of box car reporting marks, dimensional and other car data, and whatever else will fit to make up car numbers, data sets, and the like.

A better arrangement is to have decals custom made for you by a company specializing in model railroad artwork, like Rail Graphics. Though this is a fairly large initial expense, a little like having your own stationery printed up, the cost will likely average out to about $1 per car for the most expensive setups, and half that for the simplest arrangement. You can choose from a variety of type styles and three or four sizes, and numerous colors. A complete set (FIG. 9-11), that in many instances can be split up between two or more cars, might consist of the full road name, initials, number sequence, herald, slogan, and car data set, each duplicated and in two sizes. You get a lot of decals for your money, and with some planning you can make them go a long way and fulfill a lot of purposes.

Painting

Painting models is not a difficult chore, though at times it can be tedious. With a little practice you'll be able to get excellent results. Brush application is best for small parts and detailing , works very well for Z and N scale general painting, and nearly as well in HO. For small work, you'll need point-tip brushes in numbers 4/0, 3/0, 0, and 1, a number 1 square tip, perhaps a ¼-inch square tip, and whatever other sizes seem to work best for your purposes. Use top quality artist's brushes, or you'll be disappointed with the results.

Unless you desperately need certain prototypical railroad colors that are only available in solvent-based model paints, I strongly recommend that you use acrylic model and craft paints exclusively, or at least as much as possible. They flow, cover, and coat well, are available in a wide range of colors, are fast drying, feature water cleanup, and make excellent washes. Most importantly, you avoid the pungent, lingering, noxious odor, the fire hazard, and the toxic vapors that accompany all solvent based model paints. If

SILVER PLUME & UTE RIVER
SP&UR 16035827941603582794
SILVER PLUME & UTE RIVER
SP&UR 16035827941603582794

Rail
Graphics®
CUSTOM DECALS

Ride the High Rockies
Ride the High Rockies

1057

SILVER PLUME & UTE RIVER
SP&UR 16035827941603582794
SILVER PLUME & UTE RIVER
SP&UR 16035827941603582794

LEASED TO GOODSHOT MINING & MILLING	FASTEST FREIGHT IN THE WEST	PARMA LEE LUFKIN LOGGING & LUMBER	RETURN EMPTY TO UTE RIVER YARD
LEASED TO GOODSHOT MINING & MILLING	FASTEST FREIGHT IN THE WEST	PARMA LEE LUFKIN LOGGING & LUMBER	RETURN EMPTY TO UTE RIVER YARD

1900-1920's FREIGHT

36' Boxcar
CAPACITY 80000 lbs.
Wt. 46500 NEW 4.16.07
INSIDE LENGTH 36 0
INSIDE WIDTH 8.6
INSIDE HEIGHT 8.0

40, Boxcar
NOMINAL CAPACITY 100000 L.B.S.
LOAD LIMIT 125300
LIGHT WEIGHT 43700
EAVES {HEIGHT 12 Ft 5 In
{WIDTH 9 2
LENGTH {OUTSIDE 42 3
{INSIDE 40 6

50 ton Gondola
CAPACITY 1672 CU.FT.
100000 LBS.
MAX. LOAD 115200 LBS.
LIGHT WT. 39500 LBS.

50 ton Hopper
CAPY 100000 LBS.
WT. 40900 NEW 10-18
LENGTH 32 FT 1 IN
CAPY 1880 CUFT

50' Auto-Box
CAP'Y 100000
6.10.14 NEW WT. 51900

36' Reefer
CAP'Y. 60000 LBS 2077 CU FT
WT. 40000 NEW 7 17

38' Reefer
CAPY. 60000
LENGTH INSIDE 38 FT.
NEW 4.16.07 WT.42800

55 ton Hopper
CUBIC CAPACITY 1880 CU.FT.
NOMINAL CAPACITY 110000 LBS.
MAXIMUM LOAD LIMIT 110700 LBS.
LIGHT WEIGHT 41300 LBS.

40 ton Stock
CAPY. 80000
I.D. LMT. 90000
LT. WT. 35500

UNITED STATES SAFETY APPLIANCES STANDARD

HEIGHT AT EAVES 13-11
WIDTH AT EAVES 9.4
LENGTH INSIDE 50 FT.

LENGTH INSIDE 35 FT. 1 IN.
WIDTH 8 2
HEIGTH 7 3

OPEN SMALL DOOR FROM INSIDE

HEIGTH AT EAVES 12FT. 3IN.
WIDTH AT EAVES 9FT. 6IN.
LENGTH INSIDE 38 FT.

ADJUSTABLE ICE TANK
IW WROT STL. WHLS

DO NOT NAIL THIS DOOR

LENGTH 36 FT. 3 IN.
CAPY 1950 CU.FT.

EAVES {HEIGHT 12 FT. 4 IN
{WIDTH 9 FT. 3 IN.
LENGTH {OUTSIDE 38 FT 1 IN
{INSIDE 36 FT 6 IN

NEW 6-09 NEW 4-12 BUILT 10-17 NEW 4.16.07 NEW 11.20.02 NEW 9-19 NEW 2-18
BLT 6.09 BUILT 4-12 BUILT 10-17 BLT 4.16.07 BUILT 11.20.02 BLT 9-19 BLT 2-18

Rail Graphics® **H107**
AIR BRAKE MCB COUPLER
ROHN PATENT
ICE TANKS 5500 LBS. EACH
CARDWELL-FRICTION DRAFT GEAR
TYPE-G. CLASSS-25A

U.S.
U.S.
AIR BRAKE
WESTINGHOUSE
FRICTION DRAFT GEAR
K2 TRIPLE VALVE
COUPLER SHANK 6X8
KEY ATTACHMENT
NO.2 BRAKE BEAMS
DIRT COLLECTOR
NO.2 BRAKE BEAM
TYPE D COUPLER
SHANK 6"x8"
K-2 TRIPLE VALVE
KEEP DOOR SEALED WHEN EMPTY

AUTOMOBILE
FURNITURE
EASTMAN HEATER
VENTILATED
REFRIGERATOR

9-11 Custom lettering and heralds come in full sets, and add an impressive finishing touch to the motive power and rolling stock of your imaginary road. Courtesy of Rail Graphics.

you choose to use these paints, do so only with the proper precautions, including a mask and full ventilation, preferably in a spray booth or hood.

Most modelers feel that a better paint job can be obtained by spraying the paint on. That's true, but whether or not the difference is significant enough to warrant investing in spraying apparatus and going to the extra effort involved must be up to the individual. Many modelers do everything by brush and are quite content, and get exemplary results. Others prefer to use an airbrush for practically everything, and also get exemplary results. Some get mediocre results either way, which is immaterial if they are enjoying the hobby. A few model paints are available in small spray cans, all others must be thinned and sprayed with an airbrush. Using the spray cans is fairly simple, but proficiency with an airbrush takes quite a bit of practice. Neither techniques are requirements for painting models.

When painting plastic models, first wash the parts with warm water and dish washing detergent and a brush to remove mold release agents, fingerprints, and soil. If your paints are solvent based, treat the parts with a recommended prep finish that will prevent the solvents from attacking the plastic; the Floquil; product, for example, is called Barrier. Acrylic paints can be directly applied to almost any material. Some modelers start with a primer coat, often a dark gray or black under dark colors and a light gray under light colors. This is a good procedure. Flow the paint on smoothly with as large a brush as will work well. Don't overbrush or back brush, and try to avoid making brush and lap marks. Follow up with the color coats. Several thin coats are much better than a couple of thick ones. Allow at least 24 hours' curing time between coats, and in a dust-free environment.

Metal parts or models can be treated the same way as plastic ones, except that a primer should always be applied unless the part is so small or finely detailed that the primer might make the overall coating too heavy. Wood models do not need priming, but can be directly painted with full strength solvent based or acrylic colors. Thinned solvent based paints will also work well, but acrylic washes that are mostly water can cause serious problems unless applied very sparingly. Thin basswood will warp like you wouldn't believe if soaked, splitting apart and popping glue joints in the process. Although it usually will go back into its original conformation, or almost so, some damage is inevitable. For staining you can use model stains, or buy ordinary woodworking oil stains like the Minwax line at a local paint store, or mix your own alcohol based stains from stock pigments.

Transfers and Decals

Applying dry transfer lettering might seem like an easier job than applying decals, but there's not that much difference. There is nowhere near the range of selections available, either. And there are some techniques to follow. Apply the transfer to a glossy, or at least semigloss, surface that is absolutely clean and dry. If need be, brush a thin coat of clear finish on the surface area where the transfer will be. Allow at least two days' curing time. Trim the transfer carrier above or below the lettering. Align this straight edge with a guideline on the model with the lettering facing down; butting it against a lightly stuck strip of masking tape or Scotch Magic Tape. Burnish each letter individually by rubbing it gently either sideways or up and down, but not both. Preferably you should use a burnishing tool; the tip of a dull pencil, a rounded off piece of wood, or the tip of a large knitting needle will work. Too much pressure will transfer the lettering back off the model onto the carrier; too little will not make the transfer. If you goof, stick a sliver of Scotch Magic Tape over the lettering and pull it off, and start over. When you've applied a full set, cover it with the protective paper that came with the transfer and burnish the whole affair lightly. Finally, apply a clear flat protective coating, preferably by spraying but otherwise by tender brushing.

Successful decal application involves a bit more than it did when you slapped them on your bicycle as a kid. First cut from the sheet the individual item or set that you want to transfer, then trim all around it. Cut away as much extraneous clear film as possible, leaving only enough film and backing to keep everything connected for alignment. The surface to be decaled should be glossy and have a smooth, well cured finish and be perfectly clean. Put the decals in clean, lukewarm water; use tap water unless it is hard and leaves whitish deposits. In that case use bottled distilled water. Don't leave the decals to soak while you watch the weather on TV — about 15 seconds is long enough. Remove them and lay them backing-down on a paper towel. Poke an edge every few seconds to see if the film has completely loosened from the backing. When the film is loose, pick it up by an edge with tweezers and set it, backing and all, right on the spot where you want the decal. Hold the film with the point of a pin and sneak the backing out from under. Blot up any excess moisture with the edge of a paper towel, but be sure not to touch the film with anything other than your pin point; use this to make any minor position adjustment. Proper alignment right now is crucial.

After about 10 minutes check to see if there are any air bubbles under the film. If there are, prick them with a fine needle point. If the decal lies over grooves or ribs, slice the film with a new blade so it will conform. This is your last chance to make any adjustments, cuts, bubble pops. Now, with a small, fine bristled art brush, very, very gently apply a coating of decal setting fluid (a hobby shop item). Flow the solution on without letting the brush touch the decal film, and leave only a thin coating. Wait an hour and do it again, wait another hour and do it one more time. Then wait about 12 hours. Check the decal for bubbles. If there are some, prick them, then apply another coat of setting fluid. Keep this up as long as you have to in order to get rid of the bubbles. After a final 12-hour curing period, use a cotton swab to wash away any stains or old adhesive from around the decal, but don't touch it. Allow several more hours' drying time, and spray or carefully brush on a coating of clear flat finish. You're done.

Weathering

The weathering process is much the same as that used on structures, and so is the purpose (see Chapter 7). Steam locomotives don't stay clean and shiny for long — they become streaked and soot stained, splotched with oil and grease and perhaps some rust, and laced with leak stains of various sorts. Their tenders look almost as bad. Diesel locomotives fair better, with black exhaust stains near the vents. Both types accumulate road dust and dirt in a hurry.

Freight cars of the steam era got soot-grimy in short order, and all of them pick up road dust of the colors of whatever country they travel through. Only new or newly rebuilt cars can be expected to be clean and have a bit of shine. Many cars will also show traces of recently carried loads. Tank cars may have spills or streaks of tar, oil, chemicals, molasses, or numerous other substances. Coal hoppers are black, wheat cars are streaked with yellowish dust, cement hoppers with light gray dust, flat cars have all kinds of stains.

Passenger cars are likely to be cleaner than freight cars because they were frequently washed. Those used behind coal and wood-burning steamers will be soot-streaked and road-dusty, those behind oil-burning steamers and diesels will be cleaner but have some road dust and dirt. MOW rolling stock will carry most of the dirt and staining of their heavy duty service and their age, and on many roads will look faded, care-worn, and sometimes pretty shabby. Though, note that all the equipment on a prosperous, busy, well-managed railroad will look relatively clean and in good repair. The smaller, poorer, and more sloppy the road, the less likely this is to be true and the dirtier, rustier, and shabbier the equipment will look.

Study photos, and also the real thing if you can, to get an idea of what well-traveled motive power and rolling stock really looks like. Then try to make your models look the same way. The process is simple, but takes a little experimenting and practice to achieve the effects that look best to you.

Detailing

Detailing motive power and rolling stock is a task that many modelers don't bother with, but the process can add a great deal of realism. This is easiest to do as you assemble each kit, or kit bash or scratch build, but you can detail rtr models as well. In fact, they often need it the most. The best course is to detail each car and engine as you ready it for service on your line, rather than trying to wade through a couple of dozen units as a major project. That chore pales rapidly. The object of detailing is to improve the authenticity, prototypical appearance, and scale sizing of any given model in whatever way is practical. Some things, like oversized wheel flanges or door tracks that are scaled too bulky, you can't do much about. But almost always there are some improvements that you can make.

Part of this process might lie in improving or changing the lettering or painting to better conform to a prototype, as to style, letter size, color tones, or paint scheme. Another possibility is making a change in the trucks or couplers. Removing molded-on grab irons and ladders and replacing them with scale, stand-off parts is a common change that much improves a car's appearance. Operating doors or ice hatches, "glass" in caboose windows and better scaled caboose railings, changes and improvements in the braking and other underframe components, and adding vestibules to passenger cars are other possibilities, and there are plenty more. As to locomotives, they can often be upgrade by replacing the handrails and piping with scale sizes, changing the bell or air pumps or stack or feedwater heater, adding number boards, or altering sand domes, to name a few items.

STORAGE

After a time, almost all model railroaders accumulate much more rolling stock than the layout can handle, and perhaps more locomotives as well. Then comes the question of what to do with them. There are several possibilities.

In some cases, one or more storage tracks is a workable arrangement that can be used in conjunction with other methods as required. If you have some elevated scenery with the under space accessible, you can install one or more dead end tracks here for the specific purpose of storing unused cars. This has the added advantage of keeping them relatively dust free. An alternative is to install a storage track that is hidden from view by a ridge or other scenery but is accessible from above and not an operational part of the pike. The ultimate in storage tracks is to run a single track off the layout, perhaps on a narrow shelf along the wall, to a platform above the workbench containing a large storage yard with its own little control panel.

Storage cases are another possibility, although less convenient, that makes particular sense for a modeler who often transports equipment to shows or operating sessions. There are several cases commercially available that are custom-made for model railroad equipment. You can also make your own from plywood, and fit it with storage drawers or slip-in boxes. Or, you could modify such containers as a salesman's sample case, a mechanic's drawer-type tool chest, a hard bodied camera case, or an ordinary hard bodied suitcase (cheap at second-hand stores). Carved Styrofoam or other foam plastic or foam rubber can serve as protective restraining material, or you can fit in individual lined containers.

Another method is to use a small shelf set or bookcase (a glass-front barrister-type works well) or a kitchen wall cabinet. You can install additional shelves if you wish, doubling or tripling the storage space. If you install a tier of narrow shelves on each of the deep shelves and add a length of track to each, every piece of equipment will be visible, readily accessible, and easy to see.

Part of the fun of having an assortment of cars and locomotives is in being able to see them, and show them off. In the small scales, shadow box wall display cases are practical and attractive, keeping the models highly visible but dust free and right at hand. These cases are commercially available, but if you have a bent for woodworking you can easily make your own. The homemade case shown in FIG. 9-12 is for N-scale equipment; the dimensions would have to be changed for other scales. The sides, top, and bottom of the frame were ripped to width from pine S4S stock molding; at full width that material would be about right for HO scale. The shelves are standard pine door stop molding. Several stock widths are available off-the-shelf.

The back is ¼-inch-thick tempered hardboard painted gloss white (spray can); ⅛-inch hardboard, plywood, or even Formica would also work. The back is set in a rabbet cut into the frame so that it lies flush, and is attached with #4 x ¾-inch sheet metal screws into the frame and also at two points in the back edge of each shelf. The shelves, which were installed first,

9-12   One of the best ways to store not-in-service motive power and rolling stock is in a dust-free wall display case like this.

are nailed through the sides with ring-shanked panel nails in predrilled pilot holes. The forward edges of the sides are rabbeted to match a groove in the top and bottom pieces. The bottom groove is 1/16-inch deep, the top one 1/8-inch deep. Assembly of the frame requires cutting overlap butt joints at the ends of the top and bottom pieces with a hand miter box in order to cover the side rabbets. An alternative would be to make simple butt joints, then fill the gaps by gluing in small wood filler pieces.

The door is acrylic glazing plastic fitted with a pair of small cabinet door knobs as handles. To put the door in place, you tilt the top inward and slide the top corners upward along the side rabbet until the top edge slips into the upper groove, then swing the bottom edge inward and drop it into the bottom groove. It fits flush against the side rabbets and is very dust tight. The finish is two coats of satin varnish, applied before the back was installed. The track is full length Atlas flex sections, secured to the shelves after varnishing with narrow beads of clear silicone adhesive run along the tie strips directly below the rails. The finished and loaded case is heavy, so two heavy duty serrated-type picture hangers are attached to the frame with screws instead of the nails supplied. These are hooked over a pair of 50-pound capacity standard picture hanging hooks.

If you don't have the equipment to rabbet the back edges of the frame, you can attach the back directly to the frame edges. In that case, the shelves should be set back flush with the frame back edges. To avoid rabetting and dadoing the front edges of the frame for the glazing, install stops instead. Glue lengths of $\frac{3}{16}$ or $\frac{1}{4}$-inch square basswood strip (a hobby shop item) around the inside of the frame, back from the front edge a suitable distance, as back stops. Install two more strips, top and bottom face stops, spaced out from the back stops by the thickness of the door glazing you will use, plus about $\frac{1}{32}$ to $\frac{3}{64}$-inch. Cut the glazing to the height required so that the panel will slip up between the top stops, clear the bottom face stop and drop down into that slot, but not come out of the upper slot. Trim the plastic glazing panel by scoring with a knife made for the purpose, then breaking; dress the edges with a bastard file.

Glossary

ABS acrylonitrile-butadiene-sytrene, a polymeric plastic sometimes used in modeling projects.

ACC alphacyanoacrylate, a fast setting glue used for bonding nonporous materials; also, super-glue.

articulated a steam locomotive with two engines on one chassis under one boiler, such as 2-6-6-2. One set of drivers, rods, and cylinders is usually pivoted.

ashcat a locomotive fireman.

bad order out of order, broken, in need of repair; a *bad order* boxcar, etc.

bakehead a locomotive fireman.

big hook a wrecking crane, usually on a work train, a MOW piece.

block in modeling, a section or division of track, electrically isolated for control purposes.

block signal a signal at the beginning of a block that indicates whether or not a train is in the block.

bobber a caboose, often a small 4-wheel or a shop-built car.

bolster to shore up, augment. Also, the cross member of a car frame where the truck is mounted. Also, the cross member of a truck.

boomer an experienced railroad hand who goes from railroad to railroad.

brass railroad executives and officials; any bigwigs.

brass button a passenger car conductor or brakeman.

brass pounder a telegraph operator.

broad gauge any track with the width between rails more than the prototype standard 4 feet 8 ½ inches.

bug a railroad lantern.

bulls railroad police.

bumper a device placed at the end of a track siding to keep the cars from rolling off.

cab-forward a type of steam locomotive with the cab located in front.

caboose the crew car of a freight train, usually the last in line.

caboose track a storage track, double-ended, for cabooses and generally located near the yard office.

camelback a steam locomotive with the cabin built over the boiler.

cardstock a popular modeling material; stiff, laminated, fairly heavy paper sheet.

center pin   also kingpin; the steel pivot on which a truck swivels.

circus   an entire railroad.

Climax   a steam locomotive with cylinders driving a jackshaft parallel with the axles, with the trucks driven by shafts and bevel gears; commonly used on logging railroads.

coaling station   a structure, sometimes only bins, and machinery used to store coal and transfer it to steam locomotive tenders.

consist   prounounced "con'-sist"; the car makeup of a train, or a written list of the cars.

crossing   two tracks that cross but do not permit transfer from one line to the other. Also, the place where a road or highway crosses a track.

crossover   two turnouts set back to back to allow transfer of a train from one line to the other.

crummy   a caboose.

cupola   the square observation housing atop a caboose; not present in all cases.

cut   a section of roadbed that has been cut through a hill or knoll higher than the grade level.

cut of cars   a number of cars coupled together.

deadhead   a car or train traveling empty, or a passenger traveling on a pass.

deck   the walkway, also called runway, atop a boxcar.

derail   to come off the rails. Also, a device set over a rail to keep a car from rolling down the track.

die-cast   a process of molding often used in making model parts; molten metal or other material is poured or injected into a mold.

dinky   a yard switcher, or goat, because of the small size.

diorama   a scaled, detailed scene or part of a scene, set up as a display, usually static but sometimes animated.

doubleheader   a train pulled by two locomotives manned by two crews.

doubling   the process of splitting a train in two and taking the halves over a hill or pass one at a time.

draft gear   the box at each end of a car or locomotive where the coupler is mounted.

empty   An empty freight car.

engine class   A locomotive designation that depends upon traction power groupings, usually according to the weight on the drivers.

enginehouse   A special building, sometimes only a shed, where locomotives are serviced and often parked or stored.

epoxy   A two part thermosetting adhesive, very strong, for bonding non-porous surfaces, often used in modelmaking.

fiddle   to place or remove cars or locomotives on the layout tracks by hand; a fiddle yard is concealed trackage used for making up cuts on trains.

fill   a section of roadbed built up to grade above the natural grade, often with spoil dirt from a cut.

freight house track   one or more sidings or short sections of track fronting freight warehouses, for LCL cars. Also, house track.

gandy dancer   a trackworker.

grab iron   the handholds (round rod) on sides, ends, and roofs of freight cars.

grade   the upward or downward lie of the track. Also, the level of the earth at any given point. Also, the roadbed or line itself; *along the grade.*

Heisler   a geared steam locomotive used by logging railroads, with trucks driven by a driveshaft connected to a slanted V-2 engine.

helper   or helper engine; a locomotive added to a train to assist in boosting it over a steep grade. As many as five or six were sometimes used.

highball   a signal to proceed. Also, to steam along rapidly.

hog   a locomotive.

hogger   a locomotive engineer.

home guard   a man who has worked for the same railroad for many years.

hostler   a worker who services locomotives.

hotbox   a common occurrence, when a car wheel bearing becomes red hot, sometimes seizing up and/or starting a fire, from lack of lubrication.

house track   see Freight-house track.

icing track   a special track, double ended, running parallel to the icing platform at the ice plant, for icing reefers.

interchange   a track section, yard, or terminal where one railroad meets another, allowing interchange of cars or trains from one to the other.

interlocking   a system of controls that permits only one train to move through a multitrack junction.

in the hole   on a siding.

janney   to couple cars together.

johnson bar   a manual reversing lever on older steam locomotives.

journal   the end of a car or locomotive axle that rides in the bearing, located in the journal box.

king pin   a conductor. Also, any boss. Not to be confused with a truck king-pin.

kit-bash   to combine the parts of two or more model kits, resulting in a different, noncommercial model.

kitchen   the cab of a locomotive.

LCL   less than car load; said mostly of boxcars, having less than a whole load of (usually) mixed freight.

light train   a locomotive, tender, and one car, usually a caboose.

maintenance-of-way   the term used for equipment and cars employed in maintaining and repairing the track, ties, and roadbed. Also MOW, MofW.

master maniac   a master mechanic in charge of locomotive maintenance and repair.

module   a small section of a model railroad built to a standard size and configuration, portable and joinable to other modules to form a complete operating layout.

narrow gauge   any track with the width between rails less than the prototype standard 4 feet 8 ½ inches.

owl train   a late night local train.

peddler freight   a usually short local freight train that stops at every town from terminal to terminal. Also called a way freight.

piggyback truck trailers loaded on flatcars. Also called TOFC.

pike abbreviation for turnpike, and refers to a model railroad layout in general.

Pullman a sleeping or parlor car operated by the Pullman Co.

pusher a helper locomotive at the end of the train, pushing.

reefer a refrigerator car.

right-of-way the track, roadbed, and adjoining property along the lines owned by the railroad.

roadmaster a traveling railroad superintendent.

roundhouse a semicircular building with several stalls for servicing and repairing locomotives, served by a turntable or transfer table.

runaround a main and siding track arrangement where a locomotive can uncouple on the main line, back down the siding, and hook onto the rear of the train. Also, a thoroughfare bypass that allows passage through or around a yard or terminal area.

scratch building the process of constructing a model from bulk materials, standard parts, and raw stock, from scratch.

selective compression the process of reducing sizes and apparent distances and dimensions of structures and scenic details, retaining basic designs, and creating or reinforcing the illusion of realism.

Shay a type of steam locomotive having 3 vertical cylinders on the right side, driving a crankshaft geared to the axles; widely used in logging.

side-door Pullman a boxcar.

skipper a conductor.

smart Alec a Pullman conductor.

spot a car to position a car in a particular designated place.

standard gauge the standard distance (in the United States and some other countries) of 4 feet 8 ½ inches between the inside faces of the rail heads; refers to both prototype and scale.

streak of rust a railroad, or rail line.

styrene a polymeric plastic, readily workable and widely used in model making.

super elevation the process of banking up the outer rail of a track on a curve to reduce sway and counteract centrifugal force, allowing a higher safe speed.

switchback an arrangement of track that zigzags across the face of a slope, allowing an otherwise too-steep grade to be surmounted.

talgo a common style of model railroad car trucks having the coupler mounted on the truck instead of the car body.

tangent straight track.

tank engine a steam locomotive that carries its fuel and water supplies in saddle tanks slung over the boiler; it has no tender.

team track a siding or short section of track where freight cars are loaded and unloaded directly from or into trucks.

tender a car containing fuel and water attached directly behind a steam locomotive.

throat the spot in a yard where the trackage starts to diverge into the various multiple lines.

throttle jerker   a locomotive engineer.

TOFC   trailer on flatcar; see Piggyback.

truck   the wheel assembly of a car, including the bolster, sideframes, axles and bearings, and wheels; also, the pivoting leading or trailing wheel sets on a locomotive.

unit   a diesel locomotive.

USRA   the United States Railroad Administration, which took over operation of all U.S. railroads during WW I.

varnish   a passenger train, or car, from the fact that early wood cars were heavily coated with shiny varnish.

vestibule   the enclosed area at each end of a passenger car where the side doors are.

water column   a standpipe with a movable spout, usually located in a service yard or near a terminal, for filling steam locomotive water tanks.

way freight   see Peddler freight.

weathering   the process of simulating on models the visible prototypical effects of use, wear, aging, and weather, using paints, chalks, stains, etc.

wye   a triangular track pattern with a long tail for reversing locomotives or trains. Also, a type of turnout with a "Y" configuration.

yard engine   a small switching locomotive used in yards. Also, a goat or dinky.

yard master   the man in charge of a yard, with diverse duties.

yard shanty   the yard master's office. Also called "the shack," a popular gathering spot for talk.

Index